A

GLOBAL TOURISM, SUSTAINABLE TOURISM & ECO-TOURISM

GLOBAL TOURISM, SUSTAINABLE TOURISM & ECO-TOURISM
Code of Ethics, Charter, Guidelines, Resolutions

Edited by
Dr. P.C. Sinha

SBS Publishers & Distributors Pvt. Ltd.
New Delhi

ISBN : 81-89741-30-6

Global Tourism, Sustainable Tourism, Eco-Tourism: Code of Ethics, Charter, Guidelines, Resolutions

First Published in India in 2006

© Dr. P.C. Sinha

Published by:
SBS PUBLISHERS & DISTRIBUTORS PVT. LTD.
2/9, Ground Floor, Ansari Road, Darya Ganj,
New Delhi - 110002, INDIA.
Tel: 0091-11-23289119 / 41563911
Email: mail@sbspublishers.com

Printed at
Chaman Enterprises
1603, Pataudi House,Daryaganj
New Delhi 110002

Preface

This book titled "Global Tourism, Sustainable Tourism, Ecotourism: Code of Ethics, Charter, Guidelines, Resolutions" gives an in depth insight into contemporary global trends, as far as tourism ethics, charters, guidelines and resolutions are concerned. This makes this reading very beneficial for all the sectors dealing with tourism, sustainable tourism and ecotourism related activities.

The first chapter deals with the global code of ethics, both for tourism sector in general and the travelers in particular. The World Tourism Organization's code of ethics for tourism is presented in detail. As code of ethics for travelers a model guideline developed by the last frontiers for responsible tourism in Latin America is dealt in detail.

The second chapter deals with global charter for sustainable tourism, its state of affairs, principles on its implementation and management. The charter for Sustainable Tourism development at the World Conference on Sustainable Tourism in Spain during 1995 is presented. A complete overview of the state of affairs existing in global sustainable tourism today is briefly discussed. Also, the United Nations Environment Programme's principles on the implementation of sustainable tourism globally are presented including issues like integration of tourism into overall policy for sustainable development, development of sustainable tourism and its integrated management and conditions for success. The destination management approach developed for sustainable management of tourism destinations globally is discussed briefly, so is the local Agenda 21 approach.

The third chapter discusses in detail the convention on Biological Diversity's sustainable tourism development guidelines, including the guidelines for biodiversity conservation and development of vulnerable ecosystems. Concerned policy-making, development planning and management processes are covered in detail, so are the notification processes and information requirements. Focus also lies on the scope, education, capacity building and awareness raising aspects.

The last chapter discusses in detail the various resolutions, remarks, declarations and summit reports on global ecotourism. The famous Quebec Declaration on Ecotourism is presented, so is the in depth report on World Ecotourism Summit, covering aspects of ecotourism planning, regulation, product development, marketing and promotion. Issues related to monitoring aspects of ecotourism costs and benefits are also covered. All this virtually makes this book a very useful reference book.

Dr. P.C. Sinha

Contents

Glossary

Aboriginal: Refers to the original inhabitants of a country and their descendants. The term is used mainly in Australia and Canada.

ABTA: Association of British Travel Agents. The trade association of large tour operators.

All-inclusive: A resort providing accommodation, food and all facilities (e.g. beach and watersports) internally, so that visitors have no need to leave the resort.

ATOL: Air Travel Organizers Licence. A bonding scheme run by the Civil Aviation Authority. If your tour operator is a member of ATOL, you are guaranteed a refund if the company goes into liquidation.

Backpacker: A (usually young) independent traveller; typically carries a rucksack and stays in cheap, locally owned accommodation.

Canopy walkway: A constructed bridge walkway through the tree tops of a forest.

Community: A mutually supportive, geographically specific social unit such as a rural village or tribe. In an urban, Western context, the phrase is often used more loosely, to describe people with common interests, ethnic origins, etc.

Community-based tourism: Tourism that consults, involves and benefits a local community, especially in the context of rural villages in developing countries and indigenous peoples.

Conservation (nature): Protection against irreversible destruction and other undesirable changes, including the management of human use of organisms or ecosystems to ensure such use is sustainable.

Conservation enterprises: Income generating activities that focus on conserving natural resources and ecosystems.

Customised itineraries: A holiday schedule drawn up by a tour operator specifically for one client or group, usually including flight, accommodation and transport. Sometimes called tailor-made holidays.

Domestic tourism: Holidays taken within the tourist's own country. The volume of domestic tourism is hard to quantify but has been estimated at three to five times greater than international tourism.

Ecology: Originally defined by Ernst Haeckel in 1866, ecology is the study of the relationships that develop among living organisms and between these organisms and the environment.

Economic growth: The change over a period of time in the value (monetary and non-monetary) of goods and services and the ability and capacity to produce goods and services. It is economic growth which generates the wealth necessary to provide social services, health care, and education. It is the basis for ongoing job creation. However, sustainable development requires that there be a change in the nature of economic growth, to ensure that goods and services are produced by environmentally sound and economically sustainable processes.

Economy: What human beings do. The activity of managing resources and producing, distributing, and consuming goods and services.

Eco-system: A dynamic complex of plant, animal, fungal and microorganism communities and their associated non-living environment interacting as an ecological unit.

Eco-tourism: According to the US-based Eco-tourism Society, 'Eco-tourism is responsible travel to natural areas that conserves the environment and sustains the well-being of local people'.

In the UK, the phrase green travel is sometimes preferred.

Eco-tourism activities: Activities included in a tour that are designed to entertain clients and are coordinated by a professional guide or interpreter. Over 80 activities have been listed for eco-tourism, such as birdwatching, hiking, diving, kayaking, participating in cultural events, photography, and mountaineering.

Eco-tourism product: A combination of resources, activities, and services, which are sold and managed through professional tour operators.

Eco-tourism resources: Natural and cultural features that attract visitors, such as landscapes, endemic or rare flora and fauna, cultural festivals, and historical monuments.

Eco-tourism services: Tourism services such as transportation, food, lodging, guiding and interpretation services which cause minimal damage to the biological and cultural environments and promote a better understanding of the natural and cultural history of an area.

Endangered species: Species of plants or animals threatened with extinction because their numbers have declined to a critical level as a result of overharvesting or because their habitat has drastically changed. That critical level is the minimum viable population (MVP), and represents the smallest number of breeding pairs required to maintain the viability of species.

Endemism: The level of species that occur naturally only in a specific region or site.

Environment: A combination of the various physical and biological elements that affect the life of an organism. Although it is common to refer to 'the' environment, there are in fact many environments eg, aquatic or terrestrial, microscopic to global, all capable of change in time and place, but all intimately linked and in combination constituting the whole earth/atmosphere system.

Environmentally-sound: The maintenance of a healthy environment and the protection of life-sustaining ecological processes. It is based on thorough knowledge and requires or will result in products, manufacturing processes, developments, etc. which are in harmony with essential ecological processes and human health.

Escort: A person, usually employed by a tour operator, who accompanies a tour from departure to return as a guide or troubleshooter; or a person who performs such functions only at the destination. The terms host-escort or host are often used, and are preferred, to describe this service.

Escorted Tour: A pre-arranged travel programe, usually for a group, with host service. Fully escorted tours also may use local guide services.

Fair trade: Equitable, non-exploitative trade between developing world suppliers and Western consumers.

Familiarization Tour ("Fam Tour"): A complimentary or reduced-rate travel program for travel agents, airline and rail employees, or other travel buyers, designed to acquaint participants with specific destinations and to stimulate the sale of travel. Familiarization tours are sometimes offered to journalists as research trips for the purpose of cultivating media coverage of specific travel products.

First Nations: A collective term for the original, pre-European inhabitants of the US, Canada, Hawaii, Australia and New Zealand. In individual countries, different terms are sometimes used, for example, Aboriginal, indigenous, tribal, Indian, First Peoples, Native American, AmerIndian.

Foreign Independent Travel or Foreign Individual Travel (FIT): An international pre-paid, unescorted tour that includes several travel elements such as accommodations, rental cars and sightseeing. A FIT operator specializes in preparing FITs documents at the request of retail travel agents. FITs usually receive travel vouchers to present to on-site services as verification of pre-payment.

Geotourism: Focuses on preserving a destination's geographic "character"-the combination of natural and human attributes that make one place distinct from another. Geotourism encompasses cultural and environmental concerns, as well as the local impact tourism has upon communities and their individual economies and lifestyles.

Green travel: A UK alternative to the American term ecotourism.

Ground Operator: A company that provides local travel services, including transportation or guide services.

Historic Property: A site with qualities that make it significant in history, architecture, archaeology, engineering or culture; sometimes more specifically a site that is eligible for or listed on the National Register of Historic Places, or on a local or state register of significant sites.

Hostel: An inexpensive, supervised lodging, particularly used by young people or elders.

Hotel Package: A sales device offered by a hotel, sometimes consisting of no more than a room and breakfast; sometimes, especially at resort hotels, consisting of ground transportation, room, meals, sports facilities and other components.

Incentive Tour: A trip offered as a prize, usually by a company, to stimulate employee sales or productivity.

Independent traveller: Someone who travels without booking a package tour.

Indigenous people: The original inhabitants of a country and their descendants. Indigenous communities are often, but not always, tribal peoples and the two terms are often and easily confused. See also First Nations, Aboriginal.

Local communities/people: People living in tourist destinations, especially in the rural developing world.

National conservation strategies: Plans that highlight country-level environmental priorities and opportunities for sustainable management of natural resources, following the example of the World Conservation Strategy published by the World Conservation Union (IUCN) in 1980. Though governments may support preparation for the strategies, they are not bound to follow IUCN's recommendations.

Native Americans: A collective term for the indigenous people of the Americas. Also First Nations, AmerIndians, American Indians, Indians.

Net Rate: Price of goods to be marked up for eventual resale to the consumer.

NGO: Non-governmental organisation: an independent pressure group or campaigning organisation, usually non-profit.

Package Tour: Saleable travel products offering an inclusive price with elements that would otherwise be purchased separately. Usually has a pre-determined price, length of time and features but can also offer options for separate purchase.

Packager: Anyone organizing a tour including prepaid transportation and travel services, usually to more than one destination.

Person-trip: The research term for one person taking one trip of 100 or more miles, one-way, away from home.

Preservation: The conservation of the qualities and materials that make historic buildings, sites, structures, objects and districts significant. Approaches to preservation include stabilization, restoration, rehabilitation, and reconstruction.

Proper resource pricing: The pricing of natural resources at levels which reflect their combined economic and environmental values.

Pro-poor tourism: Tourism that benefits poor people in developing-world tourist destinations

Rack Rate: The official cost posted by a hotel, attraction or rental car, but usually not used by tour operators.

Receptive Operator: A tour operator or travel agent specializing in services for incoming visitors, such as meeting them at the airport and facilitating their transfer to lodging facilities.

Responsible tourism: Tourism that aims to avoid harmful impacts on people and environments. Sometimes referred to as ethical tourism. Other similar concepts include People First Tourism, reality tourism, etc.

Retail Agency: Travel company selling directly to the public, sometimes a subdivision of a wholesale and/or retail travel organization.

Stakeholders: Individuals who have a vested interest in development, including community members; environmental, social, and community NGOs; natural resource, planning, and government officials; hotel owners, tour operators, guides, transportation providers, and representatives from other related services in the private sector.

Supplier: The producer of a unit of travel merchandise, such as a carrier, hotel, sightseeing operator, or cultural organization.

Sustainable development: Sustainable development has as many definitions as subscribers. In essence, it refers to economic development that meets the needs of all without leaving future generations with fewer natural resources than those we enjoy today. It is widely accepted that achieving sustainable development requires balance between three dimensions of complementary change:

- Economic (towards sustainable patterns of production and consumption)
- Ecological (towards maintenance and restoration of healthy ecosystems)
- Social (towards poverty eradication and sustainable livelihoods)

Sustainable Tourism: The primary concern of sustainable tourism is to support balance within the ecological environment and minimize the impact upon it by mass-market tourism. The use of this term is evolving as it is also used to describe the impact of mass-tourism on cultural and historic resources.

Technical Visit: Tour designed for a special interest groups, usually to visit a place of business with a common interest. The tour usually includes part business/part leisure and is customized for the group.

Third World, the: Now generally referred to as either developing countries or *the South*.

Tour Leader: A person with special qualifications to conduct a particular travel group, such as a botanist who conducts a garden tour.

Tour Operator: A company that creates and/or markets inclusive tours and/or performs tour services.

Tour: Any prearranged (but not necessarily prepaid) journey to one or more places.

Tourists: Holiday-makers, mainly (but no longer exclusively) from the West. The term is sometimes used to distinguish package tourists from independent travellers, but can be used to mean anyone going on holiday.

Transnational corporation: Correctly, a large company with shareholders in more than one country. The term is often used more loosely to mean any large, powerful, Western-owned company.

Tribal peoples: People living in close-knit social units based on kinship ties and shared belief systems. While most remaining tribal communities are indigenous, not all indigenous peoples still live tribally. (On the other hand, for example, many 'hill-tribes' in northern Thailand migrated there fairly recently from southern China, making them tribal but not indigenous to Thailand.)

Vouchers: Documents issued by a tour operator to be exchanged for accommodations, meals, sightseeing, admission tickets, etc.

West, the: The world's rich nations: ie Western Europe, the

US, Canada, Australia, New Zealand and (economically, although perhaps not culturally) Japan. Also referred to as the , the .

Wholesaler: A company that creates and markets inclusive tours and FITS for sale through travel agents. Company usually sells nothing at retail, and does not always create his/her own product. Company also is less likely to perform local services.

World Commission on Environment and Development: Established by the United Nations General Assembly in 1983 to examine international and global environmental problems and to propose strategies for sustainable development. Chaired by Norwegian Prime Minister Gro Harlem Brundtland, the independent commission held meetings and public hearing around the world and submitted a report on its inquiry to the General Assembly in 1987.

World Summit on Sustainable Development (WSSD): The World Summit on Sustainable Development takes place from 26 August - 4 September 2002 in Johannesburg, South Africa. Governments, UN agencies, and civil society organisations will come together to assess progress since the UN Conference on Environment and Development held in Rio in 1992 (hence the title 'Rio + 10' for the Johannesburg meeting). Sustainable development is defined in the report from the Rio meeting as being 'economic progress which meets all of our needs without leaving future generations with fewer resources than those we enjoy'.

World Tourism Organisation (WTO): A UN-affiliated organisation based in Madrid and comprising government and industry representatives, that compiles statistics and guidelines and promotes global tourism.

World Travel and Tourism Council (WTTC): An organisation based in Brussels and London and made up of the chief executives of the world's largest travel companies, that lobbies on behalf of the tourism industry.

Chapter 1

Global Code of Ethics for Tourism and Travellers

GLOBAL CODE OF ETHICS FOR TOURISM

- That it had provided at its Istanbul session in 1997 for the formation of a Special Committee for the preparation of the Global Code of Ethics for Tourism and that this Committee met at Cracow, Poland on 7 October 1998, in conjunction with the Quality Support Committee meeting, in order to consider an outline of the said Code.

- That based on these initial considerations, the draft Global Code of Ethics for Tourism was prepared by the Secretary-General, with the assistance of the Legal Adviser to WTO and was studied by the WTO Business Council, the Regional Commissions and finally by the Executive Council at its sixtieth session, all of which were invited to formulate their observations.

- That the WTO Members were invited to communicate in writing the remarks or suggestions that they could not make at those meetings.

- That the principle of a Global Code of Ethics for Tourism aroused great interest among the delegations that participated in the seventh session of the Commission on Sustainable Development (CSD) in New York in April 1999.

- That after the CSD session, additional consultations were undertaken by the Secretary-General with institutions representative of the tourism industry and the workers, as well as with various non-governmental organisations interested in this process.

- That, as a result of these discussions and consultations, many written contributions were received by the Secretary-General, which have so far as possible been reflected in the draft submitted to the Assembly for consideration.

Reaffirming that the aim of the Global Code of Ethics for Tourism is to establish a synthesis of the various documents, codes and declarations of the same kind or with comparable aspirations published over the years, to complement them with new considerations reflecting the development of our societies and thus to serve as a frame of reference for the stakeholders in world tourism at the dawn of the next century and millennium, adopts the Global Code of Ethics for Tourism, which reads as follows:

Preamble

World Tourism Organisation (WTO) representatives of the world tourism industry, delegates of States, territories, enterprises, institutions and bodies that are), gathered for the General Assembly at Santiago, Chile on this first day of October 1999.

Reasserting the aims set out in Article 3 of the Statutes of the World Tourism Organisation, and aware of the "decisive and central" role of this Organisation, as recognized by the General Assembly of the United Nations, in promoting and developing tourism with a view to contributing to economic development, international understanding, peace, prosperity and universal respect for, and observance of, human rights and fundamental freedoms for all without distinction as to race, sex, language or religion.

Firmly believing that, through the direct, spontaneous and non-mediatized contacts it engenders between men and women of different cultures and lifestyles, tourism represents a vital force for peace and a factor of friendship and understanding among the peoples of the world.

In keeping with the rationale of reconciling environmental protection, economic development and the fight against poverty in a sustainable manner, as formulated by the United Nations in 1992 at the "Earth Summit" of Rio de Janeiro and expressed in Agenda 21, adopted on that occasion.

Taking into account the swift and continued growth, both past and foreseeable, of the tourism activity, whether for leisure, business, culture, religious or health purposes, and its powerful effects, both positive and negative, on the environment, the economy and the society of both generating and receiving countries, on local communities and indigenous peoples, as well as on international relations and trade.

Aiming to promote responsible, sustainable and universally accessible tourism in the framework of the right of all persons to use their free time for leisure pursuits or travel with respect for the choices of society of all peoples. But convinced that the world tourism industry as a whole has much to gain by operating in an environment that favours the market economy, private enterprise and free trade and that serves to optimize its beneficial effects on the creation of wealth and employment.

Also firmly convinced that, provided a number of principles and a certain number of rules are observed, responsible and sustainable tourism is by no means incompatible with the growing liberalization of the conditions governing trade in services and under whose aegis the enterprises of this sector operate and that it is possible to reconcile in this sector economy and ecology, environment and development, openness to international trade and protection of social and cultural identities.

Considering that, with such an approach, all the stake-holders in tourism development—national, regional and local administrations, enterprises, business associations, workers in the sector, non-governmental organisations and bodies of all kinds belonging to the tourism industry, as well as host communities, the media and the tourists themselves, have different albeit interdependent responsibilities in the individual and societal development of tourism and that the formulation of their individual rights and duties will contribute to meeting this aim.

Committed, in keeping with the aims pursued by the World Tourism Organisation itself since adopting resolution 364(XII) at its General Assembly of 1997 (Istanbul), to promote a genuine partnership between the public and private stakeholders in tourism development, and wishing to see a partnership and cooperation of the same kind extend, in an open and balanced way, to the relations between generating and receiving countries and their respective tourism industries.

Following up on the Manila Declarations of 1980 on World Tourism and of 1997 on the Social Impact of Tourism, as well as on the Tourism Bill of Rights and the Tourist Code adopted at Sofia in 1985 under the aegis of WTO. But believing that these instruments should be complemented by a set of interdependent principles for their interpretation and application on which the stakeholders in tourism development should model their conduct at the dawn of the twenty-first century.

Using, for the purposes of this instrument, the definitions and classifications applicable to travel, and especially the concepts of "visitor", "tourist" and "tourism", as adopted by the Ottawa International Conference, held from 24 to 28 June 1991 and approved, in 1993, by the United Nations Statistical Commission at its twenty-seventh session.

Referring in particular to the following instruments:

- Universal Declaration of Human Rights of 10 December 1948;
- International Covenant on Economic, Social and Cultural Rights of 16 December 1966;
- International Covenant on Civil and Political Rights of 16 December 1966;
- Warsaw Convention on Air Transport of 12 October 1929;

- Chicago Convention on International Civil Aviation of 7 December 1944, and the Tokyo, The Hague and Montreal Conventions in relation thereto;
- Convention on Customs Facilities for Tourism of 4 July 1954 and related Protocol;
- Convention concerning the Protection of the World Cultural and Natural Heritage of 23 November 1972;
- Manila Declaration on World Tourism of 10 October 1980;
- Resolution of the Sixth General Assembly of WTO (Sofia) adopting the Tourism Bill of Rights and Tourist Code of 26 September 1985;
- Convention on the Rights of the Child of 26 January 1990;
- Resolution of the Ninth General Assembly of WTO (Buenos Aires) concerning in particular travel facilitation and the safety and security of tourists of 4 October 1991;
- Rio Declaration on the Environment and Development of 13 June 1992;
- General Agreement on Trade in Services of 15 April 1994;
- Convention on Biodiversity of 6 January 1995;
- Resolution of the Eleventh General Assembly of WTO (Cairo) on the prevention of organized sex tourism of 22 October 1995;
- Stockholm Declaration of 28 August 1996 against the Commercial Sexual Exploitation of Children;
- Manila Declaration on the Social Impact of Tourism of 22 May 1997; and
- Conventions and recommendations adopted by the International Labour Organisation in the area of collective conventions, prohibition of forced labour and child labour, defence of the rights of indigenous peoples, and equal treatment and non-discrimination in the work place; affirm the right to tourism and the freedom of

tourist movements, state our wish to promote an equitable, responsible and sustainable world tourism order, whose benefits will be shared by all sectors of society in the context of an open and liberalized international economy, and solemnly adopt to these ends the principles of the Global Code of Ethics for Tourism.

Principles

Article 1: Tourism's contribution to mutual understanding and respect between peoples and societies

1. The understanding and promotion of the ethical values common to humanity, with an attitude of tolerance and respect for the diversity of religious, philosophical and moral beliefs, are both the foundation and the consequence of responsible tourism; stakeholders in tourism development and tourists themselves should observe the social and cultural traditions and practices of all peoples, including those of minorities and indigenous peoples and to recognize their worth.

2. Tourism activities should be conducted in harmony with the attributes and traditions of the host regions and countries and in respect for their laws, practices and customs.

3. The host communities, on the one hand, and local professionals, on the other, should acquaint themselves with and respect the tourists who visit them and find out about their lifestyles, tastes and expectations; the education and training imparted to professionals contribute to a hospitable welcome.

4. It is the task of the public authorities to provide protection for tourists and visitors and their belongings; they must pay particular attention to the safety of foreign tourists owing to the particular vulnerability they may have; they should facilitate the introduction of specific means of information, prevention, security,

insurance and assistance consistent with their needs; any attacks, assaults, kidnappings or threats against tourists or workers in the tourism industry, as well as the willful destruction of tourism facilities or of elements of cultural or natural heritage should be severely condemned and punished in accordance with their respective national laws.

5. When travelling, tourists and visitors should not commit any criminal act or any act considered criminal by the laws of the country visited and abstain from any conduct felt to be offensive or injurious by the local populations, or likely to damage the local environment; they should refrain from all trafficking in illicit drugs, arms, antiques, protected species and products and substances that are dangerous or prohibited by national regulations.

6. Tourists and visitors have the responsibility to acquaint themselves, even before their departure, with the characteristics of the countries they are preparing to visit; they must be aware of the health and security risks inherent in any travel outside their usual environment and behave in such a way as to minimize those risks.

Article 2: Tourism as a vehicle for individual and collective fulfillment

1. Tourism, the activity most frequently associated with rest and relaxation, sport and access to culture and nature, should be planned and practised as a privileged means of individual and collective fulfilment; when practised with a sufficiently open mind, it is an irreplaceable factor of self-education, mutual tolerance and for learning about the legitimate differences between peoples and cultures and their diversity.

2. Tourism activities should respect the equality of men and women; they should promote human rights and, more particularly, the individual rights of the most vulnerable groups, notably children, the elderly, the

handicapped, ethnic minorities and indigenous peoples.

3. The exploitation of human beings in any form, particularly sexual, especially when applied to children, conflicts with the fundamental aims of tourism and is the negation of tourism; as such, in accordance with international law, it should be energetically combated with the cooperation of all the States concerned and penalized without concession by the national legislation of both the countries visited and the countries of the perpetrators of these acts, even when they are carried out abroad.

4. Travel for purposes of religion, health, education and cultural or linguistic exchanges are particularly beneficial forms of tourism, which deserve encouragement.

5. The introduction into curricula of education about the value of tourist exchanges, their economic, social and cultural benefits, and also their risks, should be encouraged.

Article 3: Tourism, a factor of sustainable development

1. All the stakeholders in tourism development should safeguard the natural environment with a view to achieving sound, continuous and sustainable economic growth geared to satisfying equitably the needs and aspirations of present and future generations.

2. All forms of tourism development that are conducive to saving rare and precious resources, in particular water and energy, as well as avoiding so far as possible waste production, should be given priority and encouraged by national, regional and local public authorities.

3. The staggering in time and space of tourist and visitor flows, particularly those resulting from paid leave and school holidays, and a more even distribution of holidays should be sought so as to reduce the pressure of tourism activity on the environment and enhance its

beneficial impact on the tourism industry and the local economy.

4. Tourism infrastructure should be designed and tourism activities programmed in such a way as to protect the natural heritage composed of eco-systems and bio-diversity and to preserve endangered species of wildlife; the stakeholders in tourism development, and especially professionals, should agree to the imposition of limitations or constraints on their activities when these are exercised in particularly sensitive areas: desert, polar or high mountain regions, coastal areas, tropical forests or wetlands, propitious to the creation of nature reserves or protected areas.

5. Nature tourism and eco-tourism are recognized as being particularly conducive to enriching and enhancing the standing of tourism, provided they respect the natural heritage and local populations and are in keeping with the carrying capacity of the sites.

Article 4: Tourism, a user of the cultural heritage of mankind and a contributor to its enhancement

1. Tourism resources belong to the common heritage of mankind; the communities in whose territories they are situated have particular rights and obligations to them.

2. Tourism policies and activities should be conducted with respect for the artistic, archaeological and cultural heritage, which they should protect and pass on to future generations; particular care should be devoted to preserving and upgrading monuments, shrines and museums as well as archaeological and historic sites which must be widely open to tourist visits; encouragement should be given to public access to privately-owned cultural property and monuments, with respect for the rights of their owners, as well as to religious buildings, without prejudice to normal needs of worship.

3. Financial resources derived from visits to cultural sites

and monuments should, at least in part, be used for the upkeep, safeguard, development and embellishment of this heritage.

4. Tourism activity should be planned in such a way as to allow traditional cultural products, crafts and folklore to survive and flourish, rather than causing them to degenerate and become standardized.

Article 5: Tourism, a beneficial activity for host countries and communities

1. Local populations should be associated with tourism activities and share equitably in the economic, social and cultural benefits they generate, and particularly in the creation of direct and indirect jobs resulting from them.

2. Tourism policies should be applied in such a way as to help to raise the standard of living of the populations of the regions visited and meet their needs; the planning and architectural approach to and operation of tourism resorts and accommodation should aim to integrate them, to the extent possible, in the local economic and social fabric; where skills are equal, priority should be given to local manpower.

3. Special attention should be paid to the specific problems of coastal areas and island territories and to vulnerable rural or mountain regions, for which tourism often represents a rare opportunity for development in the face of the decline of traditional economic activities.

4. Tourism professionals, particularly investors, governed by the regulations laid down by the public authorities, should carry out studies of the impact of their development projects on the environment and natural surroundings; they should also deliver, with the greatest transparency and objectivity, information on their future programmes and their foreseeable repercussions and foster dialogue on their contents with the populations concerned.

Article 6: Obligations of stakeholders in tourism development

1. Tourism professionals have an obligation to provide tourists with objective and honest information on their places of destination and on the conditions of travel, hospitality and stays; they should ensure that the contractual clauses proposed to their customers are readily understandable as to the nature, price and quality of the services they commit themselves to providing and the financial compensation payable by them in the event of a unilateral breach of contract on their part.

2. Tourism professionals, insofar as it depends on them, should show concern, in co-operation with the public authorities, for the security and safety, accident prevention, health protection and food safety of those who seek their services; likewise, they should ensure the existence of suitable systems of insurance and assistance; they should accept the reporting obligations prescribed by national regulations and pay fair compensation in the event of failure to observe their contractual obligations.

3. Tourism professionals, so far as this depends on them, should contribute to the cultural and spiritual fulfilment of tourists and allow them, during their travels, to practise their religions.

4. The public authorities of the generating States and the host countries, in cooperation with the professionals concerned and their associations, should ensure that the necessary mechanisms are in place for the repatriation of tourists in the event of the bankruptcy of the enterprise that organized their travel.

5. Governments have the right—and the duty—especially in a crisis, to inform their nationals of the difficult circumstances, or even the dangers they may encounter during their travels abroad; it is their responsibility however to issue such information without prejudicing in an unjustified or exaggerated manner the tourism

industry of the host countries and the interests of their own operators; the contents of travel advisories should therefore be discussed beforehand with the authorities of the host countries and the professionals concerned; recommendations formulated should be strictly proportionate to the gravity of the situations encountered and confined to the geographical areas where the insecurity has arisen; such advisories should be qualified or cancelled as soon as a return to normality permits.

6. The press, and particularly the specialized travel press and the other media, including modern means of electronic communication, should issue honest and balanced information on events and situations that could influence the flow of tourists; they should also provide accurate and reliable information to the consumers of tourism services; the new communication and electronic commerce technologies should also be developed and used for this purpose; as is the case for the media, they should not in any way promote sex tourism.

Article 7: Right to tourism

1. The prospect of direct and personal access to the discovery and enjoyment of the planet's resources constitutes a right equally open to all the world's inhabitants; the increasingly extensive participation in national and international tourism should be regarded as one of the best possible expressions of the sustained growth of free time, and obstacles should not be placed in its way.

2. The universal right to tourism must be regarded as the corollary of the right to rest and leisure, including reasonable limitation of working hours and periodic holidays with pay, guaranteed by Article 24 of the Universal Declaration of Human Rights and Article 7.d of the International Covenant on Economic, Social and Cultural Rights.

3. Social tourism, and in particular associative tourism, which facilitates widespread access to leisure, travel and holidays, should be developed with the support of the public authorities.

4. Family, youth, student and senior tourism and tourism for people with disabilities, should be encouraged and facilitated.

Article 8: Liberty of tourist movements

1. Tourists and visitors should benefit, in compliance with international law and national legislation, from the liberty to move within their countries and from one State to another, in accordance with Article 13 of the Universal Declaration of Human Rights; they should have access to places of transit and stay a.id to tourism and cultural sites without being subject to excessive formalities or discrimination.

2. Tourists and visitors should have access to all available forms of communication, internal or external; they should benefit from prompt and easy access to local administrative, legal and health services; they should be free to contact the consular representatives of their countries of origin in compliance with the diplomatic conventions in force.

3. Tourists and visitors should benefit from the same rights as the citizens of the country visited concerning the confidentiality of the personal data and information concerning them, especially when these are stored electronically.

4. Administrative procedures relating to border crossings whether they fall within the competence of States or result from international agreements, such as visas or health and customs formalities, should be adapted, so far as possible, so as to facilitate to the maximum freedom of travel and widespread access to international tourism; agreements between groups of countries to harmonize and simplify these procedures should be

encouraged; specific taxes and levies penalizing the tourism industry and undermining its competitiveness should be gradually phased out or corrected.

5. So far as the economic situation of the countries from which they come permits, travellers should have access to allowances of convertible currencies needed for their travels.

Article 9: Rights of the workers and entrepreneurs in the tourism industry

1. The fundamental rights of salaried and self-employed workers in the tourism industry and related activities, should be guaranteed under the supervision of the national and local administrations, both of their States of origin and of the host countries with particular care, given the specific constraints linked in particular to the seasonality of their activity, the global dimension of their industry and the flexibility often required of them by the nature of their work.

2. Salaried and self-employed workers in the tourism industry and related activities have the right and the duty to acquire appropriate initial and continuous training; they should be given adequate social protection; job insecurity should be limited so far as possible; and a specific status, with particular regard to their social welfare, should be offered to seasonal workers in the sector.

3. Any natural or legal person, provided he, she or it has the necessary abilities and skills, should be entitled to develop a professional activity in the field of tourism under existing national laws; entrepreneurs and investors—especially in the area of small and medium-sized enterprises—should be entitled to free access to the tourism sector with a minimum of legal or administrative restrictions.

4. Exchanges of experience offered to executives and workers, whether salaried or not, from different

countries, contributes to foster the development of the world tourism industry; these movements should be facilitated so far as possible in compliance with the applicable national laws and international conventions.

5. As an irreplaceable factor of solidarity in the development and dynamic growth of international exchanges, multinational enterprises of the tourism industry should not exploit the dominant positions they sometimes occupy; they should avoid becoming the vehicles of cultural and social models artificially imposed on the host communities; in exchange for their freedom to invest and trade which should be fully recognized, they should involve themselves in local development, avoiding, by the excessive repatriation of their profits or their induced imports, a reduction of their contribution to the economies in which they are established.

6. Partnership and the establishment of balanced relations between enterprises of generating and receiving countries contribute to the sustainable development of tourism and an equitable distribution of the benefits of its growth.

Article 10

1. Implementation of the principles of the Global Code of Ethics for Tourism:

   (*a*) The public and private stakeholders in tourism development should cooperate in the implementation of these principles and monitor their effective application.

   (*b*) The stakeholders in tourism development should recognize the role of international institutions, among which the World Tourism Organisation ranks first, and non-governmental organisations with competence in the field of tourism promotion and development, the protection of human rights, the environment or health, with due respect for the general principles of international law.

(*c*) The same stakeholders should demonstrate their intention to refer any disputes concerning the application or interpretation of the Global Code of Ethics for Tourism for conciliation to an impartial third body known as the World Committee on Tourism Ethics.

2. Calls upon the stakeholders in tourism development— national, regional and local tourism administrations, tourism enterprises, business associations, workers in the sector and tourism bodies—the host communities and the tourists themselves to model their conduct on the principles embodied in this Global Code of Ethics for Tourism and to implement them in good faith in accordance with the provisions set out below.

3. Decides that the procedures for implementing the principles embodied in the Code will, where necessary, be subject to guidelines for application, prepared by the World Committee on Tourism Ethics, submitted to the Executive Council of WTO, adopted by the General Assembly and periodically reviewed and adjusted in the same conditions.

Recommends:

(*a*) States Members or non-members of WTO, without being obliged to do so, to accept expressly the principles embodied in the Global Code of Ethics for Tourism and to use them as a basis when establishing their national laws and regulations and to inform accordingly the World Committee on Tourism Ethics, whose creation is provided for in Article 10 of the Code and organized in paragraph 6 below.

(*b*) tourism enterprises and bodies, whether WTO Affiliate Members or not, and their associations to include the relevant provisions of the Code in their contractual instruments or to make specific reference to them in their own codes of conduct or professional rules and to report on them to the World Committee on Tourism Ethics.

5. Invites the Members of WTO to actively implement the recommendations it has previously expressed during previous sessions in the fields covered by this Code, so far as the sustainable development of tourism, the prevention of organized sex tourism, as well as travel facilitation and the safety and security of tourists are concerned.

6. Subscribes to the principle of a Protocol for implementing the Global Code of Ethics for Tourism as annexed to this resolution and adopts the guiding principles on which it is based:

   ■ Creation of a flexible follow-up and evaluation mechanism with a view to ensuring the constant adjustment of the Code to the developments of world tourism and, more broadly, to the changing conditions of international relations.

   ■ The making available to States and other stakeholders in tourism development of a conciliation mechanism to which they may have recourse by consensus of on a voluntary basis.

7. Invites the Full Members of the Organisation and all the stakeholders in tourism development to submit their additional remarks and proposed amendments to the draft Protocol of Implementation annexed to this resolution within a period of six months, so as to allow the Executive Council to study, in due time, the amendments to be made to this text and requests the Secretary-General to report back to it on this point at its fourteenth session.

8. Decides to start the process of appointing the Members of the World Committee on Tourism Ethics, so that its composition may be completed at the fourteenth session of the General Assembly.

9. Urges the States Members of WTO to publish and make known as widely as possible the Global Code of Ethics for Tourism, in particular by disseminating it among all the stakeholders in tourism development and inviting them to give it broad publicity.

10. Entrusts the Secretary-General with approaching the Secretariat of the United Nations in order to study how it might be associated with this Code, or even in what form it could endorse it, in particular as part of the process of implementing the recommendations of the recent CSVC session

Protocol of Implementation

Body responsible for interpreting, applying and evaluating the provisions of the Global Code of Ethics for Tourism:

(a) A World Committee on Tourism Ethics shall be created comprising twelve eminent persons independent of governments and twelve alternates, selected on the basis of their competence in the field of tourism and related fields; they shall not receive any orders or instructions from those who proposed their nomination or who designated them and shall not report to them;

(b) The members of the World Committee on Tourism Ethics shall be appointed as follows:

- Six members and six alternate members designated by the WTO Regional Commissions, on the proposal of the States Members of WTO.

- A member and an alternate designated by the autonomous territories that are Associate Members of WTO from among their members;—four members and four alternate members elected by the WTO General Assembly from among the Affiliate Members of WTO representing professionals or employees of the tourism industry, universities and non-governmental organisations, after conferring with the Committee of Affiliate Members.

- A chairman, who may be an eminent person not belonging to WTO, elected by the other members of the Committee, on the proposal of the Secretary-General of WTO.

The Legal Adviser of the World Tourism Organisation shall participate, when necessary, and in an advisory capacity, in the Committee meetings; the Secretary-General shall attend *ex officio* or may arrange to be represented at its meetings;

On appointing the members of the Committee, account shall be taken of the need for a balanced geographical composition of this body and for a diversification of the qualifications and personal status of its members, from both the economic and social as well as the legal viewpoint; the members shall be appointed for four years and their term of office may be renewed only once; in the event of a vacancy, the member shall be replaced by his alternate, it being understood that if the vacancy concerns both the member and his alternate, the Committee itself shall fill the vacant seat; if the Chairman's seat is vacant he or she shall be replaced in the conditions set out above.

(c) The WTO Regional Commissions shall act, in the cases provided for in paragraphs I(*d*), (*g*) and (*h*), as well as II(*a*), (*b*), (*f*) and (*g*) below of this Protocol, as regional committees on tourism ethics.

(d) The World Committee on Tourism Ethics shall establish its own Rules of Procedure, which shall apply equally, mutatis mutandis, to the Regional Commissions when these are acting as regional committees on tourism ethics; the presence of two-thirds of the Committee members shall be necessary to constitute a quorum at its meetings; in the event that a member is absent, he may be replaced by his alternate; in the event of a tie in the voting, the chairman shall have the casting vote.

(e) When proposing the candidature of an eminent person to serve on the Committee, each Member of WTO shall undertake to cover the travel expenses and daily subsistence allowances occasioned by the participation in the meetings of the person whose nomination it has proposed, it being understood that the members of the

Committee shall not receive any remuneration; the expenses incurred by the participation of the Chairman of the Committee, also unremunerated, may be borne by the WTO budget; the secretariat of the Committee shall be provided by the services of WTO; the operating costs remaining payable by the Organisation may, wholly or in part, be charged to a trust fund financed by voluntary contributions.

(f) The World Committee on Tourism Ethics shall meet in principle once a year; whenever a dispute is referred to it for settlement, the chairman shall consult the other members and the Secretary-General of WTO about the expediency of convening an extraordinary meeting.

(g) The functions of the World Committee on Tourism Ethics and the WTO Regional Commissions shall be the evaluation of the implementation of this Code and conciliation; it may invite experts or external institutions to contribute to its proceedings.

(h) On the basis of periodic reports submitted to them by Full Members, Associate Members and Affiliate Members of WTO, the WTO Regional Commissions shall, every two years, as regional committees on tourism ethics, examine the application of the Code in their respective regions; they shall record their findings in a report to the World Committee on Tourism Ethics; the reports of the Regional Commissions may contain suggestions to amend or supplement the Global Code of Ethics for Tourism.

(i) The World Committee on Tourism Ethics shall exercise a global function as a "watchdog" for the problems encountered in implementing the Code and for the proposed solutions; it shall summarize the reports drawn up by the Regional Commissions and supplement them with the information it has collected with the assistance of the Secretary-General and the support of the Committee of Affiliate Members, which shall include, should the need arise, proposals to amend or supplement the Global Code of Ethics for Tourism.

(j) The Secretary-General shall refer the report of the World Committee on Tourism Ethics to the Executive Council, together with his own observations, for consideration and transmission to the General Assembly with the Council's recommendations; the General Assembly shall decide what follow-up action to take on the report and the recommendations thus submitted to it, which the national tourism administrations and other stakeholders in the tourism development shall subsequently have the task of implementing.

* * *

Conciliation mechanism for the settlement of disputes

(a) In the event of a dispute concerning the interpretation or application of the Global Code of Ethics for Tourism, two or more stakeholders in tourism development may jointly refer it to the World Committee on Tourism Ethics; if the dispute is between two or more stakeholders belonging to the same region, the Parties should refer the matter to the competent WTO Regional Commission in its capacity as a regional committee on tourism ethics.

(b) The States, as well as tourism enterprises and bodies, may declare that they accept in advance the competence of the World Committee on Tourism Ethics or of a WTO Regional Commission for any dispute concerning the interpretation or application of this Code, or for certain categories of dispute; in this case, the Committee or the competent Regional Commission shall be considered as validly referred to unilaterally by the other Party to the dispute.

(c) When a dispute is submitted in the first instance to the World Committee on Tourism Ethics for consideration, its chairman shall appoint a sub-committee of three members who shall be responsible for examining the dispute.

(d) The World Committee on Tourism Ethics to which a

dispute has been referred shall reach a decision on the basis of the record drawn up by the Parties to the dispute; the Committee may ask these Parties for additional information and, if deemed useful, may hear them at their request; the expenses incurred by this hearing shall be borne by the Parties unless the circumstances are considered exceptional by the Committee; the failure of one of the Parties to appear even though he or she has been given a reasonable opportunity to participate, shall not prevent the Committee from making a ruling.

(e) Unless otherwise agreed by the Parties, the World Committee on Tourism Ethics shall announce its decision within three months of the date on which it was referred to; it shall present recommendations to the Parties suitable to form the basis of a settlement; the Parties shall immediately inform the chairman of the Committee that has examined the dispute of the action they have taken on these recommendations.

(f) If a dispute is referred to a WTO Regional Commission, it shall announce its decision following the same procedure, mutatis mutandis, as that applied by the World Committee on Tourism Ethics when it intervenes in the first instance.

(g) If within a period of two months after notification of the proposals of the Committee or of a Regional Commission the Parties have failed to agree on the terms of a final settlement, the Parties or one of them may refer the dispute to a plenary session of the World Committee on Tourism Ethics; when the Committee has made a ruling in the first instance, the members that served on the sub-committee that examined the dispute may not take part in this plenary session and shall be replaced by their alternates; if these intervened in the first instance, the members shall not be prevented from participating.

(h) The plenary session of the World Committee on

Tourism Ethics shall make its ruling following the procedure laid out in paragraphs II(*d*) and (*e*) above; if no solution has been found at a previous stage, it shall formulate final conclusions for the settlement of the dispute, which the Parties, if they agree with their contents, will be recommended to apply at the earliest possible opportunity; these conclusions shall be made public, even if the process of conciliation has not been successfully completed and one of the Parties refuses to accept the final conclusions proposed.

(*i*) Full Members, Associate Members and Affiliate Members of WTO, as well as States that are not members of WTO, may declare that they accept in advance as binding and, where applicable, subject to the sole reservation of reciprocity, the final conclusions of the World Committee on Tourism Ethics in the disputes, or in a private dispute to which they are party.

(*j*) Likewise, the States may accept as binding or subject to exequatur the final conclusions of the World Committee on Tourism Ethics in disputes to which their nationals are party or which should be applied in their territory.

(*k*) Tourism enterprises and bodies may include in their contractual documents a provision making the final conclusions of the World Committee on Tourism Ethics binding in their relations with their contracting parties.

CODE OF ETHICS FOR TRAVELLERS: A MODEL GUIDELINE

Last Fronties for Responsible Tourism in Lating America

1. Travel in a spirit of humility and with a genuine desire to learn more about the people of your host country. Be sensitively aware of the feelings of other people, thus preventing what might be offensive behaviour on your part.

2. Cultivate the habit of listening and observing rather than merely hearing and seeing.

3. Realise that often the people in the country you visit have time concepts and thought patterns different from your own. This does not make them inferior, only different.

4. Acquaint yourself with local customs. What is courteous in one country may be quite the reverse in another— people will be happy to help you.

5. Instead of the western practice of 'knowing all the answers', cultivate the habit of asking questions.

6. Do not make promises to people in your host country unless you can carry them through.

7. Remember that you are only one of thousands of tourists visiting this country and do not expect special privileges.

8. If you really want your experience to be a 'home away from home', it is foolish to waste money on travelling.

9. Spend time reflecting on your daily experience in an attempt to deepen your understanding.

Specifically:

- Always ask permission before photographing people.
- When you are shopping, remember that the bargain you obtained may only be possible because of the low wages paid to the maker.
- Understand that there can be no guarantees when it comes to wildlife, all sightings are a bonus.
- Ensure that your behaviour has no impact on the wildlife you so enjoy and remember that picking flowers, removing seeds and buying souvenirs such as shells and skins can only cause harm in the long run.
- Conservation begins with keeping an eye on your own consumption of such base necessities as water and energy.

Chapter 2

Sustainable Tourism: Global Charter, State of Affairs and Implementation

CHARTER FOR SUSTAINABLE TOURISM

Tourism is a worldwide pheonomenon and also an important element of socio-economic and political development in many countries, and that tourism touches the highest and deepest aspirations of all people.

Recognizing that tourism, as an ambivalent pheonomenon, since it has the potential to contribute positively to socio-economic and cultural achievement, while at the same time it can contribute to the degradation of the environment and the loss of local identity, should be approached with a global methodology. Mindful that the resources on which tourism is based are fragile and that there is a growing demand for improved environmental quality.

Recognizing that tourism can afford the opportunity to travel and to get to know other cultures, and that the development of tourism can help promote closer ties and peace among peoples, creating a conscience that is respectful of the diversity of culture and life styles. Guided by the principles set forth in the Rio Declaration on the Environment and Development and the recommendations that emanate from Agenda 21. Recalling declarations in the matter of tourism, such as the Manila Declaration on World Tourism, the Hague Declaration and the Tourism Charter and Tourist Code.

Recognizing the objective of developing a tourism that meets economic expectations and environmental requirements, and respects not only the social and physical structure of the location, but also the local population.

Taking into account the priority of protecting and reinforcing the human dignity of both local communities and visitors.

Mindful of the need to establish effective alliances among the principal actors in the field of tourism so as to build the hope of a tourism that is more responsible towards our common heritage.

URGE governments, other public authorities, decision-makers and professionals in the field of tourism, public and private associations and institutions whose activities are related to tourism, and tourists themselves, to adopt the principles and objectives of the Declaration that follows:

1. Tourism Development shall be based on criteria of sustainability, which means that it must be ecologically bearable in the long term, as well as economically viable, and ethically and socially equitable for local communities. Sustainable development is a guided process which envisages global management of resources so as to ensure their viability, thus enabling our natural and cultural capital, including protected areas, to be preserved. As a powerful instrument of development, tourism can and should participate actively in the sustainable development strategy. A requirement of sound management of tourism is that the sustainability of the resources on which it depends must be guaranteed.

2. Tourism has to contribute to sustainable development and its integration with the natural, cultural and human environment; it must respect the fragile balances that characterize many tourist destinations, in particular small islands and environmentally sensitive areas. Tourism should ensure an acceptable solution as regards the influence of tourism activity on natural

resources, biodiversity and the capability for assimilation of any impacts and residues produced.

3. Tourism must consider its effects on the cultural heritage and traditional elements, activities and dynamics of each local community. Recognition of these local factors and support for the identity, culture and interests of the local community must at all times play a central role in the formulations of tourism strategies, particularly in developing countries.

4. The active contribution of tourism to sustainable development necessarily presupposes the solidarity, mutual respect, and participation of all the actors, both public and private, implicated in the process, and must be based on efficient cooperation mechanisms at all levels: local, national, regional and international.

5. The conservation, protection and appreciation of the worth of our natural and cultural heritage afford a privileged area for cooperation. This approach implies that all those responsible must take upon themselves a true challenge, that of cultural, technological and professional innovation, and must also undertake a major effort to create and implement integrated planning and management instruments.

6. Quality criteria both for the preservation of the tourist destination and for the capacity to satisfy tourists, determined jointly with local communities and informed by the principles of sustainable development, should represent priority objectives in the formulation of tourism strategies and projects.

7. To participate in sustainable development, tourism must be based on the diversity of opportunities offered by the local economy. It should be fully integrated into and contribute positively to local economic development.

8. All options for tourism development must serve effectively to improve the quality of life of all people and must entail a positive effect and inter-relation as regards sociocultural identity.

9. Governments and the competent authorities, with the participation of NGOs and local communities, shall undertake actions aimed at integrating the planning of tourism as a contribution to sustainable development.

10. In recognition of economic and social cohesion among the peoples of the world as a fundamental principle of sustainable development, it is urgent that measures be promoted to permit a more equitable distribution of the benefits and burdens of tourism. This implies a change of consumption patterns and the introduction of pricing methods which allow environmental costs to be internalized. Governments and multilateral organisations are called upon to reorient aid related to tourism, particularly aid which leads to negative effects on the environment. Within this context, it is necessary to explore thoroughly the application of internationally harmonised economic, legal and fiscal instruments to ensure the sustainable use of resources in tourism.

11. Environmentally and culturally vulnerable spaces, both now and in the future, should be given special priority in the matter of technical cooperation and financial aid for sustainable tourism development. Similarly, special treatment should be given to zones that have been degraded by obsolete and high impact tourism models.

12. The promotion of alternative forms of tourism that are comparible with the principles of sustainable development, together with the encouragement of diversification, participate in medium-and long-term sustainability. In this respect there is a need for many small islands and environmentally sensitive areas in particular, to actively pursue and strengthen regional cooperation.

13. Governments, industry, authorities, and tourism-related NGOs should promote and participate in the creation of open networks for research, dissemination of information and transfer of appropriate tourism and environmental knowledge on tourism and environmentally sustainable technologies.

14. The establishment of a sustainable tourism policy necessarily requires the support and promotion of environmentally-compatible tourism management systems, feasibility studies for the transformation of the sector, as well as the implementation of demonstration projects and the development of international cooperation programmes.

15. Bodies, particularly associations and NGOs whose activities are related to tourism, shall draw up specific frameworks for positive and preventive actions for sustainable tourism development and establish programmes to support the implementation of such practices. They shall monitor achievements, report on results and exchange their experiences.

16. Particular attention should be paid to the role and the environmental repercussions of transport in tourism, and to the development of economic instruments designed to reduce the use of non-renewable energy and to encourage recycling and minimization of residues in resorts.

17. The adoption and implementation of codes of conduct conducive to sustainability by the principal actors involved in tourism, particularly industry, are fundamental if tourism is to be sustainable. Such codes can be effective instruments for the development of responsible tourism activities.

18. All necessary measures should be implemented in order to sensitize and inform all parties involved in the tourism industry, at local, regional, national and international level, with regard to the contents and objectives of the Lanzarote Conference.

Final Resolution

1. The Conference recommends State and regional governments to draw up urgently plans of action for sustainable development applied to tourism, in consonance with the principles set out in this Charter.

2. The Conference agrees to refer the Charter for Sustainable Tourism to the Secretary-General of the United Nations, so that it may be taken up by the bodies and agencies of the United Nations system, as well as by international organisations which have cooperation agreements with the United Nations, for submission to the General Assembly.

SUSTAINABLE TOURISM—STATE OF AFFAIRS

Introduction

There are a myriad of definitions for Sustainable Tourism, including eco-tourism, green travel, environmentally and culturally responsible tourism, fair trade and ethical travel. The most widely accepted definition is that of the World Tourism Organisation. They define sustainable tourism as *"tourism which leads to management of all resources in such a way that economic, social and aesthetic needs can be fulfilled while maintaining cultural integrity, essential ecological processes, biological diversity and life support systems."* In addition they describe the development of sustainable tourism as a process which meets the needs of present tourists and host communities whilst protecting and enhancing needs in the future (World Tourism Organisation 1996). Tourism is one of the world's largest industries. For developing countries it is also one of the biggest income generators. But the huge infrastructural and resource demands of tourism (*e.g.* water consumption, waste generation and energy use) can have severe impacts upon local communities and the environment if it is not properly managed. To reach this current state, we have witnessed an exponential growth in global tourism over the past half century. 25 million international visitors in 1950 grew to an estimated 650 million people by the year 2000 (Roe *et al.* 1997). Several factors have contributed to this rise in consumer demand in recent decades. This includes an increase in the standard of living in the developed countries, greater allowances for holiday entitlements and declining costs of travel. Tourism is an important export for a large number of developing countries, and the principal export for about a third of these. Statistics for domestic tourism are not so easily available. However it is certain that domestic tourism is also growing rapidly in many Asian and Latin American countries (Goodwin 2000).

World Travel and Tourism Council (WTTC) estimates show that in 2002 travel, tourism and related activities will contribute 11 per cent to the world's GDP, rising to 12 per cent by 2010. The industry is currently estimated to generate 1 in every 12.8 jobs or 7.8 per cent of the total workforce. This percentage is expected to rise to 8.6 per cent by 2012. Tourism is also the world's largest employer, accounting for more than 255 million jobs, or 10.7 per cent of the global labour force (WTTC 2002).

It is clear that eco-tourism, in the strictest sense of the word, still only accounts for a small proportion of the total tourism market. Current estimates are between 3-7 per cent of the market (WTTC, WTO, Earth Council 1996). Taking the WTO's full definition of tourism, there's a risk that eco-tourism alone will fail to fully realise the potential to support more sustainable development across the entire sector—suggesting that there may be real benefits trying to make all of the Travel and Tourism industry more sustainable.

Current Global and Regional Trends

Tourism and Travel Statistics and Trends

The magnitude of the tourism industry can be clearly seen from the World Travel and Tourism Council (WTTC) statistics. The WTTC estimates that in the year 2002, travel, tourism and related activities will contribute to approximately 10 per cent of the world's GDP, growing to 10.6 per cent by 2012. The industry is currently estimated to help generate 1 in every 12.8 jobs, 7.8 per cent of total employment. This will rise to 8.6 per cent by 2012 (WTTC 2002).

Tourism has helped to create millions of jobs in developing countries. For example official estimates for 2002 suggest China has 51.1 million jobs associated to tourism and India 23.7 million jobs. In terms of the relative importance of different sectors for job creation, the largest contributors in travel and tourism employment are found in island states and destinations—ranging from 76.3 per cent of the total number of people employed in Curacao, to 34.6 per cent employment in Antigua and Barbuda. The top ten countries with greatest expected relative growth in employment over the next ten years are all developing countries. Vanuatu is predicted an annual growth rate of 8.8 per cent in employment and tops the list. The balance of benefits begins to tilt toward the developed countries in terms of visitor exports and capital investments, in absolute terms. The top ten list for visitor exports is led by the US. The rest are all European countries, except for China (at number 7). On capital investments, US receives an estimated investment of US\$ 205.2 million—far ahead of all other countries. Japan with an investment of US\$ 42.7 million and China with US\$ 42.5 million follow. The expected growth rates for capital investments over the next ten years are significant for developing countries. Turkey has an annualised growth rate of 10.4 per cent (WTTC 2002). Whilst it can be argued that tourism creates an incentive for environmental conservation, tourism is also responsible for damage to the environment. The phenomenal growth of the sector has been accompanied by severe environmental and cultural damage. The projected growth for the industry frequently occurs in destinations that are close to or have exceeded their natural carrying-capacity limits. The consequences are that short term economic gain clearly incurs long term environmental and social costs (European Parliament 2002). Beyond these environmental aspects, other issues of a more social, cultural and rights-based nature have gained increased attention since the mid-1990's. These include financial leakages, disruptive impacts to local livelihoods and culture, gender bias, sexual exploitation, formal vs. informal sector, domestic vs. international tourism, the growth of "all-inclusive" package tours. Some of the key issues and challenges related to these problems are outlined in the sections below.

Table 1: Global and Regional Trends in Tourism

Global	<ul><li>*Distribution*—Tourism is a significant sector in almost half of the low income countries, and in virtually all the lower-middle income countries.</li><li>*Destinations*—The top 15 tourism destinations in the developing world (in terms of absolute numbers of arrivals or receipts) tend to be populous, low-middle income and upper middle-income countries. 5 out of these 15 destinations have a population of over 10 million living below a $ a day.</li><li>*Employment*—World-wide forecasts predict a growth in tourism employment of over 100 million jobs by 2007. Global tourism already accounts for over 250 million jobs.</li><li>*Growth*—tourism contributed to an aggregate economic growth of over 50 per cent between 1990 and 1997</li><li>*Pro-poor tourism*—In most countries with high levels of poverty, tourism is a significant contributing factor, providing over 2 per cent of GDP or 5 per cent of exports). Some 12 countries account for 80 per cent of the world's poor (living on less than a dollar a day). In 11 of these countries, each with over 10 million poor people, tourism is significant addition to the economy and this contribution is growing</li></ul>
Africa	**Central and S. Africa** <ul><li>*Economic contribution*—Travel & Tourism contribution is significantly lower for this region than for world averages (GDP 6.2 per cent as compared to 10 per cent globally). But expected growth is actually significantly higher than the world average (a predicted annual growth rate of 5.6 per cent GDP as compared to world average of 4 per cent)</li></ul>**N Africa and Middle East** <ul><li>*Economic contribution*—Economic statistics are comparable to world statistics. Cultural tourism is an important sector. Evidence suggests that in practice eco-tourism can fail to help local people *e.g.* tourism around the Maasai Mara generates approx. $18 million a year but little appears to reach local people</li><li>*Biodiversity*—there are 5 internationally recognised 'biodiversity' hotspots (areas of particularly high species richness and under threat) in this region. These areas are important attractions for tourists and valuable as a source of foreign exchange, but are increasingly under pressure from tourism, leading to environmental degradation & resource depletion.</li></ul>

- *Notable successes*—tourism is largely responsible for saving the mountain gorillas of Rwanda from extinction and protecting their forest habitat.
- *Lack of infrastructure and poverty*—are preventing potential local opportunities to gain from tourism and support for livelihoods.
- *Political insecurity*—has a direct impact on tourism levels in some countries because of the possible risks involved in visiting those areas.
- Water shortages for local people occur as a result of excessive water use by hotel developments.
- *Coastal zone*—there is currently little regulation of coastal development to prevent excessive impacts to environmental and local communities.

- *General statistics*—Current growth rates in relative terms tend to be lower than world average. With a very large population, the scenario in absolute terms is different however. Domestic and regional tourism are significant and growing in importance. Both mass and alternative tourism have grown in past & despite economic down-turns and currency fluctuations, continue to grow.

SE Asia

- *Economic contribution*—Some 21 million people are employed in tourism, its economic impact is expected to grow by 80 per cent in next decade
- *Coasts and seas*—In coastal and marine areas, tourism pressures (along with increasing urbanisation, industrialization etc) have contributed to the degradation of coastal areas, reduced water quality and increased pressures on marine resources
- Tourism pressures, industrialisation and urbanisation—are resulting in critical depletion of coastal resources.
- *Coral reefs*—More than half the world's coral reefs are located in the Pacific Island countries, and large areas are already degraded. Tourism and recreation activities are one factor that leads to this degradation *e.g.* unsafe diving activities, tourism development.
- *'Ethical tourism'*—is a growing sector. Tourists and tour companies are staying away from countries like Burma (Myanmar is the military Junta's new name for the country) where torture, human rights abuses, forced labour on tourism projects, and mass disruption for local communities from tourism developments occur.

Asia & the Pacific

- *Waste*—Litter and discarded waste in popular sites like Himalayas (Mt Everest) has been a major problem for a number of years. Parts of the Himalayas recently underwent a clean-up campaign which has been a major suc cess for the area.

N. America & W. Europe

- *Economic contribution*—In absolute terms the contribution of Travel and Tourism activities to these regions is very important. For instance, North America and EU together account for 68 per cent of the total amount of personal travel and tourism, 74 per cent of business travel, 61 per cent of visitor exports, 69 per cent of other travel and tourism related exports and 64 per cent of capital investments.
- *Trans-national companies*—Companies in the region dominate the international tourism market. However, domestic and regional tourism are important segments of the market and growing.
- *Coastal zone*—Areas along the Mediterranean coast are facing major environmental pressures (*i.e.* nitrogen loading) through a combination of urban growth, inadequate waste water treatment, tourism and intensively farmed crops. Linear coastal ribbon development in places like Cyprus is now acknowledged to have been the wrong development model.
- *Land degradation*—Degradation of land is associated with tourism development and industrialization
- *Protected areas*—e.g. US National forests and parks are set aside to maintain wildlife habitat and often serve dual tourism and recreation purposes but these require active tourism management/visitor impact management *e.g.* Yosemite.

Central Asia & E. Europe

- *Economic contribution*—Contribution to GDP is significantly lower for the region than globally. Employment statistics are comparable. Growth projections are better than world averages.
- *Coastal zone*—85 per cent of European coasts are at high or moderate risk from development-related pressures. Two thirds of Europe's tourism is centred on coastlines. In 1990 the Med. coast had 35 million tourists and is expected to receive 235-353 million tourists annually by 2025.
- Growing tourist trade in Arctic (over 1.5 million visitors in 2000) is prompting fears of environmental degradation.

Latin America & Caribbean

- Economic contribution—Statistics for current situation and for expected growth tend to be significantly higher than world average. For instance GDP contribution is estimated at 14 per cent (10 per cent globally). In several individual countries travel and tourism is a very important sector of the economy, the key catalyst for growth.
- Protected areas—More than 10 per cent of region is currently protected and the creation of private/community-managed forests are on the increase.
  Also there have been isolated successes in curbing the illegal trade in endangered species. Tourism has been linked to providing a financial incentive to maintain these areas and species.
- Urbanisation—Nearly 75 per cent of the population lives in urban areas. Urbanisation is expected to reach 85 per cent by 2025.
- Child sex tourism—There are growing concerns about tourism related paedophilic activities in several countries of the region

Sources: UNEP 2002, WTTC 1998, Ashley *et al.* 2001, Roe, *et al.* 1997.

Issues: Progress and Challenges

Tourism and the Environment

The natural environment is an important resource for tourism. With increasing urbanisation, destinations in both industrialised and developing countries with significant natural features, scenery, cultural heritage or biodiversity are becoming increasingly popular sites for tourist destinations. Efforts to preserve and enhance the natural environment should therefore be a high priority for the industry and for governments. But the reality is not quite as clear cut. Environments where past human interaction has been minimal are often fragile. Small islands, coastal areas, wetlands, mountains and deserts, all now popular as tourist destinations, are five of the six 'fragile eco-systems' as identified by Agenda 21 that require specific action by governments and international donors. The biophysical characteristics of these habitats often render them particularly susceptible to damage from human activities. As the scale of tourism grows, the resource use threatens to become unsustainable. With a degraded physical environment, the destination is in danger of losing its original attraction, increasing the levels of cheaper mass tourism and forcing more "nature-based" tourism to move on to new destinations, which are likely to be even more inaccessible and fragile. Mainstream "eco-tourism", as promoted after the Rio Earth Summit, hasn't always enjoyed a good reputation. Tour operators have used the concept merely as a "greenwash" marketing tool. In reality it often meant introducing unsustainable levels of tourism into fragile areas, having scant regard for either the environment or for the residents of the destination areas. As the International Council for Local Environmental Initiatives (ICLEI) pointed out:

"Tourism in natural areas, euphemistically called "eco-tourism," can be a major source of degradation of local ecological, economic and social systems. The intrusion of large numbers of foreigners with high-consumption and high-waste habits into natural areas, or into towns with inadequate waste management infrastructure, can produce changes to those natural areas at a rate that is far greater than imposed by local residents. These tourism-related changes are particularly deleterious when local residents rely on those natural areas for their sustenance. Resulting economic losses can encourage socially deleterious economic activities such as prostitution, crime, and migrant and child labour" (ICLEI 1999).

Some of the different kinds of impacts that tourism development and operational activities can have include:

- Threats to eco-systems and biodiversity—*e.g.* loss of wildlife and rare species, habitat loss and degradation,
- Disruption of coasts—*e.g.* shoreline erosion and pollution, impact to coral reefs and fish spawning grounds,

- Deforestation—loss of forests for fuel wood and timber by the tourist industry also impact on soil and water quality, bio-diversity integrity, reducing the collection of forest products by local communities,

- Water overuse—as a result of tourism/recreational activities *e.g.* golf courses, swimming pools, and tourist consumption in hotels,

- Urban problems—Congestion and overcrowding, increased vehicle traffic and resultant environmental impacts, including air and noise pollution, and health impacts,

- Exacerbate climate change—from fossil fuel energy consumption for travel, hotel and recreational requirements, and

- Unsustainable and inequitable resource use—Energy and water over consumption, excessive production of wastes, litter and garbage are all common impacts.

Further study could be carried out regarding the negative relationship between tourism and environment (Roe *et al.* 1997), however the many examples across the globe indicate this scenario is quite typical and widely recognised, emphasising the need to identify more mutually beneficial approaches in tourism development.

Tourism and Economics

Economic gains have been a major driving force for the growth of tourism in developing countries. The initial period of growth happened in the late 1960's and 1970's, when tourism was perceived as a key activity for generating foreign exchange and employment by both development institutions, such as the World Bank, as well as by governments (Goodwin 2000). Despite the negative economic impacts of tourism (such as inflation; dominance by outsiders in land and property markets; inward-migration eroding economic opportunities for domestic industry including the poor) the demand for travel and tourism continues to grow. The WTTC has estimated there was an approximate 40 per cent cumulative growth in tourism demand between 1990 and 2000. This demand was largely driven by economic gains at all levels, including in the communities in remote, and hitherto relatively isolated, destinations (Ashley, 2000). There is significant scope for enhancing the possible gains through addressing a number of issues that can help improve opportunities for entrepreneurs and the communities in the destinations, for the poorer sections within these communities, as well as at the macro level for the national economy. Some of these are options are discussed below.

Financial Leakages

Powerful trans-national corporations (TNCs) continue to dominate the international tourism market. Estimates suggest that about 80 per cent of international mass tourism is controlled by TNCs. These companies have an almost unhindered access to markets and use this to drive down the cost of supplies. The result is high levels of financial leakage, and limited levels of revenue retention in the destination or host countries. Financial leakages tend to occur due to various factors, including importation of foreign building material, skilled labour and luxury products, and packaged travel arranged with TNCs. This is as opposed to locally sourcing the necessary resources. It has been estimated that, on average, at least 55 per cent of tourism expenditure flows back out of the destination country, rising to 75 per cent in certain cases *e.g.* the Gambia and Commonwealth Caribbean (Ashley *et al.* 2000).

During the seventh UN Commission on Sustainable Development (CSD) meeting (1999), financial leakages was identified as a key area for stakeholders to take action and work together in order to try and assess the situation, as well as seek solutions to better support local communities in host/developing countries. The CSD called upon the UN and the World Tourism Organisation, in consultation with major groups, as well as other relevant international organisations, to jointly facilitate the establishment of an ad-hoc informal open-ended working group on tourism to:

ess financial leakages and determine how to
kimize benefits for indigenous and local
nmunities.

■ repare a joint initiative to improve information
availability and capacity-building for participation, and
address other matters relevant to the implementation
of the international work programme on sustainable
tourism development (UNCSD 1999).

Impacts on Livelihoods in Destination Communities

In most tourist destinations of developing countries, the
livelihood impacts of tourism, takes various forms. Jobs and
wages are only a part of livelihood gains and often not the most
significant ones. Tourism can generate four different types of
local cash income, involving four distinct categories of people:

■ Wages from formal employment.

■ Earnings from selling goods, services, or casual labour
(*e.g.* food, crafts, building materials, guide services).

■ Dividends and profits arising from locally-owned
enterprises.

■ Collective income: this may include profits from a
community-run enterprise, dividends from a private
sector partnership and land rental paid by an investor.

Waged employment can be sufficient to lift a household
from an insecure to a secure footing, but it may only be available
to a minority of people, and not the poor. Casual earnings may
be very small, but more widely spread, and may be enough,
for instance, to cover school fees for one or more children. Local
participation in the industry can be categorised into three
different categories; the formal sector (such as hotels), the
informal sector (such as vending) and secondary enterprises
that are linked to tourism (such as food retail and
telecommunications). Experience from Asia suggests that:

■ As a destination is developing, accommodation for

tourists can be as simple as offering home stays at the early stage, with lodges, guest houses and hotels replacing more basic options as tourism grows, and some of these may include foreign companies. Once luxury resorts start to develop, the scenario becomes more complex with international investors beginning to play a much more dominant role.

- Transport tends to fall into a grey area between formal and informal sectors. Most destinations have taxis, jeeps or other motorised forms of transport, often driven by the owners. As things expand organised associations of owners, operating on a rota system become more common.

- Data about employment in the formal sector is scattered and collection is often not very systematic. There are references of cases where high-status jobs in resorts typically go to non-locals, expatriate staff or foreign-trained nationals. However, there is almost no analysis of who is employed in middle and lower ranking jobs. The potential for employment of local staff seems to improve as one moves away from the luxury resorts into less established areas.

- The informal sector includes activities such as vending, running stalls and collecting fuel wood for the tourist industry. The informal sector often provides an easy entry into the industry for the poor, especially for women. The incomes can be substantial but unreliable as it is often a seasonal activity. However it can still provide a substantial boost to the income of the poor.

- The informal sector tends to get the least attention when interventions are planned, and interventions such as planning permissions are frequently detrimental to this sector. However, there are cases where initiatives such as flexible licensing systems and cooperatives and associations have helped the sector.

- Causal labour and self-employment provide major

opportunities for local communities to enhance their livelihood opportunities from tourism. Unlike formal employment, self-employment tends to highlight the entrepreneurial spirit of village communities. Villagers are used to stringing together a livelihood from a diverse variety of sources, often giving them a knack for enterprise. Causal labour includes porters, cooks, guides, launderers, cleaners, caterer and entertainers. Nepal, for instance, has a well organised labour market to employ porters, cooks and guides on a seasonal basis. An estimate made in 1989 showed that trekking alone generated 0.5 to 1 million person days of employment in a year in Nepal.

- Significant gains also accrue from economic linkages between tourism and other economic sectors such as agriculture, horticulture, animal husbandry and handicrafts. (Shah & Gupta 2000)

There continues to be fairly poor quantitative data available regarding the economic gains that can be generated from travel and tourism, particularly data that quantifies the impacts to formal, informal and indirect activities as touched upon above. There is a need for a standardised framework and guidelines for the collection and analysis of comparative data sets, to better identify the possible economic impacts for different segments of the market, as well as to develop policies which better reflect the needs of the informal as well as formal tourism ventures. Another gap in research about tourism relates to understanding how domestic tourism benefits formal and informal segments in a country and the degree to which the extreme poor gain at all from the industry (Ashley 2000):

- Domestic or regional tourists are particularly important clients for self-employed sellers and owners of -small establishments (the skilled poor and not-so-poor). Studies in Yogyakarta (Indonesia) and elsewhere in South East Asia show that domestic and other Asian tourists tend to buy more from local vendors than

Western tourists (Shah, 2000).

- Budget and independent tourists, particularly backpackers are also more likely than luxury tourists to use the cheaper guest houses, home-stays, transport and eating services provided by local people. They tend to stay longer at a destination than groups of tourists and interact more with the local economy, but also spend less per day, often bargaining over prices.

- Nature-based tourism (including 'eco-tourism') does not necessarily provide more opportunities for the poor than 'mass tourism'. Nature tourism does offer some potential advantages however. It takes place in less developed areas, often involves smaller operators with more local commitment. It involves a higher proportion of independent travellers, and if marketed as 'eco-tourism' can stimulate consumer pressure for ensuring domestic socio-economic benefits. But it remains a niche in the market, can be heavily dependent on imports, and can spread disruption to less developed areas.

- Mass tourism is highly competitive, and usually dominated by large suppliers who have little commitment to a destination. They are less likely to use local suppliers. However the segment does generate jobs and negative impacts are not always spread beyond immediate localities. Further knowledge is needed about how local economic opportunities can be expanded under such circumstances, as well as to identify how the negative impacts can be minimised in the mass tourism segment.

- Cruises and 'all-inclusives' are rapidly growing segments of the market, but by their nature are unlikely to generate few economic linkages. Some governments are trying to actively reduce this, for example the Gambian Government has recently decided to ban 'all-inclusives' in response to local demands.

- The informal sector is where opportunities for small-scale enterprise or labour by the poor are maximised. For example, at Bai Chay, Ha Long Bay in Vietnam, almost a dozen local families run private hotels, but local involvement in tourism spreads far beyond this, to an estimated 70–80 per cent of the population. Apart from those with jobs in the hotels and restaurants, local women share the running of noodle stalls, many women and children are walking vendors, and anyone with a boat or motorbike hires them out to tourists. However, the informal sector is often neglected by planners.

Tourism and Society/Culture

Tourism developments often stop people from having the right of access to land, water and natural resources. NGO's such as Tourism Concern and Rethinking Tourism have reported on examples worldwide where the articles in the UN Declaration of Human Rights are flouted, and where indigenous rights are lost or exploited. Adverse social impacts also include poor working conditions, low wages, child labour and sex tourism. The International Labour Organisation and International Confederation Free Trade Unions (ICFTU) note that some parts of the tourist industry still degrades labour and drives workers to the lowest levels, exhibiting the worst side of unsustainable production.

Cultural Transformation

Fears of tourism threatening local cultures can be misplaced and many cultures have proved resilient enough to be able to take rapid changes required by tourism in their stride. However it is true that popular destinations are typically transformed at a very rapid pace. Buzzing small towns can replace sleepy one lane bazaars. Areas where once only officials rode in motorised vehicles become a familiar site for traffic jams, and dealing with unknown faces can become a daily occurrence for people whose previous focus had been confined to a few score square kilometres to their home and work.

Communities visited by tourists can (or have to!) adapt surprisingly quickly. For example, they rapidly adopt business-like attitudes to maximise profits. They are creative in inventing and staging events to entertain and provide information on their culture. These attractions, while usually not explicitly developed to protect back regions (*i.e.* areas of a host society reserved only for local residents, where tourists are not welcome), can function to deflect the tourist gaze from private space and activities. Host communities take specific, active measures to protect their values and customs. This can either be covert action such as private communal functions, fencing off of domesticities but also overt action such as organised protests and even aggression to protect their interests (Harrison and Price 1996). Tourism development in remote areas can be positive however, bringing with it infrastructure, health services and education facilities. It could be a by-product, or a result of increased incomes, or as is happening increasingly, a result of corporate and customer social responsibility. Nevertheless, rapid tourism development can come at a price and often creates its own unique problems. Tourism activities can degrade the social and natural wealth of a community. The intrusion of large numbers of uninformed foreigners into local social systems can undermine pre-existing social relationships and values. This is particularly a problem where tourism business is centred in traditional social systems, such as isolated communities or indigenous peoples (ICLEI 1999). There are also examples in eco-tourism segment, of communities becoming marginalised and forced out of traditional lands as protected areas and destinations become established. Involving host and particularly local communities in all stages of tourism development, from planning right through operations, will help to alleviate some of these issues— if their needs and perspectives are properly taken into account. There is growing amount of work in this area and an expanding body of good practice examples but such approaches need to extended. In addition, programmes which aim to train and assist communities adversely affected by tourism development *i.e.* providing a social safety net need to be openly assessed for their suitability, and promoted where appropriate.

Tourism and Child Prostitution

On the darker side to global tourism, the sex trade and drug tourism remain areas that are poorly reported or regulated, especially where it concerns children. The root causes behind these growing problems may not wholly lie with growth in tourism, but it is significant and should be a real cause for concern throughout the sector. In recent years the industry has started to try and tackle such problems. In 1998 it collaborated with ECPAT (End Child Prostitution and Trafficking in Children for Sexual Purposes) to draw up a Code of Conduct for tour operators in relation to child prostitution and tourism. Signatories to ECPAT's Code of Conduct commit themselves to:

- Working against child exploitation in their policy documents;
- Training staff on how to combat child exploitation;
- Provision of information to customers;
- Putting pressure on suppliers by including a clause against the commercial sexual exploitation of children in the contract (with hotels, for example); and
- Provision of information to key local people and organisations by creating a network in destinations to raise awareness amongst local people.

The Fritidresor Group (FRG), a subsidiary of Thomson Travel Group, has risen to the challenge by following up on this initiative in a systematic manner. Since 1999 it has designed and conducted workshops, developed an elaborate customer information programme and initiated pilot programmes in five destinations where child abuse is common (Brazil, Cuba, Dominican Republic, India and Thailand). Feedback from ECPAT from one of the pilots has been positive, *e.g.* the number of paedophiles in Thailand is decreasing. There are concerns, however, that this is happening at the expense of other countries, especially in Central America, where ECPAT has a weaker presence (Tour Operators Initiatives for Sustainable Tourism Development).

Gender

Gender dis-aggregated data for the tourism sector are not easily available. Using the data for restaurant, catering and hotels as proxy, the Gender and Tourism Report prepared by Stakeholder Forum for the CSD in 1999, reached some tentative conclusions. The general picture suggests that the formal tourism industry seems to be a particularly important sector for women (46 per cent of the workforce are women, compared to 34-40 per cent in other general labour markets). However the proportion of women in the tourism workforce varies greatly—from as low as 2 per cent in some countries and up to over 80 per cent in others, depending upon the maturity of the tourism industry. For example, in countries where there is a mature industry, women generally accounted for around 50 per cent of those employed in the industry. Using data from 39 countries, the proportion of women's working hours compared to men's working hours was 89 per cent. Whilst the proportion of women's wages to men's wages is 79 per cent (based on data available from 31 countries). This suggests that women continue to receive disproportionately lower wages than their male counterparts—often in equivalent positions of status in an organisation. Furthermore the statistics, typically do not include the contribution of women employed in the informal sector. Several studies have indicated, whilst this area is frequently ignored, it also tends to be a significant contributor, particularly in developing countries (Hemmati 1999).

Solutions and Partnerships—Towards Sustainable Tourism

Tourism was only specifically mentioned in a few sections of 1992 Rio Agenda 21, despite its huge economic significance. Agenda 21 for the Travel and Tourism Industry was written in 1996 by the World Trade Organisation, the World Travel and Tourism Council and Earth Council to try and fill this gap. It noted that with a growing standing in the world economy the tourism industry has "a moral responsibility in making the transition to sustainable development. It also has a vested interest in doing so.". The document highlights the vital importance of the environment as the main base upon which the market relies. These and other activities have supported a growing awareness of the positive and negative impacts of tourism, including a growing realisation of the impact that a degrading environment has on the livelihoods of communities living in destination areas. This has contributed towards the initiation of positive actions for mitigating and minimising the more negative aspects. Various different approaches have been explored, especially in the last couple of decades. Emerging from these efforts is a better recognition of the importance of the role of local communities, their valuable knowledge base and understanding of local circumstances, as well as their strong vested interest in preserving a sustainable system. Establishing partnerships with local communities is being increasingly recognised as necessary for sustainable tourism. The trend now is moving towards more integrated approaches, which include communities working with governments. Some broad proposals and responses for moving towards more sustainable tourism, from various stakeholders, are outlined below.

International Institutions, Agreements and Action Plans

International institutions such as UNEP are working in a number of ways (often in partnership) to promote sustainable tourism (Box 1). This includes a proposal by UN Economic and Social Council to the UN General Assembly to designate 2002 the "UN International Year of Eco-tourism". Though facing some controversy regarding the definition and breadth of the term "eco-tourism", the idea was that the year would aim to recognise tourism's potential benefit as both a tool for environmental protection and development. For eco-tourism, it is particularly seen as a means to advance three basic goals of the UN Convention on Biological Diversity:

1. To conserve biological diversity;

2. To promote sustainable use of biodiversity to generate income, jobs and business opportunities in eco-tourism etc.; and

3. To share the benefits of eco-tourism developments equitably with local communities and indigenous peoples).

Other groups like the World Tourism Organisation do work to try and encourage good practice in the sector. For example the World Tourism Organisation has produced a "Global Code of Ethics for Tourism in 1999 (an extension of the WTO "Manila Declaration on the Social Impacts of Tourism" 1997), as well as a "Compilation of good practices in sustainable tourism", and a practical guide for the development and application of indicators of sustainable tourism, "What Tourism Managers Need to Know".

Business Activities and Tourism

The Rio Earth Summit 1992 was a major turning point for the tourism industry. Environmental issues subsequently became an important part of the agenda for the industry. However, the approach has not yet generally been an integrating one. Instead the focus has been on minimising environmental impacts that the industry is directly responsible for. There is growing support by lead companies throughout the private sector to implement principles of Corporate Social Responsibility (CSR), Environmental Management and Auditing Systems (EMAS), "Triple Bottom Line" accounting procedures (Environment, Society and Economics) and Sustainability Reporting. Measures are predominately based on adopting a voluntary approach to tackling impacts rather than having regulations/legislation imposed on business by governments (see Box 2 for some examples).

Box 1: UNEP and Tourism

- UNEP and Eco-tourism Society have produced a guide *Eco-tourism: Principles, Practices and Policies for Sustainability*, highlighting eco-tourism's successes and failures.
- UNEP Partnerships with hotel industry have been developed—*Sowing the Seeds of Change*, is an environmental training pack with good practice examples for hotels, published with the International Hotel and Restaurant Association and International Association of Hotel Schools.
- For tourists, UNEP (in partnership with McCann International and the French Government) has produced *It's My Choice—Coral or no Coral?*, a package of communication tools in 5 languages available free to any company or organisation willing to distribute them.
- UNEP with UNESCO World Heritage Centre and support from the United Nations Foundation is also implementing sustainable tourism components in 6 World Heritage Sites in Mexico, Guatemala, Honduras and Indonesia.
- UNEP Global Programme of Action for the Protection of the Marine Environment from Land-based activities (launched in 1995) was revitalized in 2001. A key aim is reducing untreated sewage discharges, often linked to coastal and tourism development.

UNEP has also produced a set of policy guidelines, including the *Principles for Implementation of Sustainable Tourism*, widely distributed to governments and local authorities and used as inputs to some of the multi-lateral environmental agreements. UNEP's Principles on Implementation of Sustainable Tourism (2000) include:

- *Legislative Framework:* Support implementation of sustainable tourism through an effective legislative framework that establishes standards for land use in tourism development, tourism facilities, management and investment in tourism.
- *Environmental Standards*: Protect the environment by setting clear ambient environmental quality standards, along with targets for reducing pollution from all sectors, including tourism, to achieve these standards, and by preventing development in areas where it would be inappropriate.
- *Regional Standards*: Ensure that tourism and the environment are mutually supportive at a regional level through cooperation and coordination between States, to establish common approaches to incentives, environmental policies, and integrated tourism development planning.

Source: http://www.uneptie.org/pc/tourism/policy/principles.htm

---

Box 2: Business Initiatives

1. International Hotels Environment Initiative (IHEI)—a charity programme developed by the international hotel industry whose aim is to promote the benefits of environmental management as an integral part of running a successful, efficient hotel business. http://www.ihei.org

2. Benchmarkhotel—An online bench marking tool to help hotels measure and improve their environmental performance (joint initiative of IHEI, WWF-UK and Biffa Award). http://www.benchmarkhotel.com

3. Tour Operators' Initiative for Sustainable Tourism Deve lopment— Tour operators are moving towards sustainable tourism by committing themselves to the concepts of sustainable development as the core of their business activity and to work together through common activities to promote and disseminate methods and practices compatible with sustainable development. The Initiative has been developed by tour operators for tour operators with the support of the United Nations Environment Programme (UNEP), the United Nations Educational, Scientific and Cultural Organisation (UNESCO) and the World Tourism Organisation (WTO/OMT), who are also full members of the Initiative. http://www.toinitiative.org

---

The action plan for the industry, "Agenda 21 for the Travel and Tourism Industry: Towards Environmentally Sustainable Development" contains a number of priority areas for action and suggested steps to achieve them. The importance of partnerships between government, industry and NGOs is stressed, along with the enormous benefits that will be obtained by making the tourism industry more sustainable. The document warns the industry not to under-estimate the challenge which requires "fundamental reorientation". However it also makes it clear that the long-term costs of inaction will far outweigh those for starting to act now. Companies are encouraged to set up systems and procedures to incorporate sustainable development issues into core management functions and to identify actions needed to bring sustainable tourism into being. A long-term communications programme was initiated after the document launch to increase awareness and promote regional implementation (WTTC). The 10 priority areas for action are:

- Waste minimization, re-use and recycling,
- Energy efficiency, conservation and management,
- Management of freshwater resources,
- Waste water treatment,
- Hazardous substances,
- Transport,
- Land-use planning and management,
- Involving staff, customers and communities in environmental issues,
- Design for sustainability, and
- Partnerships for sustainability.

Another major voluntary activity highlighted by many companies is the use of codes of conduct and certification (see Box 3). However, even the voluntary codes lag far behind activities for environmental performance in the area of social responsibility (UNED 1999). The World Tourism Organisation recently produced a study "Voluntary Initiatives for Sustainable Tourism" examining 104 schemes worldwide and gives recommendations to improve the conditions for voluntary initiatives and achieve better effectiveness in the operation and support of voluntary initiatives. In addition it gives a checklist for the planning and assessing of your own voluntary initiatives and makes recommendations for eco-labelling. The report states that voluntary practice has not yet had a significant impact on the mass market. The report recognises that "their current impact has been minimal across the sector as a whole". It finds that 78 per cent of tourism certificates focus on tourism within Europe and not further afield. However the report also says that:

> "they are revealing tremendous potential to move the industry towards sustainability, but not without careful nurturing and support from key industry partners" (WTO 2000).

Box 3: Voluntary Codes

A. Pacific Asia Travel Association Traveller's Code: Sustaining Indigenous Cultures

"Travel is a passage through other people's lives and other people's places."

1. Be Flexible. Are you prepared to accept cultures and practices different from your own?
2. Choose Responsibly. Have you elected to support businesses that clearly and actively address the cultural and environmental concerns of the locale you are visiting?
3. Do Your Homework. Have you done any research about the people and places you plan to visit so you may avoid what may innocently offend them or harm their environment?
4. Be Aware. Are you informed of the holidays, holy days, and general religious and social customs of the places you visit?
5. Support Local Enterprise. Have you made a commitment to contribute to the local economy by using businesses that economically support the community you are visiting, eating in local restaurants and buying locally made artisan crafts as remembrances of your trip?
6. Be Respectful and Observant. Are you willing to respect local laws that may include restrictions of your usage of or access to places and things that may harm or otherwise erode the environment or alter or run counter to the places you visit? http://www.pata.org/frame3.cfm?pageid=55

B. Green Globe scheme, Standards and Certification

Pressure to incorporate social and cultural issues as well as environmental considerations within industry-backed initiatives has resulted in a number of initiatives. One example is found in the agenda of GREEN GLOBE 21, an institution created in 1994 specifically for developing capacity for environmental management and awareness within the travel & tourism industry and for maintaining a certification process. Issues such as training and employment of local people and local sourcing of goods and services are being incorporated, though in a very tentative manner. 'Where possible' is a key phrase in some of these requirements. The GREEN GLOBE 21 standard was originally designed for a number of institutions, mostly those directly related to the industry such as hotels, airports, cruise ships and car hire companies. Beaches and natural protected areas had also been included. But now certification for communities has been added, bringing in Cumbria (UK) Jersey (Channel Islands) and Vilamoura (Portugal). More than a dozen other destinations (in both developing and developed countries) are in the process of being certified, as well as two countries, Dominica and Sri Lanka. GREEN GLOBE is therefore a source of information on lessons learned from designing and implementing measures to le ssen the detrimental impacts upon the environment and local communities. http://www.greenglobe21.com/index_cn.html

When it comes to building more mainstream corporate responsibility, the vast majority of tourist companies state that whilst they would like to do something they feel they are unable to do so because of being faced with 'cut throat' business competition. They argue that the costs involved in acting more responsibly would drive them out of the market, especially if they take unilateral action without wider industry support. Industry surveys have identified the need for establishing mandatory regulations, making it compulsory for everyone to meet the same standards and thereby incur similar costs. Legal and fiscal regulation of corporate sector includes market-based tools such as carbon trading, as supported through the Kyoto Protocol of the UN Framework Convention for Climate Change. Also environmental standards legislated by governments on water quality and waste management, labelling standards, are growing but need to be more widely implemented and effectively enforced.

NGOs are increasingly engaging with the travel sector. They have been playing an active role in addressing problems such as financial leakages and in trying to encourage greater corporate responsibility. Key activities involve consumer education about the potential impacts of tourism and about how local communities might benefit more from the industry. They actively lobby policy-makers on associated issues of trade liberalisation, fair trade and globalisation. There has also been a concerted effort to set up common certification standards, independent of the industry, along the lines of Fair Trade certification or eco-labelling. Initiatives include the International Fair Trade in Tourism Network, established by Tourism Concern (London-based) in 1999 and a feasibility study for setting up a Sustainable Tourism Stewardship Council (see Box 4) being conducted by the Rainforest Alliance, New York.

Box 4: The Sustainable Tourism Stewardship Council

The Sustainable Tourism Stewardship Council (STSC) is proposed as a global accreditation body for sustainable tourism and eco-tourism certifiers. If this body is found feasible, it will set international standards for certification of tourism industry organisations that want to claim being sustainable or practicing eco-tourism. The current project will investigate the viability of such body by consulting a wide range of stakeholders.

Why an accreditation body? The STSC will respond to the market demand to have international, comparable standards to identify and purchase sustainable holidays and to minimize false claims. There are over 100 certification schemes in tourism, many of them under-funded and generally not able to reach the international tourism market. Bringing certification schemes with high standards under one umbrella will give them competitive advantage in marketing, planning and managing their schemes; this in turn will benefit the companies they certify. Stewardship councils have been successfully implemented in industries such as forestry, organic farming, fishing and social accountability, acting as a catalyst for sustainable business to business and business to consumer purchasing.

Source: http://www.rainforest-alliance.org/programmes/sv/
stsc.html

Initiatives for Assisting Local Communities to Realise Tourism Opportunities

During the 1990's a number of initiatives emerged which aimed to help communities in destination countries make the most from opportunities provided by tourism. Many have been self initiated, locally and have continued to expand under their own steam, sometimes attracting external technical and/or financial assistance on their own terms. In others, external agents have acted as catalysts. The nature of the activities have been broad, ranging from small one-village initiatives for organising handicrafts production to building powerful networks of small accommodation providers and creating a marketing network for them. Over time, and by learning from experience and sharing knowledge, these initiatives have tended to become more complex and inclusive. Effective multi-stakeholder processes have evolved from the ground.

Backed with success and experience at the ground level and on a significant scale, lessons learnt here have the potential for wide and rapid replication. This also requires support from the international community for creating space and resources to assist the players who have been the active leaders of these processes so far to take the lead in formulating a strategy.

Local Authorities

A World Tourism Organisation report on the role of local authorities noted that local authorities have a key role to play in many aspects of tourism development and operations. As countries becomes more decentralised, they are taking on more in this area and realising that the sector may assist local areas in achieving development. Community involvement is referred to as a key part of this process—ensuring participation in planning and development, therefore increasing the possibility of achieving more local benefits from tourism *e.g.* employment, income, establishing tourism related enterprises.

The report notes that many local authorities lack in experience for planning, nurturing and developing tourism however. This can result in wasted resources and opportunities. The report states that proper planning, efficient implementation and effective management are all essential to optimise the benefits of tourism (WTO 1998).

The statement by the International Council for Local Environmental Initiatives (ICLEI) during the seventh session of the CSD said that *"in addition to their direct roles in the development process, perhaps the most important role that local authorities can play in a global economy is that of facilitator among the diverse interests seeking to influence the direction of local development"*. ICLEI also stated that *"solutions to adverse tourism impacts are to be found in the shared interest of local communities, tourism businesses, and tourism consumers to maintain the natural wealth and social heritage of the tourist destination"*. Thus a major challenge for "sustainable tourism" will be the creation of tangible and working local partnerships. One way to approach this will be through the principles espoused in Local Agenda 21.

These principles should be applied, through partnerships, to evaluate and improve efforts to address sensitive tourism development issues, including:

■ Inequitable distribution of tourism revenues and "financial leakages".

■ Displacement of pre-existing local settlements by tourism developments.

■ Equal access to local coastal and recreational resources.

■ Conflict over use and long-term protection of those areas.

■ Concerns related to lack of foreign tourist sensitivity to cultural traditions and sites.

Governments

It is fairly disappointing to say that many Governments have been slow to take the lead in ensuring the progress of sustainable tourism and much more work could be done by them to engage more pro-actively with this sector than in the past. Further engagement includes action at all levels, from international forums and negotiations, down to development of tourism plans and policy, and the enforcement of key regulation at national and local levels. A study for the European Union made some useful recommendations for governments to take action in support of sustainable tourism (see Box 5). In addition, it recommends production of regional and national tourism strategies, as well as the development and exchange of knowledge through regional networks on sustainable tourism, engaging stakeholders as well as government ministries (European Parliament 2002).

Pro-Poor Tourism (PPT) Strategies

PPT is an approach that gaining recognition by national governments and local authorities. Although PPT is still relatively new and has not been widely applied in practice, existing case studies reveal a number of lessons. These include:

Box 5: National Measures To Encourage Good Environmental Practice In Tourism Destinations

Support Local Agenda 21

- Design national and international investment, and development assistance programmes for local authorities and support locally relevant mechanisms to monitor and evaluate progress.
- National governments should ensure implementation of Local Agenda 21 Plans—through development of national action plans, and provision of resources and expertise. Establish Local Agenda 21 best practice networks—to facilitate knowledge transfer across countries.
- Use strategic environmental assessments and environmental impact assessments. These assessments should be made public, for use by all stakeholders. Maintain the integrity of SEAs and EIAs through impartial and informed entities, such as research institutes and universities.
- Land use planning and development control—The precautionary and polluter pays principles should be applied at local and regional levels. Carrying capacity studies conducted in all tourist destinations prior to further expansion.
- Integrated Coastal Zone Management strategies—Resources should be allocated to programmes for fostering ICZM projects. The release of funds for coastal areas should be dependent up-holding the principles of ICZM.

Promote Tourism in Natural and Cultural Heritage Sites

- Tourism in protected areas and heritage sites—Management plans for each specific area should be given full attention by national governments, and adequate resources and expertise made available to develop competent plans. Projects combining preservation and promotion of cultural heritage sites should be supported, provided that proposals are of a high quality and are based on a sound visitor management plan.
- Rural tourism—Measures should be taken to support development of rural tourism as a key component of sustainable development in rural areas. Rural destinations should be encouraged to adopt the principles of Integrated Quality Management, involving local communities in measures to manage and develop rural products in line with market needs, plus maximizing the proportion of income retained in the community. Loss of biodiversity and cultural heritage

caused by tourism should be offset by resources at the regional level to mitigate habitat fragmentation and maintain and restore the regional landscape.

■ Eco-tourism—Eco-tourism should be encouraged and regulated through use of eco-labels and certification schemes, to guarantee better environmental performance and progress towards sustainable development. If an activity is to be conducted in a designated protected area, then an Environmental Impact Assessment should be undertaken in advance by the responsible agency, and plans amended according to the outcomes of the assessment.

Making Tourism Enterprises More Sustainable

■ Information, training and advice—stimulate and support development of information networks for sustainable tourism. Provide the technological capacity to manage the networks efficiently. Sustainable tourism internet training should be developed for specific industry players.

■ Quality marks and labelling—Research the best ways for evolving product and service certification, through examination of which sectors to target, and of mandatory vs. voluntary certification. Use existing know-how and experience to achieve recognition and acceptance by the sector and consumers. High priority should be given to promoting the image of eco-labels, equating "environmentally friendly" with quality.

■ Financial incentives—Set up a comprehensive enquiry into green taxes for the tourism industry, taking into account both the opportunity for punitive taxes via the polluter pays principle and tax breaks for certified good practice. Greater stakeholder consultation should be conducted to investigate how the industry can access suitable funding schemes. Monitoring of projects should focus on the sustainability criteria built into a project, and ensure compliance of commitment to sustainability.

Raising Public Awareness

■ Stakeholder Participation—Reinforce current increasing environmental awareness with greater stakeholder access to information, though improvements in government educational programmes and the refinement of the availability and content of information services.

Source: Adapted from EU working paper
http://www.europarl.eu. int/toa/publi/pdf/stoa103_en.pdf

- Diverse activities—beyond community tourism it includes product development, marketing, planning, policy, and investment.
- A lead advocate for PPT is useful, but involving other stakeholders is critical. PPT can be incorporated into the tourism development strategies of government or business.
- Location: PPT works best where the wider destination is developing well.
- PPT strategies often involve development of new products, particularly products linked to local culture. These products should be integrated with mainstream markets where possible.
- Ensuring commercial viability is a priority. This requires understanding demand, product quality, marketing, investment in business skills, and involving the private sector.
- Economic measures should expand both formal and casual earning opportunities.
- Non-financial benefits (*e.g.* increased community participation, access to assets) can reduce market vulnerability.
- PPT is a long-term investment. Expectations must be prudent and opportunities for short-term benefits investigated.
- External funding may be necessary to cover substantial transaction costs of establishing partnerships, developing skills, and revising policies (Ashley *et al.* 2001).

Opportunities for Mutual Gain and Partnership

Conserving and Documenting Biodiversity

The scientific community has played a role in promoting conservation and research on biodiversity through tourism. One example is Earthwatch, an organisation that supports scientific research through volunteer tourists and funding. In the UK,

Earthwatch has a programme which sponsors teachers to be volunteers, and as a result has encouraged greater environmental education in schools in the UK. Another example is the Monteverde Cloud Forest Preserve (MCFR) in Costa Rica, a unique case of what private initiative and a spirit of internationalism can do (Box 6).

Box 6: The Monteverde Cloud Forest Preserve

Located high up in the Tilarian Mountains of Costa Rica, the Monteverde Cloud Forest Preserve is climatically influenced by both the Atlantic and the Pacific. The result is a unique bio-sphere with six major eco-zones or microclimates harbouring over 100 species of mammals, 400 bird and 120 reptile species and 2500 plant species. The primary forest cover was still extensive in the 1950s, but the area came under pressure expanding agricultural practices. Around this time a group of Quaker families emigrated from the US, in the search of an "alternative" lifestyle. They bought 1400 ha of land, setting aside 554 hectares as a watershed and dividing the rest amongst themselves for cultivation. A decade later, scientific studies began to attract tourists into the area, coinciding with a growth in the conservation movement. In 1972, a Costa Rican NGO—the Tropical Science Centre—acquired 328 hectares for a reserve in Monteverde. And in 1974 they reached an agreement with the Quakers to manage the watershed area. This was the beginning of the MCFR, which now covers a 100 sq. km area. Visitor numbers have reached 50, 000 a year and over 80 tourist-related businesses, several locally owned, have appeared (Baez 1996).

http://www.monteverdeinfo.com/

Community Based Wildlife Tourism

In Africa, Community Based Wildlife Tourism (CBWT) has succeeded in conserving the environment as well as empowering communities. The principle behind CBWT is simple—the benefits to wildlife must exceed the costs. In reality this is not so straight forward. A number of the caveats and complexities necessary for success have been identified through experiences on the ground:

- The link between tourism resource and wildlife conservation is not always obvious. It has to be emphasised through education, dialogue and negotiations. Financial incentives will be ineffective in the absence of institutions and capacity for sustainable management. Hence, responsibility for wildlife management and institutional capacity should take precedence over the benefits.

- Equitable distribution of local earnings from tourism is critical and they should be widely shared within the community managing tourism resources.
- Even if tourism creates incentives for wildlife conservation, wider impacts on eco-systems or bio-diversity maintenance should also be considered (Ashley 1998).

ICT and Alternative Technologies

The growing use of Information Communication Technology has been cited as a way to cut down on "unnecessary travel", particularly for work-related travel *e.g.* through using video conferencing instead of travelling to meetings all the time (IIIEE 2002). However for recreational tourism, the main focus of this paper, the link is less obvious. There are, however, numerous examples of web-based guides and tools, aiming to support sustainable tourism, that are springing up all over the place, a few of which have been cited in this paper. A recent study, for the Global Information Society International Research Programme, identified a number of ways that ICT can support tourism as well as protection of biodiversity:

- Helping to establish global tourism/biodiversity databases to enable more effective planning and monitoring in an inter-related and comprehensive way,
- Encouraging global exchange of information and expertise among professionals and stakeholders,
- Allowing small operators and others to be included in discussion and to gain greater access to data,
- Encouraging direct dialogue, including that of marketing and promotion, between sites and tourists, and between tourist providers and tourists, and

- Generally improving consumer and operator awareness of impacts and outcomes of tourism (Boniface 2000).

The study indicated that it is the immediacy of ICT, its capacity to retain and distribute information and its flexibility that are some of its strongest benefits. Another is that ICT can assist the creation of new connections and networks between practitioners, operators and tourists across the globe. Such groups are important to help learn and exchange good practice in sustainable tourism.

Alternative technologies are another important area. Organisations which combine alternative technology with "learning by living" holidays are growing in number. They include activities like agro-eco-tourism, which link tourism, education and promoting traditional conservation and sustainable use practices. Tourists are taught new skills for sustainable living, such as organic farming, using alternative renewable energies, through visiting eco-villages, alternative technology centres and traditional communities (ITDG 2002).

Education, Capacity Building and Participation

Education is the key to changing tourist behaviour. Some examples, such as marketing and publicity campaigns by tour operators, have already been cited. Other opportunities also exist, such as learning about sustainability in tourism through job training. These activities should be a shared responsibility between government, private sector operators and trade associations, as well as local tourist organisations, formal training institutions, unions and representative bodies (ICFTU 1999).

The Way Forward—Responsible Tourism

"Responsible tourism is the job of everyone involved—governments, local authorities, the tourist industry and tourists themselves" (UNEP 2001)

Recognising the substantial impacts of tourism yet also its potential to help implementation of Sustainable Development, the CSD addressed sustainable tourism for the first time in 1999. Many of the issues raised are already considered within this paper but a direct result was the designation of 2002 as UN 2002 UN International Year of Eco-tourism (IYE). IYE has not been without its critics (*e.g.* Third World Network, Rethinking Tourism) who expressed real concerns about assuming that Eco-tourism was already a "success", when even the World Bank (who has been supporting eco-tourism for over a decade) suggests that few projects have actually generated substantial income for local communities (Vivanco 2002). The Quebec Declaration on Eco-tourism is expected to become a major point of reference for future discussion about eco-tourism but "much work remains to be done, notably in the fight against poverty" (WTO 2002). Promoting a broader and more inclusive approach towards seeking sustainable tourism development and capacity building will be key. According to UNEP some of the conditions for a successful transition towards sustainable tourism include:

- Involvement of stakeholders: Increase the long-term success of tourism projects by involving key stakeholders in the development and implementation of tourism plans (See table 2).

- Information exchange: Raise awareness of sustainable tourism and its implementation by promoting exchange of information, between governments and stakeholders, on best practice for sustainable tourism, and establishing networks for dialogue on implementation of Sustainable Tourism Principles.

- Promote understanding and awareness: to strengthen attitudes, values and actions compatible with sustainable development.

- Capacity Building: Ensure effective implementation of sustainable tourism, through capacity building programmes to develop and strengthen human resources and institutional capacities in government at national and local levels, and amongst local communities; and to integrate environmental and human ecological considerations at all levels.

Table 2: Stakeholder Roles and Responsibilities

International Institutions	
	■ Assist host communities to manage visitation to their tourism attractions for their maximum financial benefit whilst ensuring the least negative impact on and risks for their traditions, culture and living environment. The World Tourism Organisation and other relevant agencies should facilitate the implementation in their Member States. Provide technical assistance to developing countries and countries with economies in transition to support sustainable tourism business development and investment, tourism awareness programmes to improve domestic tourism, and to stimulate entrepreneurial development. ■ Maintain productivity and biodiversity of important but vulnerable eco-systems through implementation of, and adherence to key Conventions and Agreements. ■ Interagency Coordination and Cooperation: Enhance international co-operation, foreign direct investment and partnerships with both private and public sectors at all levels. Provide investment support for processes and infrastructure. Promote opportunities for planning for sustainable tourism development. Improve the management and development of tourism by ensuring coordination and cooperation between the different agencies, authorities and organisations concerned at all levels, and that their jurisdictions and responsibilities are clearly defined and complement each other.
Government & local government	■ Ratify international agreements and implement legal mechanisms to protect habitats and communities. Undertake assessments of the existing regulatory, economic and voluntary framework to bring about sustainable tourism. ■ National strategies: Ensure that tour ism is balanced by economic, social and environmental objectives at national and local level by setting out a national tourism strategy based on environmental and biodiversity knowledge, and ensure it is integrated into national and regional sustainable development plans. ■ Interagency coordination and cooperation: Improve management and development of tourism through coordination and cooperation between the different agencies, authorities and organisations, and ensure their responsibilities are clearly defined and complementary.

Government & local government

- Integrated management: Coordinate allocation of land uses, and regulate inappropriate activities that damage ecosystems, by strengthening or developing integrated policies and management covering all activities, *e.g.* Integrated Coastal Zone Management and adoption of an ecosystem approach. Nations should warn one another of natural disasters that may affect tourism.
- Tourism development issues should be handled with the participation of concerned citizens. Planning decisions should be taken at the local level. Local communities should be involved in tourism initiatives with aim of strengthening local economies. This will require training, education and public awareness programmes. As well as initiatives for measuring progress in achieving sustainable tourism development at the local level. Assist host communities to manage visitation to their tourism attractions for optimal financial benefit whilst minimising the negative impacts on and risks to traditions, culture and the living environment. Develop programmes that encourage people to participate in sustainable tourism and enhance stakeholder co-operation in tourism development and heritage preservation to improve the protection of the environment, natural resources and cultural heritage.
- Environmental Impact Assessment (EIA): Anticipate environmental impacts by undertaking comprehensive EIAs for all tourism deve lopment programmes taking into account cumulative effects from multiple development activities of all types.
- Planning measures: Promote planning for sustainable tourism development, ensuring that tourism development remains within national and local plans for tourism and other types of activity, by implementing assessment of carrying capacity and planning controls.
- Facilitate exchange of information, skills and technology relating to sustainable tourism between developed and developing countries
- Create practical tools for implementing sustainable tourism, including action plans and strategies at local, national, regional and international levels utilising multi-stakeholder processes, with national governments taking the lead.
- Research gaps in knowledge *e.g.* livelihood impacts, gender, domestic, regional and cultural aspects.

NGO	■ Policy formulation: NGO's & civil society must play a broader role in formulating policies. ■ Monitoring role: (Tourism Concern/Rethinking Tourism etc.), research and good practice: consumer engagement. Monitor/Support the participation of all sectors of society. ■ Promote and support training, education and public awareness. ■ Support the participation of all sectors of society, assist with public awareness and education work and encourage local capacity building, including for support southern NGO initiatives.
Farming/ Indigenous Peoples	■ Participation in national policy-making processes. ■ Transfer of appropriate technologies. ■ Transfer and protection of indigenous knowledge of land, resources and environmental management. ■ Education and training: Includes independent information service, training.
Trade Unions	■ Monitoring labour standards and principles. ■ Enhancing corporate conduct and performance internally and externally, through labour consultation. ■ Promote and support training, education and public awareness. ■ Promote the protection and rights of workers who act as whistle—blowers on unsustainable practices by industry.
Business	■ Industry initiatives: Ensure long-term commitments and improvements to develop and promote sustainable tourism, through partnerships and voluntary initiatives by all sectors and stakeholders, including initiatives to give local communities a share in the ownership and benefits of tourism. ■ Monitoring: Ensure consistent monitoring and review of tourism activities to detect problems at an early stage and enable action to prevent the possibility of serious damage. ■ Compliance Mechanisms: Ensure compliance with development plans, planning conditions, standards and targets for sustainable tourism by providing incentives, monitoring compliance, and enforcement activities where necessary. Respect international/national laws protecting the environment. When developing facilities in other countries, ensure that environmental standards are as high as those in the country of origin.

- Technology: Minimise resource use and the generation of pollution and wastes by using and promoting environmentally-sound technologies for tourism and associated infrastructure. Engage in assessment and good practice certification schemes.

Business (SMEs and TNCs)

- Promote the diversification of the economic activities, including through the facilitation of access to markets and commercial information, and participation of emerging local enterprises, especially SME's
- Promote interaction between tourists and host communities. Involve local communities in tourism initiatives and development. Promote planning and engage in active partnerships for sustainable tourism development. Contribute to the economic development & improve the wellbeing of the local community *e.g.* provide economic outlets for local trades-people, use local materials an labour when constructing new facilities, offer training opportunities to other businesses in the locality. Develop programmes that encourage people to participate in eco-tourism and enhance stakeholder co-operation in tourism development and heritage preservation to improve the protection of the environment & natural resources. Tourism development should recognise and support the identity, culture and interests of indigenous peoples. Travel and Tourism should use its capacity to create employment for indigenous peoples and women
- Design for sustainability: establish company-wide policies on sustainable development, examine the potential environmental, social, cultural and economic impacts of new products, make adequate preparations for natural disasters, employ technologies and materials appropriate to local conditions in new developments and refurbishments. Design new tourism products with sustainability at their core
- The link between tourism and health in the context of the spread of contagious diseases was discussed at 7th CSD meeting in1999. Participants attached much importance to the involvement of the tourism industry in efforts to address health issues associated wit h tourism, including HIV/AIDS.

Monitoring and Measuring Progress Through Indicators

The effectiveness of sustainable tourism initiatives requires effective monitoring of progress, through collecting data around key sustainability indicators for the tourism sector. During CSD 7 participants proposed that the CSD should encourage international agencies to develop indicators to measure the environmental, cultural and social impacts of coastal tourism. The World Tourism Organisation has also done some work in this area. Their Agenda 21 for the Travel and Tourism Industry noted that indicators were a relatively new area for the industry although a number of National Tourism Authorities (including Argentina, Canada, France, Malta, Mexico, Netherlands, Spain, Turkey and the USA) had participated in the World Tourism Organisation ongoing programme to develop a key set of indicators for use by national and local authorities. Also UNESCO and UNEP's Tour Operators Initiative recently signed a Memo of Understanding with the Global Reporting Initiative (GRI) to develop Sustainability Reporting Guidelines specially targeted at tour operators. Some examples are outlined in Table 3.

Conclusions

As we've seen eco-tourism is just one approach towards seeking sustainable tourism. Responsible and pro-poor tourism are emerging as new specialist approaches. And new initiatives which aim to push the mainstream tourism industry are building. One example is a new alliance between the World Tourism Organisation and UNCTAD aimed at "poverty alleviation through tourism". The initiative was announced in July 2002 and it will be presented at the Johannesburg Summit in an attempt to gain wider support. Model projects and successful multi-stakeholder initiatives, albeit on a small-scale, are also beginning to grow. Even these few examples perhaps prove that tourism has the potential to meet many of the objectives of sustainable development—to revitalize economies, support local communities, protect the environment and even generate cost savings and efficiency gains for tourism companies.

Table 3: Examples of Tourism Indicators

Issue	Indicator
Tourism demand	■ Household consumption expenditure on recreation
National/ Domestic contribution	■ % GDP, in current international dollars, derived by tourism sector and retained in domestic economy. ■ % different products/activities supplied locally vs from out the country (*e.g.* historic—cultural tourism, sports-based, conference, explorative tourism, recreational opportunities) ■ Percentage of reporting organisation's business (by passenger carried) and market share in operating destinations. ■ Measures to maximise economic benefits to destinations. ■ Business establishments offering tourist services and owned by locals as a percentage of all business establishments, ■ Income multiplier for the touris m sector as estimated in an input-output table, ■ Revenues exported as a percentage of total revenues in the business establishments owned by foreigners
Employment	■ Number of people employed within host country for the tourism sector (per thousand persons or as a percentage of total employed in tourism sector) ■ % Females employed in the tourism labour force ■ Unemployment rates in the off-season periods ■ Implementation of core ILO conventions—policies excluding child labour, programmes combating commercial sexual exploitation of children, recognition of independent trade unions and application of collective bargaining agreements
Community/ Stakeholder involvement	■ Consultation with destination stakeholders prior to and during tourism developments to ensure sites are socially acceptable-evidence of consultation with destination stakeholders and suppliers.

The "Economic" label spans the Tourism demand, National/Domestic contribution rows; "Socio-economic" spans the Employment, Community/Stakeholder involvement rows.

Issue	Indicator
	■ Existence of educational/informational programmes for the public and tourists about local culture
	■ Existence of procedures and obligations for public and stakeholders involved to suggest changes in policies
	■ Means to invite customers' feedback on economic, environmental, and social issues related to the holiday product and actions taken to respond to feedback. % feedback related to economic, environmental and social issues.
	■ Measures taken to identify and offer commercial opportunities and assistance to non contracted suppliers that support community development.
Health	■ Number of samplings of swimming waters exceeding safe limits, as these are defined nationally or internationally
	■ Quality of water expressed as concentration of various pollutants
	■ Existence of functioning Health and Safety committees
	■ Policies and programmes to combat and mitigate the social impacts of HIV/AID
Culture	■ Policies and actions in place (by operator) to accommodate cultural customs, traditions and practices of staff throughout the organisation.
Biodiversity	■ Number of special interest sites (natural, cultural) under protection Vs to those without any protection,
	■ Existence of legis lation for species protection,
	■ Number of endangered/threatened species on the region,
	■ Monitoring of the number (*e.g.* ratio of species disappearance and/or Vs to the present numbers) and distribution of species
Consumption	■ Total quantity (tonnes or kg) of material used by type and environmental quality, for the production of promotion materials and customer documentation.

Environment

Issue	Indicator
	■ Use of renewable resources (solar, wind, etc.) used in tourist accommodations as a percentage of total fuels used % of materials which can be recycled and % which receive this kind of treatment, ■ Water/energy consumption per tourist (or bed or night). Amount of water recycled as a percentage of total water consumed Number of hotels, restaurants and other places offering tourist services which have enacted environmental sound systems for eliminating over-consumption of resources and waste generation as a percentage of all establishments.
Tourism strategies	■ Completion of national strategy for sustainable tourism with regular up-dates on progress (*e.g.* annual/bi-annual) ■ Development of regional tourism strategy to deal with trans-boundary tourism issues, including environmental pollution
Monitoring & assessment	■ Measures to control and monitor tour operators, tourism facilities, and tourists in any area ■ Adoption of Sustainability Impact Assessments, Environmental and Social Audits, prior to and during tourism development and operations
Regulation	■ Introduce or enforcement of regulations for integrated coastal zone management; protection of habitats, both marine and land-based, and other environmental law; enforcement of ILO core labour standards.
Customer relations	■ Tools and measures used by reporting organisation to: raise the awareness of consumers on suppliers'/destinations environmental, social and economic performance; on sustainable holiday making. ■ Number of complaints from destinations' stakeholders and holiday-makers regarding misleading and inaccurate representation of destinations. Actions taken to address these.

Institutional

Promotion of sustainable tourism, through the development of policy tools, capacity building and awareness-raising programmes, local involvement, guidelines for good practice and actual implementation remain essential goals. Sustainable tourism should aim to directly support poverty eradication and sustainable production and consumption—in line with the general aims of Agenda 21. Making progress on a larger scale will be a fine balancing act and will require a massive "sea-change" in approach from the entire Travel and Tourism industry but it is an approach that is clearly worthy of support from all stakeholders interested and involved in the industry.

PRINCIPLES ON THE IMPLEMENTATION OF SUSTAINABLE TOURISM

While some agreement has been reached on what sustainable tourism is, the key question is how to put sustainable development into practice in all tourism activities—from mass tourism to nature-based and specialist tourism.

The proposed UNEP Principles for implementation of sustainable tourism were presented at UNEP's 20th Governing Council Session.

Objectives

The objectives for developing the UNEP Principles for Implementation of Sustainable Tourism are:

- To help governments and intergovernmental, private-sector and other organisations apply the general concept of sustainable tourism in practice, and minimize environmental impacts from tourism.
- To facilitate the development of more specific guidelines at the regional level or in relation to specific issues, such as coral reefs and biodiversity.
- To provide a framework for the work programmes of the Convention on Biological Diversity, the Framework Convention on Climate Change, the Regional Seas Ac-

tion Plans, and other international agreements that address tourism issues.

Consultation Processes

Consultation processes were conducted in three ways: through active input collection at three regional events, on the Web, and through comments received by UNEP's regional offices.

In early 2000, the Principles were produced in final form, and have been used as reference by many inter-governmental organisations and agreements such as the Convention on Biological Diversity.

Principles

Integration of Tourism into Overall Policy for Sustainable Development

National Strategies

Ensure that tourism is balanced with broader economic, social and environmental objectives at national and local level by setting out a national tourism strategy that is based on knowledge of environmental and biodiversity resources, and is integrated with national and regional sustainable development plans.

- Establish a national tourism strategy that is updated periodically and a master plan for tourism development and management.
- Integrate conservation of environmental and biodiversity resources into all such strategies and plans.
- Enhance prospects for economic development and employment while maintaining protection of the environment.
- Provide support through policy development and commitment to promote sustainability in tourism and related activities.

Interagency Coordination and Cooperation

Improve the management and development of tourism by ensuring coordination and cooperation between the different agencies, authorities and organisations concerned at all levels, and that their jurisdictions and responsibilities are clearly defined and complement each other.

- Strengthen the coordination of tourism policy, planning development and management at both national and local levels.
- Strengthen the role of local authorities in the management and control of tourism, including providing capacity development for this.
- Ensure that all stakeholders, including government agencies and local planning authorities, are involved in the development and implementation of tourism.
- Maintain a balance with other economic activities and natural resource uses in the area, and take into account all environmental costs and benefits.

Integrated Management

Coordinate the allocation of land uses, and regulate inappropriate activities that damage eco-systems, by strengthening or developing integrated policies and management covering all activities, including Integrated Coastal Zone Management and adoption of an ecosystem approach.

- Maximise economic, social and environmental benefits from tourism and minimise its adverse effects, through effective coordination and management of development.
- Adopt integrated management approaches that cover all economic activities in an area, including tourism.
- Use integrated management approaches to carry out restoration programmes effectively in areas that have been damaged or degraded by past activities.

Reconciling Conflicting Resource Uses

Identify and resolve potential or actual conflicts between tourism and other activities over resource use at an early stage. Involve all relevant stakeholders in the development of sound management plans, and provide the organisation, facilities and enforcement capacity required for effective implementation of those management plans.

- Enable different stakeholders in the tourism industry and local communities, organisations and institutions to work alongside each other.
- Focus on ways in which different interests can complement each other within a balanced programme for sustainable development.

Development of Sustainable Tourism: The Role of Planning

Planning for Development and Land-use at Sub-National Level

Conserve the environment, maintain the quality of the visitor experience, and provide benefits for local communities by ensuring that tourism planning is undertaken as part of overall development plans for any area, and that plans for the short-, medium-, and long-term encompass these objectives.

- Incorporate tourism planning with planning for all sectors and development objectives to ensure that the needs of all areas are addressed. (Tourism planning should not be undertaken in isolation.)
- Ensure that plans create and share employment opportunities with local communities.
- Ensure that plans contain a set of development guidelines for the sustainable use of natural resources and land.
- Prevent *ad hoc* or speculative developments.
- Promote development of a diverse tourism base that is well-integrated with other local economic activities.

- Protect important habitats and conserve biodiversity in accordance with the Convention on Biological Diversity.

Environmental Impact Assessment (EIA)

Anticipate environmental impacts by undertaking comprehesive EIAs for all tourism development programmes taking into account cumulative effects from multiple development activities of all types.

- Examine impacts at the regional national and local levels.
- Adopt or amend legislation to ensure that EIAs and the planning process take account of regional factors, if necessary.
- Ensure that project proposals respond to regional development plans and guidelines for sustainable development.

Planning Measures

Ensure that tourism development remains within national and local plans for both tourism and for other types of activity by implementing effective carrying capacity programmes, planning controls and management.

- Introduce measures to control and monitor tour operators, tourism facilities, and tourists in any area.
- Apply economic instruments, such as user fees or bonds.
- Zone of land and marine as an appropriate mechanism to influence the siting and type of tourism development by confining development to specified areas where environmental impact would be minimised.
- Adopt planning measures to reduce emissions of CO_2 and other greenhouse gases, reduce pollution and the generation of wastes, and promote sound waste management.
- Introduce new or amended planning or related legislation where necessary.

Legislation and Standards

Legislative Framework

Support implementation of sustainable tourism through an effective legislative framework that establishes standards for land use in tourism development, tourism facilities, management and investment in tourism.

- Strengthen institutional frameworks for enforcement of legislation to improve their effectiveness where necessary.

- Standardise legislation and simplify regulations and regulatory structures to improve clarity and remove inconsistencies.

- Strengthen regulations for coastal zone management and the creation of protected areas, both marine and land-based, and their enforcement, as appropriate.

- Provide a flexible legal framework for tourism destinations to develop their own set of rules and regulations applicable within their boundaries to suit the specific circumstances of their local economic, social and environmental situations, while maintaining consistency with overall national and regional objectives and minimum standards.

- Promote a better understanding between stakeholders of their differentiated roles and their shared responsibility to make tourism sustainable.

Environmental Standards

Protect the environment by setting clear ambient environmental quality standards, along with targets for reducing pollution from all sectors, including tourism, to achieve these standards, and by preventing development in areas where it would be inappropriate:

- Minimise pollution at source, for example, by waste minimisation, recycling, and appropriate effluent treatment.

- Take into account the need to reduce emissions of CO_2 and other greenhouse gases resulting from travel and the tourism industry.

Regional Standards

Ensure that tourism and the environment are mutually supportive at a regional level through cooperation and coordination between States, to establish common approaches to incentives, environmental policies, and integrated tourism development planning:

- Adopt overall regional frameworks within which States may wish to jointly set their own targets, incentive and environmental policies, standards and regulations, to maximise benefits from tourism and avoid environmental deterioration from tourism activities.
- Consider regional collaboration for integrated tourism development planning.
- Develop mechanisms for measuring progress, such as indicators for sustainable tourism.
- Develop regional strategies to address transboundary environmental issues, such as marine pollution from shipping and from land-based sources of pollution.

Management of Tourism

Initiatives by Industry

Ensure long-term commitments and improvements to develop and promote sustainable tourism, through partnerships and voluntary initiatives by all sectors and stakeholders, including initiatives to give local communities a share in the ownership and benefits of tourism:

- Structure initiatives to give all stakeholders a share in the ownership, to maximise their effectiveness.
- Establish clear responsibilities, boundaries and timetables for the success of any initiative.

- As well as global initiatives, encourage small and medium-sized enterprises to also develop and promote their own initiatives for sustainable tourism at a more local level.
- Consider integrating initiatives for small and medium-sized enterprises within overall business support packages, including access to financing, training and marketing, alongside measures to improve sustainability as well as the quality and diversity of their tourism products.
- Market tourism in a manner consistent with sustainable development of tourism.

Monitoring

Ensure consistent monitoring and review of tourism activities to detect problems at an early stage and to enable action to prevent the possibility of more serious damage:

- Establish indicators for measuring the overall progress of tourist areas towards sustainable development.
- Establish institutional and staff capacity for monitoring.
- Monitor the implementation of environmental protection and related measures set out in EIAs, and their effectiveness, taking into account the effectiveness of any ongoing management requirements for the effective operation and maintenance of those measures for protection of areas where tourism activities take place.

Technology

Minimise resource use and the generation of pollution and wastes by using and promoting environmentally-sound technologies (ESTs) for tourism and associated infrastructure:

- Develop and implement international agreements which include provisions to assist in the transfer of Environmentally Sound Technologies (ESTs) for the tourism sector, such as the Clean Development Mechanism of the Kyoto Protocol for energy-related issues.

■ Promote introduction and more widespread use of ESTs by tourism enterprises and public authorities dealing with tourism or related infrastructures, as appropriate, including the use of renewable energy and ESTs for sanitation, water supply, and minimisation of the production of wastes generated by tourism facilities and those brought to port by cruise ships.

Compliance Mechanisms

Ensure compliance with development plans, planning conditions, standards and targets for sustainable tourism by providing incentives, monitoring compliance, and enforcement activities where necessary:

■ Provide sufficient resources for maintaining compliance, including increasing the number of trained staff able to undertake enforcement activities as part of their duties.

■ Monitor environmental conditions and compliance with legislation, regulations, and consent conditions

■ Use compliance mechanisms and structured monitoring to help detect problems at an early stage, enabling action to be taken to prevent the possibility of more serious damage.

■ Take into account compliance and reporting requirements set out in relevant international agreements.

■ Use incentives to encourage good practice, where appropriate.

Conditions for Success

Involvement of Stakeholders

Increase the long-term success of tourism projects by involving all primary stakeholders, including the local community, the tourism industry, and the government, in the development and implementation of tourism plans:

- Involve all primary stakeholders in the development and implementation of tourism plans, in order to enhance their success. (Projects are most successful where all main stakeholders are involved.)
- Encourage development of partnerships with primary stakeholders to give them ownership shares in projects and a shared responsibility for success.

Information Exchange

Raise awareness of sustainable tourism and its implementation by promoting exchange of information between governments and all stakeholders, on best practice for sustainable tourism, and establishment of networks for dialogue on implementation of these Principles; and promote broad understanding are awareness to strengthen attitudes, values and actions that are compatible with sustainable development:

- Exchange information between governments and all stakeholders, on best practice for sustainable tourism development and management, including information on planning, standards, legislation and enforcement, and of experience gained in implementation of these Principles.
- Use International and regional organisations, including UNEP, can assist with information exchange.
- Encourage development of networks for the exchange of views and information.

Capacity Building

Ensure effective implementation of sustainable tourism, and these Principles, through capacity building programmes to develop and strengthen human resources and institutional capacities in government at national and local levels, and amongst local communities; and to integrate environmental and human ecological considerations at all levels:

- Develop and strengthen their human resources and institutional capacities to facilitate the effective implementation of these Principles.

- Transfer know-how and provide training in areas related to sustainability in tourism, such as planning, legal framework, standards setting, administration and regulatory control, and the application of impact assessment and management techniques and procedures to tourism.

- Facilitate the transfer and assimilation of new environmentally-sound, socially acceptable and appropriate technology and know-how.

- Encourage contributions to capacity-building from the local, national, regional and international levels by countries, international organisations, the private sector and tourism industry, and NGOs.

- Encourage assistance from those involved in tourism in countries which have not yet been able to implement sustainability mechanisms in training at the local and national level in the sustainable development of tourism in co-operation with the Governments concerned.

MANAGEMENT OF TOURISM DESTINATIONS

Managing tourism destinations is an important part of controlling tourism's environmental impacts. Destination management can include land use planning, business permits and zoning controls, environmental and other regulations, business association initiatives, and a host of other techniques to shape the development and daily operation of tourism-related activities.

The term "destination" refers broadly to an area where tourism is a relatively important activity and where the economy may be significantly influenced by tourism revenues.

Destination management is complicated by the fact that a single, recognizable destination may include several municipalities, provinces, or other government entities—in island environments it may be the entire country.

Participating governance structures led by local authorities, with the involvement of local NGOs, community and indigenous representatives, academia, and local chambers of commerce, make up what are known as "Destination Management Organisations" (DMOs). Often DMOs take the form of local tourism boards, councils, or development organisations. The network of local tourism businesses (hotels, attractions, transportation services, service providers such as guides and equipment rentals, restaurants, etc.) are also a significant part of a destination.

Destination Management Approach

The needs, expectations and anticipated benefits of tourism vary greatly from one destination to the next, and there is certainly no "one size fits all" approach to destination management. As local communities living in regions with tourism potential develop a vision for what kind of tourism they want to facilitate, a comprehensive planning framework such as Local Agenda 21 has proved useful and is being used more and more often. For UNEP, promoting sustainable tourism within Local Agenda 21 processes is a way to strengthen local stewardship of the environment. UNEP works with the International Council of Local Environmental Initiatives (ICLEI) to build local capacity and to disseminate tools and useful approaches to local destination governance.

AGENDA 21 APPROACH

Agenda 21 binds local authorities to implementing at local level the commitments made towards sustainable development by the international community. It was drawn up in 1992 at the "Earth Summit" in Rio de Janeiro—and has since become the main mechanism for community planning for sustainability.

A local Agenda 21 is an approach through which a local community defines a sustainable development strategy and an action programme to implement it. A local authority initiates and provides leadership for the process; its success hinges on close cooperation between the population, NGOs, and economic and social players.

ICLEI estimates that more than three thousand local communities worldwide are now implementing local Agendas 21. In the coming years their numbers will continue to rise, thanks to inter-community networking and to the information campaigns being conducted by international organisations, states and NGOs. The approach is also spreading through teaching tools and methodologies for communities, in particular through training and guides produced by ICLEI.

Experience has proven that the success of a local Agenda 21 depends directly on the involvement of the population, and on the partnerships between the various players. Such partnerships encourage a balance between economic development, social development and the protection of natural resources and the environment.

UNEP has produced a study called Promoting Sustainable Tourism Within Local Agenda 21 that looks at how tourism has been taken into account in local Agenda 21 programmes. It is partly based on a study of the hands-on experience gained by local communities that are involved to varying degrees in tourist activity, and that have adopted a local Agenda 21 approach. It examines:

- The position of tourism within local Agenda 21 programmes.
- The usefulness of the local Agenda 21 process in dealing with problems posed by tourism and in defining a tourism strategy.
- Recommendations for improving the way in which specific tourism-related aspects are taken on board in local Agenda 21 processes.

Chapter 3

UNEP, CBD, Biological Diversity and Tourism: Global Guidelines on Conservation and Development

INTRODUCTION

Tourism is one of the world's fastest growing industries as well as the major source of foreign exchange earning and employment for many developing countries, and it is increasingly focusing on natural environments. However, tourism is a double-edged activity. It has the potential to contribute in a positive manner to socio-economic achievements but, at the same time, its fast and sometimes uncontrolled growth can be the major cause of degradation of the environment and loss of local identity and traditional cultures. Biological and physical resources are in fact the assets that attract tourists. However, the stress imposed by tourism activities on fragile eco-systems accelerates and aggravates their depletion. Paradoxically, the very success of tourism may lead to the degradation of the natural environment: by depleting natural resources tourism reduces the site attractiveness to tourists, the very commodity that tourism has to offer.

As far as economic benefits are concerned, tourism certainly constitutes an opportunity for economic development, economic diversification and the growth of related activities, in developing countries especially, contributing around 1.5 per cent of world gross national product. Tourism is also a major source of income and employment. Tourism based on the natural environment (eco-tourism) is a vital growing segment of the tourism industry and, despite the negative impacts, and given the fact that tourism generates a large proportion of income and that a growing percentage of the activities are nature-based, tourism does present a significant potential for realizing benefits in terms of the conservation of biological diversity and the sustainable use of its components.

Among the benefits are direct revenues generated by fees and taxes incurred and voluntary payments for the use of biological resources. These revenues can be used for the maintenance of natural areas and the contribution of tourism to economic development, including linkage effects to other related sectors and job-creation. Sustainable tourism can make positive improvements to biological diversity conservation especially when local communities are directly involved with operators. If such local communities receive income directly from a tourist enterprise they, in turn, increase their evaluation of the resources around them. This is followed by greater protection and conservation of those resources as they are recognized as the source of income. Moreover, sustainable tourism can serve as a major educational opportunity, increasing knowledge of and respect for natural eco-systems and biological resources. Other benefits include the provision of incentives for maintaining traditional arts and crafts, traditional knowledge, and innovations and practices that contribute to the sustainable use of biological diversity.

In considering the role of tourism in the sustainable use of biological resources and their diversity, it is important that the potential adverse impacts of tourism are fully considered. These are roughly divided into environmental impacts and socio-economic impacts, the latter generally being those imposed on local and indigenous communities. Although such impacts on biological resources may be less easy to quantify and analyze systematically, they may be at least as important as, if not more important than, environmental impacts in the long term.

Direct use of natural resources, both renewable and non-renewable, in the provision of tourist facilities is one of the most significant direct impacts of tourism in a given area. Land use for accommodation and infrastructure provision, the choice of the site, the use of building materials are all essential factors. Deforestation and intensified or unsustainable use of land also cause erosion and loss of biodiversity. Direct impact on the species composition and on wildlife can be caused by incorrect behaviours and unregulated tourism activities (*e.g.* off-road driving, plant-picking, hunting, shooting, fishing, scuba diving). Moreover, tourists and tourist transportation means can increase the risk of introducing alien species and the manner and frequency of human presence can cause disturbance to the behaviour of animals. Construction activities related to tourism can cause enormous alteration to wildlife habitats and ecosystems.

Tourism has for many years been focused on mountain and coastal areas. Pressures from tourism activities on biological resources and their diversity are enormous and includes: erosion and pollution from the construction of hiking trails, bridges in high mountains, camp sites, chalet and hotels. Tourism activities have a major impact also on the marine and coastal environment, the resources they host and the diversity of those resources. Most often, those impacts are due to inappropriate planning, irresponsible behaviour by tourists and operators and/or lack of education and awareness of the impacts by, for example, tourist resorts along the coastal zones.

Tourism is also a water-intensive activity with a large production of waste. The extraction of groundwater by some tourism activities can cause desiccation, resulting in loss of biological diversity. Moreover, the disposal of untreated effluents into surrounding rivers and seas can cause eutrophication and it can also introduce a large amount of pathogens into the water body. Disposal of waste produced by the tourism industry may cause major environmental problems.

Socio-economic and cultural impacts of tourism include influx of people and related social degradation, impacts on local communities and on cultural values. Increased tourism activities can cause an influx of people seeking employment or entrepreneurial opportunities, but who may not be able to find suitable employment, thus causing social degradation. Sudden loss of income and jobs can also be experienced in times of downturn, if the economy is not diversified and it heavily relies on tourism. When tourism development occurs, economic benefits are usually unequally distributed among members of local communities. In the case of foreign direct investment, much of the profit may be transferred back to the home country. Therefore, tourism can actually increase inequalities in communities, and thus relative poverty.

Tourism has a highly complex impact on cultural values. Tourism activities may lead to intergenerational conflicts and may affect gender relationships. Traditional practices and events may also be influenced by the tourist preferences. Tourism development can lead to the loss of access by indigenous and local communities to their land and resources as well as sacred sites.

Sustainable tourism is therefore in everybody's interest. Given that a high percentage of tourism involves visits to naturally and culturally distinguished sites, generating large amounts of revenue, there are clearly major opportunities for investing in the maintenance and sustainable use of biological resources. Along with the efforts to maximize benefits, efforts must be made to minimize the adverse impacts of the tourism industry on biological diversity.

In this context, one the challenges for the Convention on Biological Diversity is to develop, promote and disseminate guidelines for the sustainable planning and management of tourism activities in vulnerable terrestrial, marine and coastal eco-systems and habitats of major importance for biological diversity.

THE PROCESS

At its fourth meeting in 1999 the Conference of the Parties decided to consider "Sustainable use including tourism" as one of the three themes for in-depth consideration at its fifth meeting. Accordingly, a note was prepared by the Executive

Secretary for the fourth meeting of the Subsidiary Body on Scientific, Technical and Technological Advice (SBSTTA 4), in order to assist SBSTTA in its consideration of the development of approaches and practices for the sustainable use of biological resources, including tourism.

Conference of the Parties took note of the Programme for the further implementation of Agenda 21, adopted at the nineteenth special session of the United Nations General Assembly, held in June 1997. With regard to sustainable tourism, the General Assembly specifically directed the Commission on Sustainable Development (CSD) to develop an action-oriented international programme of work to be defined in cooperation with the Conference of the Parties together with other relevant organisations, including the World Tourism Organisation (WTO), the United Nations Conference on Trade and Development (UNCTAD) and the United Nations Environment Programme (UNEP). Accordingly, the seventh session of the CSD considered tourism and sustainable development and adopted an international work programme on sustainable tourism development. In its decision, the CSD invited the Conference of the Parties to further consider existing knowledge and best practice on sustainable tourism development and biological diversity with a view to contributing to international guidelines for activities related to sustainable tourism development in vulnerable eco-systems and habitats.

At its fourth meeting, in June 1999, SBSTTA focused on tourism as one example of sustainable use and developed and recommended for adoption by the Conference of the Parties an assessment of the interlinkages between tourism and biological diversity.

The Conference of the Parties accepted the invitation to participate in the international work programme on sustainable tourism development under the Commission on Sustainable Development process with regard to biological diversity, in particular, with a view to contributing to international guidelines for activities related to sustainable tourism development in vulnerable terrestrial, marine and coastal eco-systems and habitats of major importance for biological diversity and protected areas, including fragile riparian and mountain eco-systems, bearing in mind the need for such guidelines to apply to activities both within and outside protected areas, and taking into account existing guidelines".

The Conference of the Parties further requested the Executive Secretary "to prepare a proposal for the contribution on guidelines, for example by convening an international workshop".

A workshop on tourism and biodiversity was subsequently held in Santo Domingo in June 2001. The workshop resulted in the "International Guidelines on Sustainable Tourism in Vulnerable Eco-systems", which have been forwarded to the tenth session of the Commission on Sustainable Development serving as the Preparatory Committee for the World Summit on Sustainable Development. With the same recommendation SBSTTA also requested the Secretariat to submit the draft guidelines to the preparatory process for the World Summit on Eco-tourism (WES) to be held in Quebec City, in May 2002 and to open an electronic consultation inviting further reactions to the guidelines. Comments received have been compiled and made available to the sixth conference of the Parties.

Conference of the Parties, the draft guidelines were revised by the Secretariat of the Convention on Biological Diversity taking into account comments submitted to the Secretariat by Parties and Organisations through two rounds of electronic consultations as well as the outcome of the World Eco-tourism Summit, which took place in Quebec City in May 2002.

The revised version of the guidelines was submitted to the eighth session of the Subsidiary Body on Scientific, Technical and Technological Advice in March 2003 for its consideration. SBSTTA 8 forwarded it to the seventh meeting of the Conference of the Parties for final adoption. The seventh meeting of the Conference of the Parties adopted the CBD Guidelines for Biodiversity and Tourism Development.

The Conference of the Parties also requested the Executive Secretary, in order to increase clarity and facilitate the detailed understanding of the guidelines and the implementation by Parties and to identify and address specific stakeholders, to:

(a) Develop a user's manual, checklists and, on the basis of experience gained, including the contribution of indigenous and local communities, produce and make available a streamlined and user-friendly core set of improved voluntary guidelines.

(b) Prepare a glossary and definitions of terms used in the Guidelines.

(c) Promote the use of the clearing-house mechanism to collect and disseminate information on:

(i) Specific case-studies on the implementation of the Guidelines that make clearer reference to the use and application of specific analytical management tools; and

(ii) Best practices, lessons learned and case-studies on the involvement of indigenous and local communities embodying traditional lifestyles in sustainable-tourism and eco-tourism activities and projects.

SUSTAINABLE TOURISM DEVELOPMENT GUIDELINES

UNEP Principles on the implementation of sustainable tourism and the CBD sustainable tourism development guidelines for vulnerable eco-systems.

With a total of 692.7 million international arrivals, and international receipts of $462.2 billion in 2001, tourism is one of the biggest industries in the world. Biodiversity is one of its main assets. Tourism, on the other hand, can impact biodiversity both in negative and in positive ways. For this reason, the Convention on Biological Diversity, has accepted a recommendation of CSD to produce a set of guidelines. These guidelines were based on a number of existing documents, and on an expert workshop. (Please find, "the compilation and analysis of existing codes, guidelines, principles and position papers on sustainable tourism", on the bottom of the page under "Information Documents").

The CBD is the most successful Multilateral Environment Agreement ever, with 156 signatories. Along with GATS/WTO, it may become one of the most efficient intergovernmental agreements to regulate tourism.

The CBD Guidelines focus specifically on biodiversity but do refer to much broader topics such as water and waste pollution, energy consumption, coastal resource management, participation of local communities, biological diversity, including economic, social and environmental impacts. The introduction refers to "impacts of tourism on biological diversity, including economic, social and environmental impacts". The document clearly acknowledges that biodiversity is just one of the many important aspects of sustainability. The guidelines cover all forms and activities of tourism, which all come under the framework of sustainable development, in all geographic regions. These include conventional mass tourism, eco-tourism, nature- and culture-based tourism, cruise tourism, leisure tourism and sport tourism.

For these reasons, and given the significant political support, the CBD Guidelines enjoy in the process on CoP7, UNEP DTIE collaborates closely with the CBD Secretariat to support the guidelines and implement them on the ground based on practical projects.

CBD GUIDELINES ON BIODIVERSITY AND TOURISM DEVELOPMENT

International guidelines for activities related to sustainable tourism development in vulnerable terrestrial, marine and coastal eco-systems and habitats of major importance for biological diversity and protected areas, including fragile riparian and mountain eco-systems.

Scope

International guidelines for activities related to sustainable tourism development in vulnerable terrestrial, marine and coastal eco-systems and habitats of major importance for biological diversity and protected areas, including fragile riparian and mountain eco-systems

The present Guidelines are voluntary and represent a range of opportunities for local, regional, national governments, indigenous and local communities and other stakeholders to manage tourism activities in an ecological, economic and socially sustainable manner. They can be flexibly applied to suit different circumstances and domestic institutional and legal settings.

The Guidelines will assist Parties to the Convention on Biological Diversity, public authorities and stakeholders at all levels, to apply the provisions of the Convention to the sustainable development and management of tourism policies, strategies, projects and activities. They will provide technical guidance to policy makers, decision makers and managers with responsibilities covering tourism and/or biodiversity, whether in national or local government, the private sector, indigenous and local communities, non-governmental organisations or other organisations, on a process for working together with key stakeholders involved in tourism and biodiversity.

The Guidelines cover all forms and activities of tourism. These activities should be consistent with the principles of conservation and sustainable use of biological diversity. These include, but are not limited to, conventional mass tourism, eco-tourism, nature- and culture-based tourism, heritage and traditional tourism, cruise tourism, leisure and sports tourism. Although the primary focus of the Guidelines is vulnerable eco-systems and habitats, they are also appropriate for tourism with impact on biodiversity in all geographical locations and tourist destinations. The Guidelines on Biodiversity and Tourism Development can also play a crucial role in incorporating sustainable use and equity strategies within and around protected areas. Furthermore the Guidelines recognize the need for collaboration between originating and receiving countries and should be used to balance local interests and national, regional and international policies.

The Policy-making, Development Planning and Management Process

The main elements considered in developing the Guidelines are:

(a) Framework for management of tourism and bio-diversity;

(b) Notification process in relation to such a management framework; and

(c) Public education, capacity-building and awareness-raising concerning tourism and biodiversity.

Policy-making, development planning and the management process need to be undertaken through a multi-stakeholder process. Governments will normally coordinate this process at national level. This process may also be undertaken at more local levels by local government, and should ensure strong involvement of indigenous and local communities throughout the management and decision-making process. In addition, those responsible for tourism development and activities are encouraged to consult with and involve all relevant stake-holders, and especially those who are or may be affected by such developments and activities. The process applies to both new tourism development and the management of the existing tourism operations. Institutions

In order to ensure coordination between the levels of decision-making in government departments and agencies concerned with management of biological diversity and tourism as well as agencies responsible for broader national economic development, inter- and intra-departmental and inter-organisational structures and processes should be established, if they do not already exist, to guide policy development and implementation.

There is a need to improve awareness and exchange of knowledge between those responsible for and affected by tourism and nature conservation at a national, subnational and local level. In addition, national biodiversity strategies and action plans should include consideration of tourism issues, and tourism plans should likewise include full consideration of biodiversity issues. Existing documents, strategies and plans should be coherent or revised and amended to that effect as applicable.

A consultative process should be established to ensure ongoing and effective dialogue and information-sharing with stakeholders, as well as to resolve conflicts that might arise in relation to tourism and biological diversity and build consensus. To assist in this process, a multi-stakeholder body should be established including government departments, the tourism sector, non-governmental organisations, indigenous and local communities and other stakeholders, to ensure their engagement and full participation in the whole process, and encourage the establishment of partnerships.

The institutional arrangements should provide for the comprehensive involvement of stakeholders in the management process described in these Guidelines.

Authorities and managers of protected areas have a special role for the management of tourism and biodiversity. To this end, there is a need for government support and resources for managers, including training to perform their role effectively. In addition, it is necessary to establish and review mechanisms and funding policies to ensure the availability of adequate resources for maintaining biodiversity and promoting sustainable tourism. International institutions and development agencies should be involved as appropriate.

To be sustainable, tourism development in any destination requires coordinated policy-making, development planning and management. This process comprises the following steps:

Baseline Information

Baseline information is necessary to enable informed decisions to be taken on any issue. A minimum of baseline information is needed to enable impact assessment and decision-making and it is recommended that its compilation follow the ecosystem approach.

For tourism and biodiversity, the baseline information should include information, as appropriate, on:

(*a*) Current economic, social and environmental conditions at national and local level, including current and planned tourism development and activities and their overall positive and negative impacts, as well as development and activities in other sectors;

(*b*) Structure and trends within the tourism sector, tourism policy and tourism markets and trends, at national, regional and international level, including information based on market research as necessary;

(*c*) Environmental and biodiversity resources and processes, including any special features and sites of particular importance and protected areas, and identifying those resources that may be off bounds to development due to their particular fragility and those resources identified by existing analysis of threats;

(*d*) Culturally sensitive areas;

(*e*) Benefits from, and costs of, tourism to indigenous and local communities;

(*f*) Information on damage done to the environment in the past;

(*g*) National biodiversity strategies, action plans and reports and other sectoral plans and policies relevant for tourism development and biodiversity; and

(*h*) National, subnational and local sustainable-development plans.

Baseline information should take into consideration all sources of knowledge. The adequacy of the baseline information available will need to be reviewed, and where necessary, further research and information-gathering can be undertaken to fill gaps that may be identified.

All stakeholders may contribute relevant information to this process, including indigenous and local communities. To this end, there is a need for capacity-building and training to assist stakeholders in documenting, accessing, analysing and interpreting baseline information.

Collation and synthesis of information provided will need to be undertaken by an appropriately qualified team, drawing on a range of expertise, including expertise in tourism and in biodiversity issues, and in traditional knowledge and innovation systems.

In order to ensure that all relevant information, its credibility and reliability, are considered, all stakeholders should be involved in review of the collated baseline information available, and in the synthesis of this information.

Baseline information should include maps, geographical information systems and other visual tools, including already identified zoning schemes.

The baseline information-gathering and review process should make full use of the clearing-house mechanism under the Convention on Biological Diversity, as well as other relevant networks such as the World Network of Biosphere Reserves, World Heritage sites and Ramsar sites.

Requirements for site-specific information in relation to proposals for tourism development and activities at particular locations are set out in the notification process, and its compilation should follow the ecosystem approach. To enable impact assessment and decision making, the basic information required includes:

(*a*) Site-specific aspects:

(*i*) The various laws and regulations and plans that may be applicable to the specific site, including overviews of:

■ Existing laws at local, subnational and national levels.

■ Existing uses, customs and traditions.

- Relevant regional and international conventions or agreements and their status, and cross-boundary agreements or memoranda of understanding (MoUs).

(*ii*) Identification of various stakeholders involved in or potentially affected by the proposed project—including stakeholders in governmental, non-governmental, and private sectors (particularly those from the tourism sector), and indigenous and local communities—along with details concerning their participation in and/or consultation on the proposed project during its design, planning, construction and operation.

(*b*) Ecological aspects:

(*i*) Detailed indication of the protected and biodiversity significant areas.

(*ii*) Specifications on the eco-systems, habitats, species.

(*iii*) Quantitative and qualitative information on the loss of habitats and species (main reasons, trends).

(*iv*) Indexing of species.

(*v*) Identified threats.

(*vi*) Existing zones, ecological zones and existing tourism zones within the ecological zones.

(*vii*) Ecologically sensitive zones and zones where ecological disasters have or will most likely take place.

(*c*) Development aspects:

(*i*) Summary of the proposed project, why and by whom it is proposed, estimated outcomes and possible impacts (including impacts on the surrounding areas and transboundary impacts), and quantitative and qualitative data on these aspects.

(*ii*) Description of the stages of development and the various structures and stakeholders that may be involved at each stage.

(*iii*) Description of current land-uses, infrastructures, tourism facilities and services and their interaction with proposed operations.

Vision and Goals

Vision

An overall vision for sustainable tourism development in harmony with the goals and objectives of the Convention on Biological Diversity and other related conventions, such as the World Heritage Convention, is important for the effective management of tourism and biodiversity, and for ensuring that this also contributes to income generation and poverty reduction and a reduction of threats to biodiversity. The vision developed at the local level, while reflecting local priorities and realities, should take into account, as appropriate, national and regional tourism development strategies, policies and plans for economic and social development and for land-use, as well as the baseline information and review. It should be based on a multi-stakeholder process including indigenous and local communities that are or may be affected by tourism development.

Goals

The main goals are established to maximize the positive benefits of tourism to biodiversity, eco-systems, and economic and social development, and of biodiversity to tourism, while minimizing negative social and environmental impacts from tourism, and can cover, *inter alia*:

(*a*) Maintenance of the structure and functioning of eco-systems;
(*b*) Sustainable tourism compatible with biodiversity conservation and sustainable use;
(*c*) Fair and equitable sharing of benefits of tourism activities, with emphasis on the specific needs of the indigenous and local communities concerned;
(*d*) Integration and interrelation with other plans, developments or activities in the same area;

(e) Information and capacity-building;

(f) Poverty reduction, through the generation of sufficient revenues and employment to effectively reduce threats to biodiversity in indigenous and local communities;

(g) Protection of indigenous livelihoods, resources and of access to those resources;

(h) Diversification of economic activities beyond tourism to reduce dependency on tourism;

(i) Prevention of any lasting damage to biological diversity, eco-systems, and natural resources, and of social and cultural damage, and restoration of past damage where appropriate;

(j) Supporting the effective participation and involvement of representatives of indigenous and local communities in the development, operation and monitoring of tourism activities on lands and waters traditionally occupied by them

(k) Zoning and control of tourism developments and activities, including licensing and overall targets for and limits to the scale of tourism, to provide a range of activities for user groups that meet overall visions and goals;

(l) Empowerment through participation in decision-making;

(m) Access by indigenous and local communities to infrastructure, transport, communications and health-care provisions laid on for tourists;

(n) Increased safety for indigenous local communities;

(o) Increased social pride; and

(p) Control of tourism development and activities including licensing and clear indication on the limits to the scale and type of tourism development.

In relation to sharing of benefits arising from tourism and the conservation of biodiversity with indigenous and local communities, it should be noted that benefits may take various forms, including: job creation, fostering local enterprises, participation in tourism enterprises and projects, education, direct investment opportunities, economic linkages and ecological services. Appropriate mechanisms need to be established/evolved to capture the benefits.

The vision and goals will form the basis of national strategies or master plans for sustainable development of tourism in relation to biodiversity. Such plans should also incorporate consideration of biodiversity strategies and plans. In addition, biodiversity strategies and plans should include consideration of tourism issues.

Governments will normally coordinate this process at national level. This process may also be undertaken at more local levels by local government, and by communities at community level. Where local and community level vision and goals for tourism and biodiversity have been set, these may be taken into account by governments when preparing the national level vision and goals, for example through workshops at the local level.

Objectives

The objectives focus on actions to implement specific elements of the overall vision and goals, and may include clear activities and the time by which these will be achieved. Objectives should be performance-based (*e.g.*, construction of an interpretative trail to aid development of local guide services) and process-based (*e.g.*, establishment of an operational management system for tourism and biodiversity). As with the vision and goals, it is important to involve and consult with all relevant stakeholders, and especially the tourism industry and indigenous and local communities that are or may be affected by tourism development, in the process for setting objectives.

Objectives should be specific and should include specific areas identified in clearly delineated zones listing the types of activities and infrastructure that would be acceptable and should be developed. It should also outline the impact management measures that would be appropriate, and intended markets (with greater detail, as set out in the notification process, being required for proposals for tourism development or activities at specific locations).

Governments may also wish to consider:

(a) Measures to ensure that sites designated at international level, such as Ramsar or World Heritage sites or Biosphere Reserves, are accorded appropriate legal recognition and government assistance at the national level;

(b) Establishing reserves based on the biosphere reserve concept and incorporating sustainable-development objectives, generating income and employment opportunities for indigenous and local communities, and promoting appropriate product development;

(c) Measures to ensure that sites, at the national level, such as national parks, reserves and marine conservation areas are accorded appropriate legal recognition, have management plans and are provided necessary government support;

(d) Strengthening the protected area network and encouraging the role of protected areas as key locations for good practices in the management of sustainable tourism and biodiversity, taking into account the full range of protected area categories;

(e) Use of political and economic tools and measures to encourage the channelling of part of total tourism revenues towards supporting the conservation and sustainable use of biodiversity, such as conservation of protected areas, education, research programmes, or local community development; and

(f) Encouraging all stakeholders, as well as the private sector, to actively support the conservation of biodiversity and the sustainable use of its components.

Governments will normally coordinate this process at

national level. This process may also be undertaken at more local levels by local government, and by communities at community level. Where local- and community-level objectives for tourism and biodiversity have been set, these may be taken into account by governments when preparing national level objectives.

Legislation and Control Measures

Respect for existing national legislation and appropriate regulatory mechanisms and tools, such as land-use planning, protected area management plans, environmental assessment, building regulations and standards for sustainable tourism, are essential for the effective implementation of any overall vision, goals, and objectives. A review of legislation and control measures could consider, as appropriate, the legislation and control measures available for implementation of the overall vision, goals and objectives for tourism and biodiversity, their effectiveness, including enforcement, and any gaps that may need to be addressed for example, by revision of—or the development of additional—legislation and control measures.

The review of legislation and control measures may include, *inter alia*, assessment of the effectiveness of any provisions for resource management, access, and/or ownership by communities, especially indigenous and local communities in relation to tourism development or operations on lands and waters traditionally occupied or used by them; addressing legally established rights of indigenous and local communities; and enabling these groups to make decisions about tourism development and activities, amongst other forms of development and activities, in these areas.

Legislation and control measures considered could include measures for:

(*a*) Effective enforcement of existing laws, including the participation of all stakeholders.

(*b*) Approval and licensing processes for tourism development and activities.

(*c*) Controlling the planning, siting, design and construction of tourism facilities and infrastructures.

(*d*) Management of tourism in relation to biodiversity and eco-systems, including vulnerable areas.

(*e*) Application of environmental assessment, including assessment of cumulative impacts and effects on biodiversity, to all proposed tourism developments, and as a tool to develop policies and measure their impacts.

(*f*) Setting national standards and/or criteria for tourism that are consistent with overall national or regional plans for sustainable development and national biodiversity strategies and action plans:

    (*i*) Environmental quality and land-use criteria in and around tourism sites, and

    (*ii*) Development of a decision-making process with environmental and cultural sustainability guidelines for new and existing tourism development within the designated goals and objectives of the site's different zones and within the limits of acceptable change.

(*g*) Integrated land-use management.

(*h*) Ensuring inter-linkages between tourism and cross-cutting issues, including agricultural development, coastal zone management, water resources, etc.

(*i*) Mechanisms to resolve any inconsistencies between policy objectives and/or legislation in a manner that takes into account the interests of all stakeholders.

(*j*) Application of economic instruments, including tiered user fees, bonds, taxes or levies, for the management of tourism and biodiversity.

(*k*) Creating incentives for sustainable tourism development in line with the provisions of the Convention on Biological Diversity and Agenda 21 through relevant economic mechanisms.

(*l*) Supporting private sector voluntary initiatives consistent with these Guidelines, such as certification schemes and providing opportunities for the private tourism sector to contribute to management initiatives through direct donations, in-kind services, and other voluntary initiatives consistent with these Guidelines, and relevant policies.

(*m*) Avoiding tourism development or activities outside those areas set out in the objectives.

(*n*) Monitoring, control of and provision of information on activities related to collection and trade of biological and related cultural resources within tourism sites.

Governments will normally coordinate this process at the national level. It is important to involve and consult with all relevant stakeholders, and especially indigenous and local communities that are or may be affected by tourism development, in the process for reviewing legislation and control measures, assessing their adequacy and effectiveness, and proposing development of new legislation and measures where necessary.

Impact Assessment

Impact assessment for sustainable tourism development in ecosystems should be based on the "Guidelines for incorporating biodiversity-related issues into environmental impact assessment legislation and/or processes and in strategic environmental assessment" developed by the Convention on Biological Diversity.

At national level, Governments should normally undertake assessment of impacts associated with the overall vision, goals and objectives for tourism and biodiversity. In addition, this process may also be undertaken at more local levels by local government, and by indigenous and local communities.

Proposers of tourism developments or activities should assess the potential impacts of their proposals and provide information on this through a notification process.

Governments will normally undertake evaluations of the

adequacy of impact assessments submitted by proposers of tourism developments or activities. These evaluations will need to be undertaken by an appropriately qualified team, drawing on a range of expertise, including expertise in tourism and in biodiversity management, and also involving those indigenous and local communities that would be affected by the proposals. There should be public access to the documentation.

If the information provided is not sufficient, or the impact assessment inadequate, then further impact assessment studies may need to be undertaken. The proposer may be requested to undertake such studies, or the Government may decide to undertake these studies, and may request funds from the proposer for this purpose, as appropriate. Other stakeholders, including biodiversity managers and indigenous and local communities that may be affected by a proposed development, may also provide their assessments of impacts associated with specific proposals for tourism developments or activities, and provisions may be needed to ensure that any such assessments are taken into account by decision-makers.

Indigenous and local communities concerned should be involved in impact assessment. Their traditional knowledge should be acknowledged and considered for impact assessment in particular tourism projects that affect their sacred sites or lands and waters traditionally occupied or used by them.

Sufficient time should be allowed considering the different conditions and circumstances to ensure that all stakeholders are able to participate effectively in the decision-making process for any project using information provided by the impact assessment. Such information should be provided in forms that are accessible and comprehensible to all the various stakeholders involved.

Impacts of tourism in relation to the environment and biological diversity may include:

(a) Use of land and resources for accommodation, tourism facilities and other infrastructure provision, including road networks, airports and seaports;

(b) Extraction and use of building materials (*e.g.*, use of sand from beaches, reef limestone and wood);

(c) Damage to or destruction of eco-systems and habitats, including deforestation, draining of wetlands, and intensified or unsustainable use of land;

(d) Increased risk of erosion;

(e) Disturbance of wild species, disrupting normal behaviour and potentially affecting mortality and reproductive success;

(f) Alterations to habitats and eco-systems;

(g) Increased risk of fires;

(h) Unsustainable consumption of flora and fauna by tourists (*e.g.*, through picking of plants; or purchase of souvenirs manufactured from wildlife, in particular such endangered species as corals and turtle shells; or through unregulated hunting, shooting and fishing);

(i) Increased risk of introduction of alien species;

(j) Intensive water demand from tourism;

(k) Extraction of groundwater;

(l) Deterioration in water quality (freshwater, coastal waters) and sewage pollution;

(m) Eutrophication of aquatic habitats;

(n) Introduction of pathogens;

(o) Generation, handling and disposal of sewage and waste-water;

(p) Chemical wastes, toxic substances and pollutants;

(q) Solid waste (garbage or rubbish);

(r) Contamination of land, freshwater and seawater resources;

(s) Pollution and production of greenhouse gases, resulting from travel by air, road, rail, or sea, at local, national and global levels; and

Socio-economic and cultural impacts related to tourism may include:

(a) Influx of people and social degradation (*e.g.* local prostitution, drug abuse, etc.);

(b) Impacts on children and youth;

(c) Vulnerability to the changes in the flow of tourist arrivals which may result in sudden loss of income and jobs in times of downturn;

(d) Impacts on indigenous and local communities and cultural values;

(e) Impacts on health and the integrity of local cultural systems;

(f) Intergenerational conflicts and changed gender relationships;

(g) Erosion of traditional practices and lifestyles; and

(h) Loss of access by indigenous and local communities to their land and resources as well as sacred sites, which are integral to the maintenance of traditional knowledge systems and traditional lifestyles.

The potential benefits of tourism may include:

(a) Revenue creation for the maintenance of natural resources of the area.

(b) Contributions to economic and social development, for example:

    (i) Funding the development of infrastructure and services;

    (ii) Providing jobs;

    (iii) Providing funds for development or maintenance of sustainable practices;

    (iv) Providing alternative and supplementary ways for communities to receive revenue from biological diversity;

    (v) Generating incomes;

    (vi) Education and empowerment;

    (vii) An entry product that can have direct benefits for developing other related products at the site and regionally; and (*viii*) Tourist satisfaction and experience gained at tourist destination.

Impact Management and Mitigation

Impact management is essential to avoid or minimize any potential damage to biodiversity conservation and sustainable use that tourism development or activities might cause. Proposals for tourism development or activities may incorporate proposals for impact management, but these may not necessarily be judged sufficient to deal with potential impacts on biodiversity. Therefore all stakeholders, and especially Governments that exercise overall control over tourism development and activities, will need to consider the various impact management approaches that may be necessary in any given situation. In particular, Governments should be aware that the tourism industry could provide a direct impetus for conservation of vulnerable eco-systems by supporting sustainable tourism activities that have a direct commercial interest in maintaining the vulnerable ecosystem in a good condition.

Tourism should be planned and managed using the internationally accepted planning methodologies (such as the Recreation Opportunity Spectrum and the Limits of Acceptable Change). In vulnerable eco-systems, based on these methodologies and relevant background information, tourism should be restricted and where necessary prevented.

Impact management can include, *inter alia*, measures for the siting of tourism development and activities, including establishing appropriate activities in different designated zones, differentiation between the impacts of different types of tourism, and measures to control tourist flows in and around tourist destinations and key sites, to promote appropriate behaviour by tourists so as to minimize their impacts, and to establish limits to numbers of visitors and their impacts within Limits of Acceptable Change at any site.

Impact management in relation to transboundary eco-systems and migratory species requires regional cooperation.

There is a need to identify those who will be responsible for implementing impact management and the resources that will be required for impact management.

Impact management for tourism development and activities can include the adoption and effective implementation of policies, good practices and lessons learned that cover, *inter alia*:

(*a*) Controlling impacts of major tourist flows including excursions, cruise ships, etc., which can cause serious effects on destinations even though they are visited for only short periods;

(*b*) Reducing impacts of activities outside tourism areas on adjacent and other eco-systems of importance for tourism (*e.g.*, pollution from nearby farming activities or extractive industries may affect areas of tourism development);

(*c*) Responsible use of natural resources (*e.g.*, land, soil, energy, water);

(*d*) Reducing, minimizing and preventing pollution and waste (*e.g.* solid and liquid waste, emissions to air, transport);

(*e*) Promoting the design of facilities that are more eco-efficient, which adopt the cleaner production approach, and use environmentally sound technologies, in particular to reduce emissions of carbon dioxide and other greenhouse gases and ozone-depleting substances, as set out in international agreements;

(*f*) Conserving flora, fauna and eco-systems;

(*g*) Preventing the introduction of alien species as a result of the construction, landscaping and operating of tourism activities, including for example from shipping associated with tourism;

(*h*) Conserving landscapes, cultural and natural heritage;

(*i*) Respecting the integrity of local cultures and avoiding negative effects on social structures, involving, and cooperating with, indigenous and local communities, including measures to ensure respect for sacred sites and customary users of these sites, and to prevent negative impacts on them and on lands and waters traditionally occupied or used by them, as well as on their subsistence resources;

(*j*) Using local products and skills, and providing local employment;

(*k*) Promoting appropriate behaviour by tourists so as to minimize their adverse impacts, and to promote positive effects through education, interpretation, extension, and other means of awareness raising;

(*l*) Alignment of marketing strategies and messages with the principles of sustainable tourism;

(*m*) Contingency plans for handling accidents, emergencies or bankruptcies that may occur during construction and use of facilities and which may threaten the environment and the conservation and sustainable use of biodiversity;

(*n*) Environmental and cultural sustainability audits and review of existing tourism activities and developments and of the effectiveness with which impact management is being applied to existing tourism activities and developments; and

(*o*) Mitigation measures for existing impacts, and appropriate funding to support them. Such measures should include development and implementation of compensation measures in cases when tourism has resulted in negative environmental, cultural, and socio-economic effects, taking into consideration the range of redress and compensation measures.

Governments, in cooperation with biodiversity managers, those communities that would be affected by the proposals, and other stakeholders, would normally assess the need for impact management in addition to any management measures included in the proposals under consideration. All stakeholders should understand the importance of such impact management.

The tourism industry can assist in promoting corporate policies on sustainable tourism and biodiversity, with defined goals, monitoring and reporting their progress publicly on a regular basis.

Decision-making

Decisions will be made concerning approval or otherwise of, *inter alia*:

(a) National strategies and plans for tourism and bio-diversity;

(b) Proposals for tourism development and activities at particular locations in relation to biodiversity, which are to be submitted through the notification process;

(c) Adequacy of impact management measures in relation to anticipated impacts from tourism development and activities; and

(d) Adequacy and frequency of monitoring and reporting.

Such decisions will ultimately be taken by Governments (or specific authorities designated by Governments). It is recognized, however, that effective consultation with and participation of the communities and groups affected, including specific input from biodiversity managers, and from indigenous and local communities as well as the private sector in a broad sense, is an important foundation of the decision-making process and critical to sustainable development. Decision makers should consider using multi-stakeholder processes as a tool for the decision-making process.

The decision-making process should be transparent, accountable, and apply the precautionary approach. Legal mechanisms should be put in place for notification and approval of tourism development proposals and for ensuring implementation of the conditions of approval of development proposals.

For proposals for tourism development and activities at particular locations, the proposers will normally be required to provide the information set out in the notification process. This should apply equally to public-sector development and infrastructure projects, as well as to private-sector development. Impact assessment should be a component of any decision-making process.

Measures should be taken to ensure full and timely disclosure of project information concerning tourism development proposals. Consistent with Article 8(*j*), decision-making should include meaningful consultation with indigenous and local communities affected by projects in order to ensure, *inter alia*, respect for the customs and traditional knowledge, innovations and practices of indigenous and local communities, and adequate funding and technical support for effective participation. Where the national legal regime requires prior informed consent of indigenous and local communities with respect to decisions identified in paragraph 52, such prior informed consent must be obtained.

Decisions should include a review of the adequacy of information available, that could cover, *inter alia*, baseline information, impact assessment, and information on the proposed tourism development or activity, its nature and size, the type(*s*) of tourism involved, and information on human settlements and communities that may be affected.

In cases where there is not sufficient contextual/baseline information available at the time, or where the overall vision, goals and objectives for tourism and biodiversity have not been developed sufficiently to make a decision, decisions may be deferred pending sufficient information being obtained, and/or completion of overall plans/goals.

In making a decision, conditions may be attached to any approvals that may be granted, including conditions regarding management of tourism in relation to avoidance or minimization of adverse impacts on biodiversity, and for appropriate decommissioning of tourism activities should the development cease. Decision makers may also, as appropriate, request further information from a proposer; defer a decision pending further baseline research by other agencies; or refuse a proposal.

Implementation

Implementation follows a decision to approve a particular proposal, strategy or plan. Unless otherwise stated, the developer and/or operator will be responsible for complying with the conditions for granting the approval; and, as part of this process, they can also be required to notify the designated government authority of any failures to comply with conditions attached to an approval, including conditions for decommissioning, and/or of any changes in circumstances, including unforeseen environmental conditions and/or biodiversity issues (*e.g.*, detection of rare or endangered species not recorded in the original proposal and impact assessment).

Any revisions or changes to an approved project, including additions and/or variations of activities, must be approved by the designated authorities before construction.

Implementation plans should recognize that indigenous and local communities and other relevant stakeholders may require assistance as actors in implementation, and should ensure that sufficient resources are available for implementation and for effective participation.

Local stakeholders should be given an ongoing opportunity to express their wishes and concerns to those managing tourism facilities and activities. As part of this process, clear and adequate information regarding implementation should be provided for review by the stakeholders, in forms that are accessible and comprehensible to them.

Availability of information on policies, programmes, projects, and their implementation, including information on existing and future guidelines, should be ensured and exchange of information fostered, for example, through the clearing house mechanism of the Convention on Biological Diversity.

Monitoring and Reporting

It is necessary to establish a monitoring and control system for the management of tourism activities and biological diversity. Long-term monitoring and assessment are necessary in relation to the impacts of tourism on biodiversity, and will need to take into account the timescale for ecosystem changes to become evident. Some effects may develop quickly, while others may take place more slowly. Long-term monitoring and assessment provide a means for detecting adverse effects that may arise from tourism activities and development in relation to biodiversity, so that action can be taken to control and mitigate such effects.

Monitoring and surveillance in relation to management of tourism and biodiversity includes, *inter alia*, the following main areas:

(*a*) Implementation of approved tourism developments or activities, and compliance with any conditions attached when approval was granted, and taking appropriate actions in cases of non-compliance;

(*b*) Impacts of tourism activities on biodiversity and eco-systems, taking appropriate preventative actions as necessary;

(*c*) Impacts of tourism on the surrounding population, especially indigenous and local communities;

(*d*) General tourism activities and trends, including tour operations, tourism facilities, and tourist flows in originating and receiving countries, including progress towards sustainable tourism;

(*e*) Clearly defined objectives, actions and targets for conservation or mitigation of threats to biodiversity, maintenance or restoration of eco-systems and for tourism; and

(*f*) Compliance with, and enforcement as necessary, of conditions attached to any approval. Communities and other interested stakeholders may also monitor and report their findings to the designated government authorities.

Developers and operators of tourism facilities and activities should be required to report periodically to designated authorities and to the public on compliance with conditions set out in approvals, and on the condition of biodiversity and the environment in relation to the tourism facilities and activities for which they are responsible.

Prior to the commencement of any new tourism development or activities, an inclusive monitoring and reporting system should be put in place, with indicators to track how tourism actions are mitigating threats to biodiversity, along with agreed upon quantifiable standards indicating thresholds of acceptable change. These should be developed in conjunction with all key stakeholders including indigenous and local communities.

Indicators to cover aspects of management of biodiversity and sustainable tourism, including socio-economic and cultural aspects, should be identified and monitored at global, national, and local levels, and should include, but not be limited to, the following:

(*a*) Conservation of biodiversity;

(*b*) Generation of income and employment from tourism (long-term and short-term);

(*c*) Proportion of tourism income retained in the local community;

(*d*) Effectiveness of multi-stakeholder processes for management of biodiversity and sustainable tourism;

(*e*) Effectiveness of impact management;

(*f*) Contribution of tourism to the well-being of the local population; and

(*g*) Visitor impacts and visitor satisfaction.

Monitoring results depend largely on the appropriate set of data to be collected. Guidelines on how to collect data in a way that can be used to evaluate change over time should be developed. Monitoring could follow a standard process and format, and be based on a framework including parameters on social, economic, environmental and cultural impact.

Monitoring and surveillance in relation to biodiversity impacts should include activities undertaken to ensure respect for endangered species under relevant international agreements, prevention of the introduction of alien species as a result of tourism activities, compliance with national rules concerning access to genetic resources, and prevention of illegal and unauthorised removal of genetic resources.

In relation to indigenous and local communities, monitoring and evaluation should include development and use of appropriate tools to monitor and evaluate tourism impacts on the economy of indigenous and local communities, particularly their food and health security, traditional knowledge, practices and customary livelihoods. Use of indicators and early warning systems should be developed as appropriate, taking into account traditional knowledge, innovation and practices of indigenous and local communities, and guidelines developed under the Convention on Biological Diversity relating to traditional knowledge. Measures should also be taken to ensure that indigenous and local communities involved in, or affected by tourism, have the opportunity to be involved effectively in monitoring and evaluation.

Monitoring of general environmental and biodiversity conditions and trends, as well as tourism trends and impacts, can be undertaken by Governments, including designated biodiversity managers. Management measures may need to be adjusted, as appropriate, where adverse impacts on biodiversity and eco-systems are detected. The need for and nature of such adjustments will be based on the results of monitoring, and it is important for these to be determined in dialogue with all relevant stakeholders, including the developers and/or operators of tourism facilities and activities, communities affected by those facilities and activities, and other interested stakeholders. The monitoring process needs to be multi-stakeholder and transparent.

Adaptive Management

The ecosystem approach requires adaptive management to deal with the complex and dynamic nature of eco-systems and the absence of complete knowledge or understanding of their functioning. Eco-system processes are often non-linear, and the outcome of such processes often shows time-lags. The result is discontinuities, leading to surprise and uncertainty. Management must be adaptive in order to be able to respond to such uncertainties and contain elements of "learning-by-doing" or research feedback. Measures may need to be taken even when some cause-and-effect relationships are not yet fully established scientifically.

Eco-system processes and functions are complex and variable. Their level of uncertainty is increased by the interaction with social constructs, which need to be better understood. Therefore, ecosystem management must involve a learning process, which helps to adapt methodologies and practices to the ways in which these systems are being managed and monitored. Adaptive management should also take the precautionary approach fully into account.

Implementation programmes should be designed to adjust to the unexpected, rather than to act on the basis of a belief in certainties.

Eco-system management needs to recognize the diversity of social and cultural factors affecting natural-resource use and sustainability.

Similarly, there is a need for flexibility in policy-making and implementation. Long-term, inflexible decisions are likely to be inadequate or even destructive. Eco-system management should be envisaged as a long-term experiment that builds on its results as it progresses. This 'learning-by-doing" will also serve as an important source of information to gain knowledge of how best to monitor the results of management and evaluate whether established goals are being attained. In this respect, it would be desirable to establish or strengthen capacities of Parties for monitoring. In addition, adaptive management learning portfolios should be developed between different sites so that comparison can be made and lessons learned.

Implementing adaptive management in relation to tourism and biodiversity will require the active cooperation of all stakeholders in tourism, and especially those in the private sector, with biodiversity managers. Impacts on biodiversity at a particular location may require rapid curtailment of visits by tourists to prevent further damage, and to allow for recovery, and in the longer-term, may necessitate an overall reduction in tourist flows. It may be possible for tourists to be redirected to less sensitive areas in such cases. In all cases, maintenance of the balance between tourism and biodiversity will require close interaction between tourism managers and biodiversity managers, and appropriate frameworks for management and dialogue are likely to need to be established.

Governments, including designated biodiversity managers, in conjunction with all other stakeholders will therefore need to take actions, as appropriate, to address any problems encountered and to keep on track towards agreed goals. This may include changes and additions to conditions set in the original approval, and will require participation of and consultation with the developer and/or operator of the tourism facilities and activities concerned, and with local communities.

Adaptive management can also be undertaken by all those who have management control over any specific site, including local governments, indigenous and local communities, the private sector, non-governmental organisations and other organisations.

Where necessary, legal frameworks may need to be reviewed and amended to support adaptive management, taking into account experience gained.

Notification Process and Information Requirements

Proposals for tourism development and activities at particular locations in relation to biodiversity are to be submitted through the notification process. As such, this process provides the link between proposers of tourism activities and development, and the management process steps outlined above. In particular, the notification process makes specific links to the steps in the management process for impact assessment and decision-making and should take into account local, regional and national impacts. Proposers of tourism projects, including government agencies, should provide full and timely advance notice to all stakeholders who may be affected, including indigenous and local communities, of proposed developments.

Information to be provided as part of the notification could include:

(*a*) Scale and types of tourism development or activities proposed, including a summary of the proposed project, why and by whom it is proposed, estimated outcomes and possible impacts, and a description of the stages of development and the various structures and stakeholders that may be involved at each stage.

(*b*) Analysis of market for proposed tourism development or activities, based on market conditions and trends.

(*c*) Geographical description including recreation opportunity zones, outlining tourist activities and infrastructure development, and location of the site of tourism development or activities, the identity and any special features of the surrounding environments and biodiversity.

(*d*) Nature and extent of human-resource requirements and plans for their procurement.

(*e*) Identification of various stakeholders involved in or potentially affected by the proposed project—including stakeholders in governmental, non-governmental, and private sectors, and indigenous and local communities —along with details concerning their participation in and/or consultation on the proposed project during its design, planning, construction and operation.

(*f*) The perceived roles of local stakeholders in the proposed development.

(*g*) The various laws and regulations that may be applicable to the specific site, including overviews of existing laws at local, subnational and national levels, of existing uses and customs, of relevant regional and international conventions or agreements and their status, and cross-boundary agreements or memoranda or understanding and any proposed legislation.

(*h*) The proximity of the site to human settlements and communities, sites used by people from those settlements and communities as part of their livelihoods and traditional activities, and heritage, cultural or sacred sites.

(*i*) Any flora, fauna and eco-systems that could be affected by the tourism development or activities, including keystone, rare, endangered or endemic species.

(*j*) Ecological aspects of the site and its surroundings, including indication of any protected areas; specifications on the eco-systems, habitats, and species; quantitative and qualitative information on the loss of habitats and species (main reasons, trends), and indexing of species.

(*k*) Training and supervision of personnel carrying out the tourism development or activities.

(*l*) Likelihood of impacts beyond the immediate area of the tourism development or activities, including transboundary impacts and effects on migratory species.

(*m*) A description of current environmental and socio-economic conditions.

(*n*) Expected changes to environmental and socio-economic conditions as a result of the tourism development or activities.

(*o*) Proposed management measures to avoid or minimize adverse impacts from the tourism development or activities, including verification of their functioning.

(*p*) Proposed measures for mitigation, decommissioning and compensation in the event of problems arising with the tourism development or activities.

(*q*) Proposed measures to maximize the local benefits of the tourism development or activities on surrounding human settlements and communities, biodiversity and eco-systems, which may include, but are not limited to:

(*i*) Using local products and skills,

(*ii*) Employment, and

(*iii*) Restoration of biodiversity and eco-systems.

(*r*) Relevant information from any previous tourism development or activities in the region, and information on possible cumulative effects.

(*s*) Relevant information from any previous tourism development or activities by the proposer.

Categories of responses that Governments may wish to consider making in response to notification of proposals for, and requests for permission to undertake, tourism development, include, *inter alia*:

(*a*) Approval without conditions,

(*b*) Approval with conditions,

(*c*) Request for further information,

(*d*) Deferral pending further baseline research by other agencies, and

(*e*) Refusal of the proposal.

Education, Capacity-Building and Awareness-Raising

Education and awareness-raising campaigns need to be addressed to both the professional sectors and the general public and should inform them about the impacts of tourism on biological diversity, and good practices in this area. The private sector, and, especially, tour operators, could provide information more widely to their clients—the tourists—about tourism and biodiversity issues, and encourage them to conserve, and avoid adverse impact on, biodiversity and cultural heritage to respect national legislation of the visited country, as well as traditions of indigenous and local communities of that country, and to support actions in conformity with the present guidelines.

Awareness campaigns explaining the link between cultural diversity and biological diversity will need to be tailored for various audiences, particularly stakeholders including consumers of tourism, developers and tourism operators.

Education and awareness-raising is required at all levels of government. This should include processes for increasing mutual understanding between relevant ministries, including joint and innovative approaches for dealing with tourism and environmental issues.

Awareness should also be increased within and outside government that vulnerable eco-systems and habitats are often located within lands and waters occupied or used by indigenous and local communities.

The tourism sector as a whole, along with tourists should be encouraged to minimize any negative impacts and maximize positive impacts on biodiversity and local cultures associated with their consumption choices and behaviour, for example through voluntary initiatives.

It is also important to raise awareness within the academic sector responsible for training and research on issues regarding the interaction between biological diversity and sustainable tourism, of the role that they can play concerning public education, capacity-building and awareness-raising on these issues.

Capacity-building activities should aim to develop and strengthen the capacities of Governments and all stakeholders to facilitate the effective implementation of the present guidelines, and may be necessary at local, national, regional and international levels.

Capacity-building activities can be identified through the adaptive management process and can include strengthening human resources and institutional capacities, the transfer of know-how, the development of appropriate facilities, and training in relation to biological diversity and sustainable tourism issues, and in impact assessment and impact management techniques.

Such activities should include ensuring that local communities are equipped with the necessary decision-making abilities, skills and knowledge in advance of future tourist in-flows, as well as with relevant capacity and training regarding tourism services and environmental protection.

Capacity-building activities should include, but not be limited to:

(*a*) Capacity-building and training to assist all stakeholders, including Governments, and indigenous and local communities, in accessing, analysing and interpreting baseline information, undertaking impact assessments and evaluations, impact management, decision-making, monitoring and adaptive management.

(*b*) Development or strengthening of mechanisms for impact assessment with the participation of all stakeholders, including for the approval of the approach, content and scope of impact assessment.

(*c*) Establishment of multi-stakeholder processes involving government departments, tourism sector, non-governmental organisations, indigenous and local communities and other stakeholders.

(*d*) Training of tourism professionals in conservation and biodiversity issues.

Information exchange and collaboration regarding sustainable tourism implementation through networking and partnerships between all stakeholders affected by, or involved in tourism, including the private sector, should be encouraged.

Chapter 4

Global Eco-Tourism: Resolution, Remark, Declaration and Final Summit Report

RESOLUTION 1998/40—DECLARING THE YEAR 2002 AS THE INTERNATIONAL YEAR OF ECO-TOURISM

United Nations Economic and Social Council

46th Plenary Meeting
30 July 1998

Recalling its resolution 1980/67 of 25 July 1980 on international years and anniversaries in which the Council recognized the contribution of international years to the furtherance of international cooperation and understanding.

Recalling also Agenda 21, 1/which was adopted by one hundred and eighty-two Governments at the United Nations Conference on Environment and Development (Earth Summit), on 14 June 1992, and the conclusions of the General Assembly at its nineteenth special session relative to sustainable tourism.

Stressing that the implementation of Agenda 21 requires the full integration of sustainable development in the tourism industry in order to ensure, *inter alia*, that travel and tourism provide a source of income for many people; that travel and tourism contribute to the conservation, protection and restoration of the Earthþs ecosystem; that international trade in travel and tourism services takes place on a sustainable basis;

and that environmental protection is an integral part of tourism development.

Stressing also the need to promote the implementation of international conventions on environment and development, including those on biodiversity and climate change.

Bearing in mind the need for international cooperation in promoting tourism within the framework of sustainable development so as to meet the needs of present tourists and host countries and regions while protecting and enhancing opportunities for the future, managing resources to fulfil economic, social and aesthetic needs, and maintaining cultural integrity, essential ecological processes, biological diversity and life-support systems.

Recognizing the support of the World Tourism Organisation for the importance of eco-tourism, and particularly of the designation of the year 2002 as the International Year of Eco-tourism, in fostering better understanding among peoples everywhere, in leading to greater awareness of the rich heritage of various civilizations and in bringing about a better appreciation of the inherent values of different cultures, thereby contributing to the strengthening of world peace.

Considering that the designation of the year 2002 as the International Year of Eco-tourism will encourage the intensification of cooperative efforts by Governments and international and regional organisations, as well as non-governmental organisations, to achieve the aims of Agenda 21 in promoting development and the protection of the environment:

1. Recommends to the General Assembly that it declare the year 2002 as the International Year of Eco-tourism.
2. Invites States Members of the United Nations, and members of the specialized agencies and pertinent intergovernmental and governmental organisations, to exert all possible efforts on behalf of the success of the Year, in particular regarding eco-tourism in developing countries.

3. Requests the Commission on Sustainable Development, in the framework of its discussion of tourism during its seventh session, to recommend to the General Assembly, through the Economic and Social Council, supportive measures and activities which will contribute to a successful Year.

4. Requests the Secretary-General to provide, in accordance with the guidelines for future international years as contained in the annex to Economic and Social Council resolution 1980/67, necessary support to ensure the success of the Year, including widespread dissemination of pertinent information.

5. Requests the Secretary-General, in cooperation with all relevant entities of the United Nations system, including the United Nations Environment Programme as well as the World Tourism Organisation and the World Travel and Tourism Council, to submit to the General Assembly at its fifty-eighth session a report containing:

   (a) Programmes and activities undertaken by Governments and interested organisations during the Year,

   (b) An assessment of the results achieved in realizing the aims and objectives of the Year, particularly in terms of encouraging eco-tourism in developing countries, and

   (c) Recommendations to further advance the promotion of eco-tourism within the framework of sustainable development.

SPEECH AND REMARKS BY KLAUS TOEPFER, UNEP EXECUTIVE DIRECTOR IN THE FIRST PLENARY SESSION—WORLD ECO-TOURISM SUMMIT

Monday, 20 May 2002, Quebec City, Canada

Excellencies, distinguished delegates, ladies and gentlemen.

Welcome to the plenary session of the World's first Summit on Eco-tourism.

I am delighted to see that we have over 1,100 delegates, from all over the world. It bodes well for our work over the coming days. It confirms support for the UN's declaration of 2002 as the International Year of Eco-tourism.

I believe that the partnerships forged here, and the outcome of our deliberations, will create a solid foundation for building up eco-tourism in the future.

Why did UNEP and the World Tourism Organisation decide to organize this Summit?

To raise the awareness among all stakeholders of eco-tourism's capacity to contribute:

- To the conservation of the natural environment and cultural heritage in remote areas.
- To the improvement of standards of living in those areas.
- To share lessons learned on planning, management, regulation and monitoring of eco-tourism.
- To finalize the Quebec City Declaration on Eco-tourism, for the World Summit on Sustainable Development in Johannesburg.
- To forge multistakeholder alliances that will help us implement Johannesburg's recommendations.

We plan to examine a number of themes that encompass key issues raised by the development of eco-tourism.

They are:

- Policy and planning.
- Regulation and institutional responsibilities.
- Product development and promotion.
- Monitoring costs and benefits of eco-tourism, ensuring equitable distribution of benefits.

I would just like to share with you briefly UNEP's vision and expectations on each of these themes. I hope that in a spirit of cooperation and partnership, we will be able to develop these ideas together and take them forward.

Policy and Planning

Eco-tourism cannot exist and grow in a vacuum, it has to be integrated into sustainable development plans, land use plans and especially plans for the use of natural protected areas.

Although governments will take a leading role, local communities have to be involved in policy development and planning—they are the guardians of natural assets at present, they should retain responsibility for these assets

Local people must be involved in all decisions to open up an area to eco-tourism.

Proper planning and management is needed, to avoid threatening the biological diversity upon which eco-tourism depends.

Planning should always take account of the future sustainability of the project-only initiatives that will flourish after donor-funding dries up, should be developed.

- The recently published Eco-tourism Guide (Eco-tourism: Practices, and Policies for Sustainability), by UNEP and the International Eco-tourism Society, and the "Sustainable Tourism in Protected Areas" manual with IUCN and WTO should assist this process.

Regulation and Institutional Responsibilities

One of the problems which eco-tourism has encountered is the lack of internationally recognized standards.

"Greenwashing" has occurred all too often, devaluing the whole concept of eco-tourism.

It is therefore imperative, and in the interest of all stakeholders, to ensure that there are guidelines, certification and codes of conduct, which are agreed and accepted as binding.

Principles and guidelines such as the WTO Global Code of Ethics, the UNEP Principles for Sustainable Tourism and the Convention on Biological Diversity Guidelines for Sustainable Tourism in Vulnerable Eco-systems have to be translated into concrete standards for eco-tourism.

This meeting offers us all a unique opportunity to develop such instruments, and to commit to their adoption.

UNEP is working with other partners in the Sustainable Tourism Stewardship Council, to examine the feasibility of an international accreditation body for eco-tourism and sustainable tourism.

Product Development and Promotion

Eco-tourism operates in a fragile environment-often it is this fragility, which is the main attraction for tourists.

Therefore, there is a need to balance the demands of the tourists, the needs and concerns of the local community, and the interests of the tourism industry, with care for the environment.

The tourists must be made aware of the delicate environment into which they are about to venture—their demands must be in line with the availability of local resources

In eco-tourism, the role of locally owned micro-, small and medium enterprises is essential.

We need to find ways to build their capacity to survive, and maintain their social and environmental standards, thereby increasing economic benefits to local communities, and helping to address poverty.

Local communities should be alerted to the value of their natural environment and their culture preservation of the asset is vital to retaining the interest of tourists

The industry also has a duty to educate the tourists, and local people, and increase understanding between them—to ensure that expectations are in line with reality.

It must be recognized that some places are too fragile for shoe leather—mountain bikes—or motor vehicles—or indeed any kind of tourism-these places therefore remain out of bounds.

We look forward to working with the tourism industry to develop new products in connection with some of our conservation initiatives, such as the International Coral Reef Action Network (ICRAN), the Mountain Commons Project, and the Great Apes Survival Project (GRASP).

Monitoring Costs and Benefits of Eco-tourism

Many of the areas that have potential for eco-tourism are underdeveloped and poor.

In the local community incomes are often limited, and income-generating activities can even be at the expense of the environment, a valuable resource (*e.g.* Koroyanitu project, a National Park, Fiji—there the people were looking for alternatives to logging native forest, and land clearing for pine tree planting—they needed to secure a sustainable income—the area was important for conservation because of high natural and cultural values).

Ideally, tourism should support the protection of the natural resource—landowners should come to understand the value of their asset, and want to preserve it.

Visitors' interest in the nature and culture of an area can renew local people's pride in their stories and heritage.

The tour operators and those marketing the eco-tourism product must do everything possible to remain true to the ideals of eco-tourism-especially when it comes to involving the community and returning benefit to them.

Concrete local community development benefits can include improved services for local people (roads, communications, sanitation), poverty alleviation, and employment opportunities (including for women and young people).

Ongoing research and monitoring is needed, not only from academia, but from all affected stakeholders:

What are the lessons learned in these last 15 years of eco-tourism?

How can they be applied?

Conclusion

We Are All Responsible

The environment is the major asset of the developing world—the poor have little else—it must be preserved and used responsibly for sustainable development. Eco-tourism can play a role in ensuring the preservation and use of natural assets.

Responsibility to act now, rests with all stakeholders—Governments, local communities, tourists, the tourism industry and international organisations, such as my own.

Many of you here have good and bad experiences, to share over the coming days. We all look forward to learning from you. I echo the hopes of Kofi Annan, that in here and Johannesburg we will see all stakeholders come together in a new coalition, "A coalition for responsible prosperity"—a coalition to fight poverty and change unsustainable consumption patterns".

In our case, I hope that it will also be a coalition:

1. To establish guidelines and standards for eco-tourism.
2. To improve the environmental and social record of eco-tourism, through concrete projects on the ground.
3. To bring the lessons learned here on eco-tourism to the attention of the international community at the Johannesburg World Summit on Sustainable Development (WSSD).
4. To ensure that the Quebec Declaration on Eco-tourism is more than a piece of paper, it is a document, which should be implemented.

QUÉBEC DECLARATION ON ECO-TOURISM

In the framework of the UN International Year of Eco-tourism, 2002, under the aegis of the United Nations Environment Programme (UNEP) and the World Tourism Organisation (WTO), over one thousand participants coming from 132 countries, from the public, private and non-governmental sectors met at the World Eco-tourism Summit, hosted in Québec City, Canada, by Tourisme Québec and the Canadian Tourism Commission, between 19 and 22 May 2002.

The Québec Summit represented the culmination of 18 preparatory meetings held in 2001 and 2002, involving over 3,000 representatives from national and local governments including the tourism, environment and other administrations, private eco-tourism businesses and their trade associations, non-governmental organisations, academic institutions and consultants, intergovernmental organisations, and indigenous and local communities.

This document takes into account the preparatory process, as well as the discussions held during the Summit. It is the result of a multistakeholder dialogue, although it is not a negotiated document. Its main purpose is the setting of a preliminary agenda and a set of recommendations for the development of eco-tourism activities in the context of sustainable development.

The participants at the Summit acknowledge the World Summit on Sustainable Development (WSSD) in Johannesburg, August/September 2002, as the ground-setting event for international policy in the next 10 years, and emphasize that, as a leading industry, the sustainability of tourism should be a priority at WSSD due to its potential contribution to poverty alleviation and environmental protection in endangered eco-systems. Participants therefore request the UN, its organisations and member governments represented at this Summit to disseminate the following Declaration and other results from the World Eco-tourism Summit at the WSSD.

The participants to the World Eco-tourism Summit, aware of the limitations of this consultative process to incorporate the input of the large variety of eco-tourism stakeholders, particularly non-governmental organisations (NGOs) and local and indigenous communities.

Recognize that eco-tourism embraces the principles of sustainable tourism, concerning the economic, social and environmental impacts of tourism. It also embraces the following specific principles which distinguish it from the wider concept of sustainable tourism:

Contributes actively to the conservation of natural and cultural heritage.

Includes local and indigenous communities in its planning, development and operation, and contributing to their well-being.

Interprets the natural and cultural heritage of the destination to visitors.

Lends itself better to independent travellers, as well as to organized tours for small size groups.

Acknowledge that tourism has significant and complex social, economic and environmental implications, which can bring both benefits and costs to the environment and local communities.

Consider the growing interest of people in travelling to natural areas, both on land and sea.

Recognize that eco-tourism has provided a leadership role in introducing sustainability practices to the tourism sector.

Emphasize that eco-tourism should continue to contribute to make the overall tourism industry more sustainable, by increasing economic and social benefits for host communities, actively contributing to the conservation of natural resources and the cultural integrity of host communities, and by increasing awareness of all travellers towards the conservation of natural and cultural heritage.

Recognize the cultural diversity associated with many natural areas, particularly because of the historical presence of local and indigenous communities, of which some have maintained their traditional knowledge, uses and practices many of which have proven to be sustainable over the centuries.

Reiterate that funding for the conservation and management of biodiverse and culturally rich protected areas has been documented to be inadequate worldwide.

Recognize further that many of these areas are home to peoples often living in poverty, who frequently lack adequate health care, education facilities, communications systems, and other infrastructure required for genuine development opportunity.

Affirm that different forms of tourism, especially eco-tourism, if managed in a sustainable manner can represent a valuable economic opportunity for local and indigenous populations and their cultures and for the conservation and sustainable use of nature for future generations and can be a leading source of revenues for protected areas.

Emphasize that at the same time, wherever and whenever tourism in natural and rural areas is not properly planned, developed and managed, it contributes to the deterioration of natural landscapes, threats to wildlife and biodiversity, marine and coastal pollution, poor water quality, poverty, displacement of indigenous and local communities, and the erosion of cultural traditions.

Acknowledge that eco-tourism development must consider and respect the land and property rights, and, where recognized, the right to self-determination and cultural sovereignty of indigenous and local communities, including their protected, sensitive and sacred sites as well as their traditional knowledge.

Stress that to achieve equitable social, economic and environmental benefits from eco-tourism and other forms of tourism in natural areas, and to minimize or avoid potential negative impacts, participative planning mechanisms are needed that allow local and indigenous communities, in a transparent way, to define and regulate the use of their areas at the local level, including the right to opt out of tourism development.

Understand that small and micro businesses seeking to meet social and environmental objectives are key partners in eco-tourism and are often operating in a development climate that does not provide suitable financial and marketing support for eco-tourism.

Recognize that to improve the chances of survival of small-, medium-, and micro enterprises further understanding of the eco-tourism market will be required through market research, specialized credit instruments for tourism businesses, grants for external costs, incentives for the use of sustainable energy and innovative technical solutions, and an emphasis on developing skills not only in business but within government and those seeking to support business solutions.

Accept the need to avoid discrimination between people, whether by race, gender or other personal circumstances, with respect to their involvement in eco-tourism as consumers or suppliers.

Recognize that visitors have a responsibility to the sustainability of the destination and the global environment through their travel choice, behaviour and activities, and that therefore it is important to communicate to them the qualities and sensitivities of destinations.

In light of the above, the participants to the World Eco-tourism Summit, having met in Québec City, from 19 to 22 May 2002, produced a series of recommendations, which they propose to governments, the private sector, non-governmental organisations, community-based associations, academic and research institutions, inter-governmental organisations, international financial institutions, development assistance agencies, and indigenous and local communities, as follows:

To National, Regional and Local Governments

Formulate national, regional and local eco-tourism policies and development strategies that are consistent with the overall objectives of sustainable development, and to do so through a wide consultation process with those who are likely to become involved in, affect, or be affected by eco-tourism activities.

Guarantee-in conjunction with local and indigenous communities, the private sector, NGOs and all eco-tourism stakeholders—the protection of nature, local and indigenous cultures and specially traditional knowledge, genetic resources, rights to land and property, as well as rights to water.

Ensure the involvement, appropriate participation and necessary coordination of all the relevant public institutions at the national, provincial and local level, (including the establishment of inter-ministerial working groups as appropriate) at different stages in the eco-tourism process, while at the same time opening and facilitating the participation of other stakeholders in eco-tourism-related decisions. Furthermore, adequate budgetary mechanisms and appropriate legislative frameworks need to be set up to allow implementation of the objectives and goals set up by these multistakeholder bodies.

Include in the above framework the necessary regulatory and monitoring mechanisms at the national, regional and local levels, including objective sustainability indicators jointly agreed with all stakeholders and environmental impact assessment studies to be used as feedback mechanism. Results of monitoring should be made available to the general public.

Develop regulatory mechanisms for internalization of environmental costs in all aspects of the tourism product, including international transport. Develop the local and municipal capacity to implement growth management tools such as zoning, and participatory land-use planning not only in protected areas but in buffer zones and other eco-tourism development zones.

Use internationally approved and reviewed guidelines to develop certification schemes, ecolabels and other voluntary initiatives geared towards sustainability in eco-tourism, encouraging private operators to join such schemes and promoting their recognition by consumers. However, certification systems should reflect regional and local criteria. Build capacity and provide financial support to make these schemes accessible to small and medium enterprises (SMEs).

In addition, monitoring and a regulatory framework are necessary to support effective implementation of these schemes.

Ensure the provision of technical, financial and human resources development support to micro, small and medium-sized firms, which are the core of eco-tourism, with a view to enable them to start, grow and develop their businesses in a sustainable manner.

Define appropriate policies, management plans, and interpretation programmes for visitors, and earmark adequate sources of funding for natural areas to manage visitor numbers, protect vulnerable eco-systems, and the sustainable use of sensitive habitats. Such plans should include clear norms, direct and indirect management strategies, and regulations with the funds to ensure monitoring of social and environmental impacts for all eco-tourism businesses operating in the area, as well as for tourists wishing to visit them.

Include micro, small and medium-sized eco-tourism companies, as well as community-based and NGO-based eco-tourism operations in the overall promotional strategies and programmes carried out by the National Tourism Administration, both in the international and domestic markets.

Encourage and support the creation of regional networks and cooperation for promotion and marketing of eco-tourism products at the international and national levels. Provide incentives to tourism operators and other service providers (such as marketing and promotion advantages) for them to adopt eco-tourism principles and make their operations more environmentally, socially and culturally responsible.

Ensure that basic environmental and health standards are identified and met by all eco-tourism development even in the most rural areas. This should include aspects such as site selection, planning, design, the treatment of solid waste, sewage, and the protection of watersheds, etc., and ensure also that eco-tourism development strategies are not undertaken by governments without investment in sustainable infrastructure and the reinforcement of local/municipal capabilities to regulate and monitor such aspects.

Institute baseline environmental impact assessment (EIA) studies and surveys that record the social environmental state of destinations, with special attention to endangered species, and invest, or support institutions that invest in research programmes on eco-tourism and sustainable tourism.

Support the further implementation of the international principles, guidelines and codes of ethics for sustainable tourism (*e.g.* such as those proposed by UNEP, WTO, the Convention on Biological Diversity, the UN Commission on Sustainable Development and the International Labor Organisation) for the enhancement of international and national legal frameworks, policies and master plans to implement the concept of sustainable development into tourism.

Consider as one option the reallocation of tenure and management of public lands, from extractive or intensive productive sectors to tourism combined with conservation, wherever this is likely to improve the net social, economic and environmental benefit for the community concerned.

Promote and develop educational programmes addressed to children and young people to enhance awareness about nature conservation and sustainable use, local and indigenous cultures and their relationship with eco-tourism.

Promote collaboration between outbound tour operators and incoming operators and other service providers and NGOs at the destination to further educate tourists and influence their behaviour at destinations, especially those in developing countries.

Incorporate sustainable transportation principles in the planning and design of access and transportation systems, and encourage tour operators and the travelling public to make soft mobility choices.

To the Private Sector

Bear in mind that for eco-tourism businesses to be sustainable, they need to be profitable for all stakeholders involved, including the projects' owners, investors, managers and employees, as well as the communities and the conservation organisations of natural areas where it takes place.

Conceive, develop and conduct their businesses minimizing negative effects on, and positively contributing to, the conservation of sensitive eco-systems and the environment in general, and directly benefiting and including local and indigenous communities.

Ensure that the design, planning, development and operation of eco-tourism facilities incorporates sustainability principles, such as sensitive site design and community sense of place, as well as conservation of water, energy and materials, and accessibility to all categories of population without discrimination.

Adopt as appropriate a reliable certification or other systems of voluntary regulation, such as ecolabels, in order to demonstrate to their potential clients their adherence to sustainability principles and the soundness of the products and services they offer.

Cooperate with governmental and non-governmental organisations in charge of protected natural areas and conservation of biodiversity, ensuring that eco-tourism operations are practised according to the management plans and other regulations prevailing in those areas, so as to minimize any negative impacts upon them while enhancing the quality of the tourism experience and contribute financially to the conservation of natural resources.

Make increasing use of local materials and products, as well as local logistical and human resource inputs in their operations, in order to maintain the overall authenticity of the eco-tourism product and increase the proportion of financial and other benefits that remain at the destination. To achieve this, private operators should invest in the training of the local workforce. Ensure that the supply chain used in building up an eco-tourism operation is thoroughly sustainable and consistent with the level of sustainability aimed at in the final product or service to be offered to the customer.

Work actively with indigenous leadership and local

communities to ensure that indigenous cultures and communities are depicted accurately and with respect, and that their staff and guests are well and accurately informed regarding local and indigenous sites, customs and history.

Promote among their clients an ethical and environmentally conscious behaviour vis-à-vis the eco-tourism destinations visited, such as by environmental education or by encouraging voluntary contributions to support local community or conservation initiatives.

Generate awareness among all management and staff of local, national and global environmental and cultural issues through ongoing environmental education, and support the contribution that they and their families can make to conservation, community economic development and poverty alleviation.

Diversify their offer by developing a wide range of tourist activities at a given destination and by extending their operations to different destinations in order to spread the potential benefits of eco-tourism and to avoid overcrowding some selected eco-tourism sites, thus threatening their long-term sustainability. In this regard, private operators are urged to respect, and contribute to, established visitor impact management systems of eco-tourism destinations.

Create and develop funding mechanisms for the operation of business associations or cooperatives that can assist with eco-tourism training, marketing, product development, research and financing.

Ensure an equitable distribution of financial benefits from eco-tourism revenues between international, outbound and incoming tour operators, local service providers and local communities through appropriate instruments and strategic alliances.

Formulate and implement company policies for sustainability with a view to applying them in each part of their operations.

To Non-governmental Organisations, Community-Based Associations, Academic and Research Institutions

Provide technical, financial, educational, capacity building and other support to eco-tourism destinations, host community organisations, small businesses and the corresponding local authorities in order to ensure that appropriate policies, development and management guidelines, and monitoring mechanisms are being applied towards sustainability.

Monitor and conduct research on the actual impacts of eco-tourism activities upon eco-systems, biodiversity, local and indigenous cultures and the socio-economic fabric of the eco-tourism destinations.

Cooperate with public and private organisations ensuring that the data and information generated through research is channeled to support decision-making processes in eco-tourism development and management. Cooperate with research institutions to develop the most adequate and practical solutions to eco-tourism development issues.

Inter-governmental Organisations, International Financial Institutions and Development Assistance Agencies

Develop and assist in the implementation of national and local policy and planning guidelines and evaluation frameworks for eco-tourism and its relationships with biodiversity conservation, socio-economic development, respect of human rights, poverty alleviation, nature conservation and other objectives of sustainable development, and to intensify the transfer of such know-how to all countries. Special attention should be paid to countries in a developing stage or least developed status, to small island developing States and to countries with mountain areas, considering that 2002 is also designated as the International Year of Mountains by the UN.

Build capacity for regional, national and local organisations for the formulation and application of eco-tourism policies and plans, based on international guidelines.

Develop or adopt, as appropriate, international standards and financial mechanisms for eco-tourism certification systems that take into account the needs of small and medium enterprises and facilitates their access to those procedures, and support their implementation.

Incorporate multistakeholder dialogue processes into policies, guidelines and projects at the global, regional and national levels for the exchange of experiences between countries and sectors involved in eco-tourism.

Strengthen efforts in identifying the factors that determine the success or failure of eco-tourism ventures throughout the world, in order to transfer such experiences and best practices to other nations, by means of publications, field missions, training seminars and technical assistance projects; UNEP, WTO and other international organisations should continue and expand the international dialogue after the Summit on Sustainable Tourism and eco-tourism issues, for example by conducting periodical reviews of eco-tourism development through international and regional forums.

Adapt as necessary their financial facilities and lending conditions and procedures to suit the needs of micro-, small- and medium-sized eco-tourism firms that are the core of this industry, as a condition to ensure its long term economic sustainability. Develop the internal human resource capacity to support sustainable tourism and eco-tourism as a development sub-sector in itself and to ensure that internal expertise, research, and documentation are in place to oversee the use of eco-tourism as a sustainable development tool.

Develop financial mechanisms for training and capacity building, that takes into account the time and resources required to successfully enable local communities and indigenous peoples to participate equitably in eco-tourism development.

To Local and Indigenous Communities

As part of a community vision for development, that may include eco-tourism, define and implement a strategy for improving collective benefits for the community through eco-tourism development including human, physical, financial, and social capital development, and improved access to technical information.

Strengthen, nurture and encourage the community's ability to maintain and use traditional skills, particularly home-based arts and crafts, agricultural produce, traditional housing and landscaping that use local natural resources in a sustainable manner.

To the World Summit on Sustainable Development (WSSD)

Recognize the need to apply the principles of sustainable development to tourism, and the exemplary role of eco-tourism in generating economic, social and environmental benefits.

Integrate the role of tourism, including eco-tourism, in the outcomes expected at WSSD.

FINAL SUMMIT REPORT THE WORLD ECO-TOURISM SUMMIT

Introduction

The World Eco-tourism Summit, was held in Quebec City, Canada from 19 to 22 May, 2002. This was the principal event to mark 2002 as the International Year of Eco-tourism. The Summit was an initiative of the World Tourism Organisation (WTO) and the United Nations Environment Programme (UNEP). It was hosted by Tourisme Québec and the Canadian Tourism Commission. These four organisations were the partners responsible for the Summit.

The purpose of the Summit was to bring together governments, international agencies, NGOs, tourism enterprises, representatives of local and indigenous communities, academic institutions and individuals with an interest in eco-tourism, and enable them to learn from each other and identify some agreed principles and priorities for the future development and management of eco-tourism.

Main Themes

UNEP and WTO, in consultation with other organisations and eco-tourism stakeholders, had defined and adopted the following main discussion themes for the International Year of Eco-tourism and for the Summit.

- *Theme A—Eco-tourism policy and planning: the sustainability challenge*: Sustainable eco-tourism plans, policies and programmes at international, national and local levels; integration of eco-tourism policies into sustainable development plans and frameworks; land use planning; use of natural parks and protected areas; balance between development and conservation objectives in policies; development agency programmes on eco-tourism and their role in funding related pipeline investments; plans for human resource development in eco-tourism.

- *Theme B—Regulation of eco-tourism: institutional responsibilities and frameworks*: Legislation, norms and other regulations for eco-tourism activities; voluntary schemes and self regulation; certification, accreditation and ecolabels; international and inter-governmental guidelines, principles and codes; roles of different stakeholders in ensuring compliance with regulations or voluntary schemes.

- *Theme C—Product development, marketing and promotion of eco-tourism: fostering sustainable products and consumers*: Building sustainable eco-tourism products; multi-stakeholder cooperation for product development especially in protected areas and biosphere reserves; market research, marketing techniques and promotional methods; information to tourists; ethical behaviour; environmental education for consumers; public-private sector relationships for marketing and promotion; co-operative marketing for small eco-tourism operations.

- *Theme D—Monitoring costs and benefits of eco-tourism: ensuring equitable distribution among all stakeholders*:

Measuring economic, ecological and social costs and benefits of eco-tourism; contribution to conservation; assessing potential and actual environmental and socio-cultural impacts of eco-tourism; taking precautionary measures at local, national, regional and international levels; integrating monitoring and evaluation procedures; research needs and adaptive management systems.

Cross-cutting Themes

Throughout the discussions on the four themes the focus was on two main cross-cutting issues:

- The sustainability of eco-tourism from the environmental, economic and socio-cultural points of view.
- Involvement and empowerment of local communities and indigenous people in the eco-tourism development process, in management and monitoring of eco-tourism activities, and in the sharing of benefits resulting from it.

The Preparatory Process for the Summit

During the latter half of 2001 and the first four months of 2002, 18 preparatory conferences were held. These conferences took place in all the regions of the world, either under the aegis of WTO or of UNEP (in association with The International Eco-tourism Society). A list of the conferences can be found later, in the reports of the regional panels. The preparatory conferences provided an opportunity for all kinds of stakeholders in eco-tourism to come together to present their experiences and discuss matters of local, regional or international concern. In total over 3,000 delegates attended the conferences and over 300 papers were presented at them.

The preparatory conferences addressed each of the four main themes of the Summit. The combined results of the conferences were summarised in four papers, one for each of the themes, which together formed a discussion paper circulated at the start of the Summit.

Participants and Presentations

A total of 1,169 delegates attended the World Eco-tourism Summit, from 132 different countries. The range of delegates included:

- International agencies engaged in supporting conservation, tourism and sustainable development.
- National ministries of tourism, culture and the environment. In total 30 ministers of state attended the Summit.
- Non-governmental organisations working at an international or local level, representing conservation, indigenous communities, travellers and other interests.
- Private sector enterprises engaged directly or indirectly in eco-tourism.
- Academics, consultants and other experts in the field of eco-tourism.

Registered delegates were invited to submit statements relating to the Summit themes. A total of 180 statement proposals were received. From these, 120 were selected for presentation during the event, considering time limitations of the three-day programme. The selection was based on the relevance and originality of the contribution and on the need to achieve a representative balance of presentations from different types of organisation and parts of the world. In addition to the registered statements, participants had the opportunity to intervene freely throughout the debate sessions.

Structure of the Summit

Following introductory presentations from the partners, the Summit consisted of the following elements:

- A plenary session at which four panels reported on the preparatory conferences held, respectively, in Africa, Asia, the Americas and Europe.

- Four parallel working group sessions, covering the four main themes of the Summit.

- A ministerial forum, and two special forums covering the business perspective and development cooperation in eco-tourism.

- A plenary session to receive and debate reports from the four thematic working groups.

Reports from the Regional Panels

The opportunities presented by eco-tourism and the need for its careful management are apparent in all regions of the world. Evidence from the preparatory conferences suggested that the fundamental principles and issues relating to the development of eco-tourism are similar in all areas. However, it was also apparent that differences in resources, eco-systems, markets and socio-economic structures, mean that priorities and practicalities vary from region to region.

These similarities and differences were brought out during the reports of the regional panels at the Summit. During each panel session, short presentations were made by selected spokespersons on the preparatory conferences held in that region. In the main, these conferences had focused on the region in which the conference was held, but in a few cases the conferences covered types of destination (*e.g.* islands, deserts, Arctic lands) irrespective of continent.

Following the presentations on the preparatory conferences, the sessions were opened up to interventions from the floor and a discussion. At the end of each session, the key points that had arisen were identified by the rapporteurs.

Session on Preparatory Meetings Held in Africa

Four reports were presented to the Summit on the preparatory meetings held in the following locations:

- Maputo, Mozambique, March 2001—for all African states with an emphasis on planning and management.

- Nairobi, Kenya, March 2002—for East Africa.
- Mahé, Seychelles, December 2001—for Small Island Developing States (SIDS) and other Small Islands.
- Algiers, Algeria, January 2002—for Desert Areas.

The presentations in this panel demonstrated that eco-tourism is one of the main forms of tourism in which Africa has a comparative advantage.

Africa features extensive protected areas hosting a variety of eco-systems and traditional cultures that are major attractions for nature-oriented tourism. In many African countries, vast national and wildlife parks count for many forms of eco-tourism activities.

Eco-tourism seems the best way to prevent controversial effects and negative impacts on prevailing eco-systems, local communities and traditional cultures and to be a viable source of economic benefits for African countries, if developed and managed in a sustainable manner.

The specific circumstances and needs for different areas were separately identified.

Africa's International Comparative Advantage: National Parks and Protected Areas

Eco-tourism is a great opportunity for African countries and its parks, reserves and protected areas are an international level resource. Thus, many African countries can base their tourism development on exploiting their natural assets on the condition that the rules of sustainable development—the basis of eco-tourism—are respected. Conservation of natural resources can become mainstream to socio-economic development in Africa. National parks and reserves in Africa should be considered as a basis for regional development, involving communities living within and adjacent to them. Given their strong international recognition, parks and reserves can be turned to sort of brands, providing advantage in tourism marketing and promotion.

Small Islands and Coastal Zones

Particular attention must be focused on tourism development in small islands as development, even eco-tourism development, can be at the origin of environmental and social problems—even before large number of tourist arrivals. This is the case of coastal zones in small islands where eco-systems, notably lagoons, are particularly vulnerable. Appropriate liquid and solid waste treatment systems must be put in place whenever any eco-tourism activity is created.

Moreover, ecolabels are particularly important for small insular countries as shown in the example of the Seychelles. Ecolabels can be very useful for achieving landscaping and beautification objectives, such as by encouraging better use of gardens, and for stimulating environmental management, such as energy conservation, waste treatment plants and recycling systems.

Due to the natural and economic specificities of tourism in small islands it is not realistic to focus on eco-tourism in the stricter sense. Rather, the broader concept of "sustainable tourism" is often a more effective policy position, though eco-tourism plays an important role in further setting the standards for the protection of the natural and cultural environment.

The fragility of island eco-systems must be the cornerstone of any eco-tourism plan and any action must respect the island's local, natural and cultural environments.

Desert Areas

Desert areas represent comparative and even absolute advantages for Africa, which has the largest desert in the world. Deserts are also some of the largest conservation areas in the world. The seminar in Algiers concluded that there are great opportunities for eco-tourism in desert areas—particularly for Africa because of its location near the large tourist generating markets of Europe. Desert areas represent complex eco-tourism attractions, showcasing natural, geological, and archaeological features, nomad and other specific cultures and traditions. A special attention should be paid in eco-tourism development and management in desert areas to the fragility of eco-systems, the extreme meteorological conditions, the presence of unique archaeological and geological remains, the scarcity of water resources and the difficulties of access.

Importance of Trans-boundary Cooperation

Many natural zones cross the political borders of several countries and this must be taken into account when developing eco-tourism. Indeed, it is impossible to envisage diverging or even opposed development policies in zones shared by several States where there is natural, human and social unity. In this case, trans-boundary cooperation is fundamental for all types of eco-tourism development, which implies common policies between countries in the same region. This cooperation is particularly necessary in areas where wildlife crosses administrative and political borders.

The development and management of trans-boundary natural resources and parks has to become a central issue in Africa, recognizing the need to maintain ecological integrity and free movement of wildlife in certain territories that are divided by country frontiers.

The Need to Find Commercial and Financial Solutions

The commercial viability of eco-tourism initiatives is a recurring theme in the debates such as in the case studies presented in the preparatory seminars, specifically in Maputo. Participants emphasised the importance of strengthening small and medium enterprises and particularly micro enterprises to enable them to successfully engage with the tourism industry in Africa. The importance of identifying and demonstrating to funding sources the value of conservation and of eco-tourism to national economies in Africa has to be recognised.

The Need to Reinforce Capacity Building

There is a lack of awareness of tourism among African local communities. Local communities need to appreciate the benefits and the demerits of tourism. It is important for governments to ensure that communities are trained to administer joint ventures, as without capacity building it is difficult to sustain an equitable approach to management. Capacity building is essential if local communities are to be real stakeholders in the development of eco-tourism in Africa.

African Necessity to Focus on Benefits for Local People

Speakers and participants identified the need to generate local community benefits from Africa's natural heritage tourism as the critical issue. Eco-tourism as a concept has most to offer in the African development context, linking to the rural economy to avoid leakages and maximise local economic benefit from tourism. In Africa, national parks, wildlife reserves and other protected areas have to play a significant role in encouraging local economic development by sourcing food and other locally produced resources.

Session on Preparatory Meetings Held in Asia and the Pacific

Five reports were presented to the Summit on the preparatory meetings held in the following locations:

- New Delhi, India, September 2001—International NGO Workshop Tourism Towards 2002.
- Gangtok, India, January 2002—Conference for South Asia.
- Maldives, February 2002—Asia-Pacific Ministerial Conference on Sustainable Development of Eco-tourism.
- Chiang Mai, Thailand, March 2002—Conference for Southeast Asia.
- Fiji, April 2002—Conference on Sustainable Development of Eco-tourism in the South Pacific Islands.

The papers and debates from the Session on Asia and the Pacific highlighted a number of issues and perspectives, as follows.

Need for Baseline Studies

The importance of baseline studies was highlighted, in order to provide a better knowledge on ground conditions, and changes over time. It was recommended that innovative approaches be examined, instead of reliance on government, particularly in under-resourced areas. Suggestions included involving volunteer organisations (*e.g.*, those that provide programmes in which conservation and community development work is combined with educational, cultural exchange and tourist activities), or involving educational institutions.

Commoditisation in Tourism

Particular mention was made of commoditisation in tourism in the region, in large part due to poverty. Commoditisation refers to the degradation of the intrinsic value of cultural items, beliefs, goods, and practices, and may even refer to treating a human being as a good for sale. This trivialisation of culture is demonstrated by the sale of culturally related trinkets, and even by people selling themselves (sexually) to visitors. Organisations developing or managing eco-tourism are urged to focus on the improvement of basic human conditions.

Managing Impacts

A range of approaches were mentioned for managing impacts, from pricing and fees, to diversification of product offers (to alleviate crowding). However, a serious impact with no solutions offered, was that of global warming in the region.

The Need to Integrate a Range of Perspectives, with Communications being Key

In some Asia-Pacific destinations, ministries try to push their own agendas on other departments and vice versa (*e.g.*, Tourism and Forestry). This achieves very little except resistance. There needs to be awareness and capacity building in government departments, to understand that eco-tourism can be a force to assist both mandates.

It was observed by some participants that some NGOs always feel government actions are wrong, and governments tend to pay less attention to constant criticism. Other participants felt that NGOs have some valid perspectives whether in critique of governments or not, and that NGO comments deserve appropriate attention. It was also felt that some NGOs or governments actually undermine private business. The issue that emerged was: how to integrate the range of perspectives, and how to cooperate to mutually beneficial ends.

Improved communications are required. In particular, it was recommended that:

- Governments should establish an open dialogue with local communities, private companies and NGOs;
- Governments should develop transparent communication, consultation and decision making processes; and
- Public-private partnerships should be seen as a key facilitating mechanism, particularly for informing and educating the travelling public about the consequences of their travels as well as their potential for beneficial action.

Challenges of Implementing Community Participation

The challenge of how to implement sustainability through empowerment and participation was discussed, since local participation has an important role in preserving biodiversity.

Bottom-up participatory processes were recommended (*e.g.*, as in Fiji, where the Fiji Eco-tourism Association was formed, so that government and others could more easily communicate with an umbrella industry organisation).

Top-down participatory mechanisms were also recommended, as well as a mechanism for multi-sectoral involvement. It was suggested that communities should be consulted on a range of topics, from product development to elements of marketing.

It was acknowledged that time is required for awareness

and capacity building, so that communities are able to participate effectively and make decisions.

Community control of local resources was said to be a key need in the Asia-Pacific region. It was suggested that communities should be involved in all levels of activity, including management.

Participatory management was said to be a key tool in ensuring participation in planning, decision-making and management. An example was given of Sri Lanka, where both poachers and policemen communicate together, and although it has taken five years (as well as time, patience, energy, and the efforts of the Eco-Development Committee), both parties now have confidence in the process, and poachers are using their locally-developed skills in a more sustainable way.

It was agreed that eco-tourism is best developed to enhance and complement current community lifestyles and economic activities, rather than basing community economies solely or predominantly on eco-tourism, or introducing a completely new activity. It was also frequently stated and agreed that communities should have control over eco-tourism, including whether they wanted to have it at all, and if so how much, where, when and of what type.

Human Resource Development is Required

It was recommended that there should be a bigger emphasis on training for local people. In the Asia-Pacific region there is a very great need to incorporate local indigenous peoples into any training programmes. It was also felt that communities in general need to have awareness training or information related to eco-tourism, and also to be made aware that they may have a choice about tourism or other activities.

A challenge related to this topic was how to develop mechanisms to ensure that revenues from eco-tourism activities are invested in training (*e.g.*, on-the-job training, management training, or sending workers to attend conferences).

Regulation and Monitoring is Required

Regulations can either have a positive role in facilitating movements of tourists and foreign exchange in SE Asia, or can be restrictive. It was suggested that very often poor planning has had adverse consequences and needs to be improved. Also, the lack of enforcement of current regulations is a problem.

Session on Preparatory Meetings Held in The Americas

Six reports were presented to the Summit on the preparatory meetings held in the following locations:

- Cuiabá, Brazil, August 2001, for all American states.
- Belize City, Belize, November 2001, for Mesoamerica.
- Lima, Peru, February 2002, for the Andean region.
- Oaxaca, Mexico, March 2002, Oaxaca Declaration on Indigenous Tourism.
- Buenos Aires, Argentina, April 2002, First National Conference on Eco-tourism.
- Web Conference on the Sustainable Development of Eco-tourism, April 2002.

The Americas are probably one of the regions in the world where eco-tourism is developing fastest. There is also an increasing concern about the involvement of indigenous peoples and local communities both in the planning and development of eco-tourism.

The preparatory conference reports showed clearly three main concerns about the development of eco-tourism: the involvement of local communities; the need for certification schemes easily accessible to everybody regardless of their economic capacity; and much needed training at all levels. In general, there is consensus about the fact that eco-tourism can and is contributing actively to nature conservation in the region, and also to a better quality of life for local people. It has also been recognised that it is very important to learn from past mistakes as well as successes.

Planning

One of the issues raised around planning was the specific problem of trans-boundary areas where there is a need for international regulations. Another important point was that very often not all available scientific information is used for planning.

A further concern was that it is important to have a diverse range of activities besides eco-tourism such as agriculture, livestock, forest non-timber products, and others, thus avoiding over-dependence on eco-tourism. Shifting from traditional sustainable use of resources (when these uses are sustainable, which is not always the case) to eco-tourism is a high-risk strategy for local communities. Besides, in areas where eco-tourism products mix with other kinds of tourism, it is agreed that there is a need to increase the sustainability of all tourism products.

Regulation and Certification

A suitable approach regarding regulation is to follow a process leading from optional guidelines to obligatory regulations. Codes of conduct need to be established as well as procedures and all stakeholders should adopt these. The importance of ethics among operators, the community and consumers was also identified as one of the key issues.

Another important point raised was that regulation of eco-tourism needs stakeholders sharing a similar concept of eco-tourism.

It was agreed that there is a need for more transparency in certification processes and that these should relate both to environmental aspects as well as quality and participation of local communities. International certification systems are believed to be too expensive and it was suggested that local initiatives should be recognised by international systems. It was suggested that certification should occur at different levels that are more suited to specific regional and local conditions and allow community-based companies to take part in the process.

There were proposals to establish incentives for certified companies. Finally it was recognised that in some areas there is a risk of a proliferation of eco-labels.

Participation of Indigenous and Local People

One of the main concerns was the lack of public participation in the process of planning for eco-tourism in many places. It was stressed that local communities need to be the main actors and that they must take part not only in the planning process but also in the management of eco-tourism products, which generally means also taking risks. A particularly sensitive issue was the concern among indigenous people about the fact that in some of their lands eco-tourism development is being imposed by governments and private companies, without proper consultation and participation.

Capacity Building and Training

Capacity building and training were identified as key points in the proper development of eco-tourism in the region. This included the need for capacity building of local communities, training and technical support. An important point raised was that training needs to be realistic, not creating too high expectations for local communities.

Policy makers were also identified as important targets for training and it was shown that they need to learn about eco-tourism in the field. Very often policies are in the hands of people with very little practical experience in the subject. Another target much in need of education about eco-tourism is the media in general, who very often cover eco-tourism but without reflecting properly its real essence.

Marketing

A fairly common problem in the Americas is that marketing generally focuses in landscape, wildlife and cultural issues and does not put enough emphasis in social, environmental and sustainability aspects, which should be part of responsible marketing communications and very often can be of interest to potential visitors.

In recent years there has been a great development of communications within the region and the Internet has become an important tool for marketing, even for small companies and communities, as well as in remote areas where Cybercafés can be accessible. The Internet can fulfil its potential only if capacity-building and access to modern technology is provided in order to empower eco-tourism stakeholders for the adequate use of this media.

Session on Preparatory Meetings Held in Europe

Four reports were presented to the Summit on the preparatory meetings held in the following locations:

- St. Johann/Pongau and Werfenweng, Salzburg, Austria 12-15 September 2001—for mountain areas, with an emphasis on European eco-tourism.
- Almaty, Kazakhstan, 17-18 October 2001—for the transitional economies of the CIS countries, Mongolia and China.
- Thessaloniki, Greece, 2-4 November 2001—for European, Middle East and Mediterranean countries.
- Hemavan, Sweden, April 2002—for the Arctic countries, including North America and Asia as well as Europe.

In addition, a paper was presented by the Minister of Tourism of Turkey.

Although the term 'eco-tourism' is less frequently used in Europe than in other continents, the presentations showed that the principles and concepts associated with it are equally important here as elsewhere. Europe has many wilderness areas, yet in much of the continent attractive rural landscapes and biodiversity are dependent on traditional land management practices. There is increasing recognition within Europe of the important and mutually supporting relationship between tourism, agriculture, viable rural communities and the conservation of nature.

The preparatory conference reports demonstrated the contrasts to be found within Europe, in terms of landscapes, climate, culture and management priorities. The specific circumstances and needs of different areas were separately identified.

Mountains

Mountains are important locations for eco-tourism. The report from the conference in Austria recognised the important linkages between the objectives of the International Year of Mountains and the International Year of Eco-tourism, both declared for 2002 by the UN. Mountainous areas often display a particular cultural richness, economic fragility, a decline in traditional populations and activities, and sensitive biodiversity. Mountain communities can use eco-tourism to address these issues. There is a close relationship between the needs and opportunities of eco-tourism and sustainable activity tourism in mountains.

The Mediterranean

This area receives some of the largest volumes of tourist arrivals in the world, concentrated on the coastal belt. Yet, this is an area of rich biodiversity and also has immense cultural resources. The report from the conference in Greece identified the opportunity for eco-tourism in the coastal hinterland and more remote inland areas, as a way of improving the image of Mediterranean destinations, diversifying the offer, reducing seasonality and bringing economic benefits to areas suffering depopulation. Careful planning will be essential.

The CIS Countries

These countries have extensive natural areas including forests, wetlands, plains and mountains. Potential for eco-tourism is considerable. However, as economies and societies in transition they have particular needs, especially in terms of the general services and infrastructure for tourism. Important issues include clarifying national objectives for eco-tourism, stimulating and catering for the domestic market, filling knowledge gaps, easing visa restrictions and promoting cross-border cooperation.

The Arctic

This is a sensitive area with its own particular needs. The traditional values and practices of the indigenous peoples of the Arctic, in protecting and using natural resources, should be recognised, as should their rights over land and water. The report from the conference held in Sweden identified the need for certification programmes for eco-tourism which take account of the particular circumstances of the Arctic. Appropriate codes of conduct for visitors and operators need to be applied. A restructuring of the cruise ship licensing system was called for, with local people having control over the use of their areas for eco-tourism.

In addition to these priorities relating to specific areas or eco-systems, a number of general themes of particular importance in the European context can be identified from the presentations and the subsequent discussion.

Taking an Integrated Approach to Destination Planning

There is strong recognition in Europe of the need for a holistic approach to the planning and development of destinations for sustainable tourism, both in terms of providing a quality experience for visitors and addressing all the impacts of tourism. Eco-tourism should be seen within this context. There should be concern about physical infrastructure, destination marketing and information services, linkages with other economic sectors, and relationships with other forms of tourism.

The important role of local authorities in supporting the development and management of sustainable tourism, including eco-tourism, is well understood in Europe. This is helped by well-established local democratic structures, effective land use planning and development control processes. At the same time, the need to foster a participative approach at a local level, for example through engaging village communities, is recognised.

Addressing Transport and Other Access Issues

The use of transport to, and within, the destination was a key concern of the preparatory conference in Austria. Where possible, eco-tourism should be based on forms of mobility which have low environmental impact. Discussion at the Summit widened the debate on access, with a call for more attention to be paid to facilitating access to rural and natural areas, including mountains, for example through networks of hiking trails.

Being Concerned About Demand and Equity Amongst Users

Demand management was felt to be an important issue in the European context. Points made about this during the discussion included:

- avoiding discrimination and increasing access to eco-tourism experiences for people with disabilities and disadvantages;
- promoting opportunities to domestic visitors, ensuring that they are not put off by high prices (*e.g.* in the CIS countries); and
- influencing larger tour operators as well as more specialist operators (*e.g.* in the Mediterranean).

Showing Responsibility in Promoting Eco-tourism in Less Developed Countries

Europe is a source region for much global eco-tourism. The responsibility of European governments and operators in encouraging more sustainable forms of eco-tourism, and in providing technical advice and support in this field, is recognised.

Reports from the Thematic Working Groups

The second full day of the Summit was devoted to four separate working groups on the four Summit themes.

Each working group meeting started with the presentation of a report from an expert, appointed by WTO and UNEP, which summarised the results of the preparatory conferences and served as discussion paper for the Summit concerning the theme in question.

A total of 71 presentations were made to the four working groups. These were restricted in time, to enable a range of topics to be covered and to give as many people as possible a chance to speak. Two presentations from the host country, Canada, were made during the first session of each group. The presentations were grouped into four sessions throughout the day, and after each one at least half an hour was allowed for interventions from the floor and for debate. In the closing session, the WTO/UNEP experts summed up the main points to be taken forward to the final day of the Summit, and these were further discussed and expanded by delegates during a final hour of debate.

On the third and final day, a report from each working group was made to a full plenary session of the Summit. This was followed by a discussion period which enabled all delegates to have a chance to make further points about each theme, and to comment on the conclusions of the working groups.

The four reports which follow set out the issues discussed and the key points and recommendations arising from the working groups, while also taking account of the points raised in the final plenary session.

These reports build on the summary reports of the preparatory conferences, adding to, illustrating and emphasising points made in them. A short resume of the key points arising from the preparatory conferences is given, before the points arising from the Summit are presented.

Many of the points made were repeated in more than one workshop. This is inevitable as most of the principles of eco-tourism relate to all of the themes and each of the topics are interdependent. For example, eco-tourism planning needs to take account of product development and regulation issues, and vice versa.

Eco-tourism Policy and Planning:
The Sustainability Challenge

Eco-tourism is a complex activity, often seeking to meet a range of objectives, involving a variety of stakeholders and taking place in environmentally and economically fragile locations. It therefore needs careful planning. This working group was concerned with the frameworks, structures and processes of eco-tourism planning and policy-making to maximise sustainability and local benefit.

There were eighteen presentations to the working group, which covered:

- National eco-tourism planning, policy-making and strategy development—Botswana, Chile, Cote d'Ivoire, Haiti, Rwanda, France, Brazil, Senegal, Tanzania, the Mayan World.
- Eco-tourism planning systems in federal and provincial parks—Canada.
- A case study of ecosystem changes in tourist destinations—Nepal.
- Guidelines to minimise negative impacts of eco-tourism in vulnerable eco-systems (the Convention on Biological Diversity) or small islands (Seychelles).
- Integrated planning and management in rural areas—Greece, Chile.
- Policies developed by origin countries for minimising tourism impacts in destinations—The Netherlands.

Issues Discussed

The main issues discussed were:

- The best structures and tools for effective eco-tourism planning, which relate to all objectives,
- Planning for environmental conservation,
- Planning for economic development,
- Gaining social and cultural benefits, and
- Multi-stakeholder participation.

The following specific issues arose throughout the debates:

The Relationship between Eco-tourism and Sustainable Tourism

It was suggested that planning and policy development for sustainable tourism was the appropriate context for eco-tourism planning, since eco-tourism embraces the principles of sustainable tourism concerning the economic, social and environmental impacts of tourism. On the other hand, it was also suggested that there was merit in highlighting the particular characteristics of eco-tourism, bringing positive benefits for conservation and communities and not simply avoiding negative impacts. It was recognised that eco-tourism products may vary considerably, but that all should adhere to basic eco-tourism principles.

Lack of Appropriate Infrastructure and Services in Destinations

In many destinations with eco-tourism potential, it is felt that there is a lack of infrastructure (*e.g.*, accommodation) and services (*e.g.*, well-trained guides).

Foreign Ownership or Low Levels of Local Jobs Minimise Local Benefits

The issue of foreign ownership draining many of the benefits at the local level was raised. This is particularly the case with respect to infrastructure. In addition, the level and quality of jobs in which local people are employed is too often inadequate (*e.g.*, in Senegal).

Eco-tourism Brand

The themes of the Summit are in many cases strongly interrelated. Within the Planning and Policy Development sessions, there were discussions about the desire to prevent the use of the word eco-tourism by those who do not adhere to its principles, through some type of trademark or branding protection, although the difficulties in this were also acknowledged. This whole topic was the focus of considerable discussion in Session B, and reference to that section provides further insight.

Uncontrolled Penetration of Eco-tourism Activities Into New Areas

The penetration of eco-tourism (or other forms of tourism) to remote areas can create management and monitoring problems. For example, in Egypt treks go to very remote areas of the country, which are mostly desert. The difficulty of monitoring tourism operations in remote areas enables the stealing of artefacts, fossils, etc.

Key Points and Recommendations

A number of key points and recommendations arising from the working group were specifically related to conservation, economic development, social benefits and stakeholder participation. However, there were many points that cut across these issues and these are presented first.

Key Crosscutting Recommendations

Main recommendations from the preparatory conferences:

- Integrate eco-tourism policies and planning across national boundaries,
- Ensure national governments provide necessary leadership and guidance,
- Create a planning framework for protected areas,
- Formulate eco-tourism plans jointly between public

agencies, NGOs and other stakeholders, with a long term vision and clear goals,

- Develop tools to assist in planning and management of eco-tourism (*e.g.* appropriate land use planning and visitor management techniques),
- Provide adequate and appropriate funding for projects, protected areas and partnerships,
- Involve governments, development agencies, NGOs, private businesses and others in building local capacity, to encourage participation and employment of local people, and
- Ensure careful consultation and participation of all stakeholders in planning and policy development processes.

Key points arising from the Summit:

Transboundary management approaches: The need for transnational policies was emphasised, related to many aspects of tourism, such as easier movement of peoples between regions, and cooperation with respect to shared ecosystem management.

Humans should be recognised and acknowledged as being a part of the ecosystem (as opposed to only using eco-systems). Transboundary movement possibilities should be built into plans and policies.

There was a recommendation that a world fund be established to enable appropriate eco-tourism development particularly at the trans-national level, with the focus intended to be on enhancing cooperative activities between jurisdictions. However, no specific proposal was made on the nature and source of the fund.

It was proposed that global regions (*e.g.*, the Caribbean) should come together for a range of planning and policy development functions (*e.g.*, to highlight issues which have regional relevance).

Collaborative approach to planning and policy development: There should be an overall national vision of how eco-tourism can serve biodiversity, as well as how biodiversity can serve eco-tourism. One of the biggest problems is lack of a sectoral planning perspective (*e.g.*, the frequent divorce in dialogue between tourism agencies and environmental agencies). All agencies need to work together. It is recommended that lessons and failures be taken from such planning processes as Integrated Coastal Zone Management Studies, for integrating eco-tourism planning. Integrated planning should be actively pursued, including collaboration with stakeholders.

Government must take a holistic perspective when developing sustainability strategies, which is both spatial and sectoral (*e.g.*, as in Greece). Eco-tourism planning should be conducted within the context of sustainable tourism planning, which in turn should relate to the wider context of planning for sustainable development. Eco-tourism planning, actions and policies should be developed with the knowledge that they are likely to be applicable to other forms of tourism, and in all likelihood will be a force for positive change throughout tourism, considering the trends towards mainstreaming eco-tourism values and principles. For example, in Tanzania, there are major policy reforms stimulated by the International Year of Eco-tourism, which are focussing on poverty reduction through a range of sectoral perspectives such as developing economic opportunities and empowering communities through community participation.

Sectoral integration should be a foundation of all planning and policy development (not only in eco-tourism). For example, Chile's National Action Plan is based on an integrated approach, and has been done with the private sector, in a bottom-up manner. Another example is found in the Seychelles, where there are not only various topical themes within their National Environmental Management Plan (including tourism and aesthetics), but there are significant cross-cutting themes (education, awareness and advocacy; partnerships, public consultation and civil society participation; training and capacity-building; management; science, research and technology; monitoring and assessment; vulnerability and global climate change).

It was recommended that whatever the mechanisms, all decision-making be transparent, and also accountable.

Appropriate tools for planning and management: It was recommended that appropriate scale in eco-tourism development be a part of planning considerations. For example, some destinations build in development controls ahead of time (*e.g.*, Botswana has, as part of its planning framework, deliberately stipulated small-sizes for their ecolodges and camps, or temporary facility structures to enable them to be moved in the future).

There was a comment that in many areas, policies and regulations may exist, but are not implemented. While appropriate planning and policy development is one requirement, rigorous implementation is fundamental.

Planning systematically for protected areas: It was emphasised in debates that a protected area system must form a key part of planning and policy making for eco-tourism, and that protected area managers be involved in planning initiatives (not only senior government officials).

A severe problem for protecting biodiversity and protected areas was felt to be the fragmentation of eco-systems. It was recommended that the issue of adequate size of protected areas be addressed in development and planning. It was suggested that a useful educational and management tool is the creation of maps to illustrate locations, threats, or other spatial variables, so indicating where it is most necessary to conserve biodiversity.

Committing adequate financial and other resources: Some countries lack the ability to mobilize the resources necessary to address significant eco-tourism planning and policy development needs. Multilateral aid is required in the form of various types of assistance. One recommendation was that there be support for centres of development and dissemination of knowledge and cooperation; another was that there be a fund for trans-national eco-tourism development.

The public may be encouraged to contribute funds. It was suggested that visitors and others should be able to donate funds to projects, and should receive some recognitions and benefits which reinforce the value of their donation. For example, the Coral Reef Action Network offers donors a range of educational reminders: stickers to heighten awareness, CD with a tool kit for customers, wall calendar, passport, poster, boaters' chart, quiz and similar items. These educate and keep donors involved with the project. In addition, they give donors guarantees that all their contributions will go to the chosen project.

It was suggested that some funding for education, in schools and elsewhere, be set aside from eco-tourism revenues.

Capacity building: Training and capacity building is required for those professionals who are involved in planning and policy development. It is recommended that the WTO and other international institutions support or fund programmes which train public officials who will be planning and developing policies, in order to build capacity within ministries and similar institutions (*e.g.*, this could be through national level training institutions). This suggestion of appropriate training was also made for the personnel of park and protected area authorities.

At a more local level, it was suggested that the WTO and other institutions should continue to expand training programmes, such as for local authorities, indigenous people and other stakeholders. Another suggestion was that a range of types of support be examined to develop capabilities locally, such as guiding skills.

It was recommended that tour operators also be involved in education and training.

Education and awareness-building is recommended as a significant tool for all players, from lodge owners and tour operators to local communities and young people. Suggestions included such innovative ideas as developing education caravans for community awareness building, or creating coursework for schools to better understand the concept of impact.

The views and perspectives of youth are a key influence on positive future directions. It is recommended that sustainable tourism education of young people be built into educational programmes and ministry curricula in all countries.

It was recommended that the Internet be better used for information exchange. International agencies should collaborate to compile a database of information, which is web accessible, continually updated, and includes information on best practice for sustainable tourism and for eco-tourism. It was suggested that qualified websites with useful information should be able to link to this site.

Building multi-stakeholder participation into policy and planning processes: Mechanisms should be developed to include a range of stakeholders in planning and policy development. It is always easier for governments to deal with umbrella organisations than with operators directly, thus developing industry organisations may assist. For example, Parks Canada and the Tourism Industry Association of Canada have developed an accord concerning heritage-based tourism, which is currently focussed on agreement about principles, which acknowledge shared stewardship in managing and protecting national heritage places.

Indigenous peoples' representatives (*e.g.*, Shushwap Nation, in Canada) emphasised the need to build targeted participative mechanisms into planning and policy development. Since indigenous peoples tend not only to be the poorest members of society, but also to have land based economies and cultures (involving hunting, fishing and gathering), it is critical to involve them early in any processes.

Other suggestions for including stakeholder participation came from Tourism Quebec, who suggests that integrated management requires that there be government centres close and accessible to citizens.

It was also emphasised that past experience should be brought into the planning and policy development processes (*e.g.*, South Africa) so that there is greater integration of eco-tourism activities into the way of life of communities. It was recommended that the Global Code of Ethics developed by the WTO should be adopted by all stakeholders, to promote a balanced perspective in different forms of tourism development, including eco-tourism.

It was also agreed that eco-tourism should not be developed if consultation revealed that local communities did not want to have it.

Recommendations for Environmental Conservation

Main recommendations from the preparatory conferences:

- Conserve energy, water, and other resources, reduce waste and favour materials that are not imported.
- Plan more sustainable transport options.
- Promote awareness of conservation and biodiversity amongst local people and visitors.
- Use appropriate tools to identify limits to use and to manage impacts.
- Seek to influence demand as well as managing visitors who do come.
- Use economic tools, information and interpretation in visitor management.

Educating communities about biodiversity and conservation: It was felt that many local communities did not understand the value of biodiversity very well, and that education was needed. Visitors should also be educated about the value of biodiversity and that natural resources belong to local peoples and should not be removed by visitors (souveniring, biopiracy, or removal of fossils, etc.).

Managing impacts: Primarily, it is essential to ensure that eco-tourism does not have negative impacts, and that operations adopt minimum impact practices and guidelines (*e.g.*, in the St Laurent or Yukon areas of Canada). Other options are planning in the destination to exclude certain activities (*e.g.*, in the Seychelles, where there are certain banned activities). In some locations, government regulations are required (*e.g.*, to ensure that cruise ships adhere to minimum environmental standards where ships do not take voluntary action).

It is recommended that management decision-making be

built into plans, together with other techniques (such as forecasting, environmental and social impact assessments or monitoring), to address potential problems or impacts as a preventative measure.

Managing visitors: Overall, it was recommended that an integrated approach is applied for the management of many variables, including supply and demand. Supply considerations, such as resources or culture, should be of primary concern, but management should also take full account of markets and demand.

Recommendations for Economic Development

Main recommendations from the preparatory conferences:

- Provide training, micro-credit and other assistance to small, medium and micro-enterprises.
- Provide incentives for enterprises to pursue sustainability.
- Provide infrastructure, such as access and telecommunications, to assist communities in eco-tourism development.
- Emphasise the role of governments as facilitators rather than operators.
- Place an emphasis on increasing retained economic value per visitor rather than expanding visitor volumes.

Providing government and other support for community level eco-tourism: It was confirmed that the state should be a partner, not a developer of eco-tourism operations.

In recognition that there is a spectrum of market interests, and a spectrum of tourism opportunities, there may be scope to link nature to cultural tourism and even to mass tourism (*e.g.*, in Greece) particularly in areas where there are fewer pristine environments, in order to heighten the attraction of the destinations, and to generate community benefits.

Communities need a source of funds which can be linked

to development. There may be opportunities to create community institutions and link them to forms of income generation; or to create Community Conservation Funds for donors, so eco-tourism is viewed as a business by communities.

International assistance should be targeted more towards eco-tourism projects. Assistance can be given in the form of finance, technology, training, information, mentorship, or in other ways. Loans might be given to countries, for example for training. Assistance could be targeted and conditional upon performance (*e.g.*, demonstrating environmental protection). It is recommended that international agencies coordinate sources and conditions of assistance, and provide centralised and up to date information (*e.g.*, on a website) for easy access by needy destinations.

Other forms of assistance may include staffing and human resources, and volunteer labour. This can provide a sense of ownership of the project by participants (*e.g.*, in Senegal there are agreements between Parks and volunteers).

Recognising mutual benefits: Often, there are contributions which local communities bring to eco-tourism or other developments, which are not viewed in terms of having conventional value (*e.g.*, in Uganda, these might be spiritual, medicinal, or other information or cultural activities). It was felt that while eco-tourism development can bring value to local communities, at the same time local communities can contribute valuable knowledge and information, practices, traditions, etc. to agencies, entrepreneurs, visitors, or others. In some cases, local people provide such information or knowledge without any recompense or benefit. It was recommended that such local contributions and sharing should be valued through financial or similar means. In this way there is likely to be more understanding that contributions are mutual, rather than the view that benefit flows are uni-directional to communities.

Exchanges of information can be of equal value to communities and to planners and policy makers. For example, imported technologies must be appropriate to the communities. However, indigenous technologies must also be acknowledged (such as India's Care and Share programme), since traditional ecological and other knowledge and technologies will also have great value. For example, the Austrian Parliament has just called for a respect for the knowledge of indigenous peoples as a basis for sustainable development, and for indigenous land rights as a basis for human rights.

Recommendations for Social and Cultural Benefits

Main recommendations from the preparatory conferences:

- Use historic buildings and other heritage resources, thereby contributing to their protection.
- Involve communities in social and cultural pro-grammes, to ensure local control, ownership and authenticity.
- Mount community awareness campaigns.
- Ensure that tour operators and other external companies are aware of their responsibilities towards communities.

Involving communities and ensuring local ownership: A number of areas have problems due to overpopulation (*e.g.*, European coastal areas) while other areas (*e.g.*, mountains) may suffer from depopulation. It was suggested that eco-tourism may provide some benefits to both areas, by alleviating pressures on the coast, while attracting visitors (and development) to rural areas. For example, in Greece the planning process aims to link natural areas with cultural tourism and to link these to mass tourism destinations.

It is recommended that governments consider providing communities with land or resources which can enable them to act as partners in eco-tourism operations. Botswana has allocated wildlife management areas to local communities for consumptive or non-consumptive use in tourism, so they can share in eco-tourism benefits. An additional benefit is that this has led to decreased poaching.

Communities should have input to planning processes through, for example, local narratives and guides, wherein they provide information to visitors, plus develop their own self-esteem.

Communities should be involved and empowered, such that there is no eco-tourism development where there is no desire for involvement in tourism. Opportunities should be sought to build on current economic and community activities rather than developing some totally new product.

Recommendations for Multi-stakeholder Participation

Main recommendations from the preparatory conferences:

- Build support for joint ventures into planning and policy initiatives.
- Facilitate community-level joint ventures, such as co-management of protected areas.
- Encourage strategic alliances between private businesses and local communities.

Encouraging joint ventures: Origin-destination joint ventures were suggested. One innovative example is in the Netherlands, where there is increasing awareness by tourists or tour operators that they may be the source of problems when they visit other destinations. An outgoing tourism policy has been developed, and moves to link outgoing tourism with NGOs in receiving destinations.

It was emphasised by Tanzania that there needs to be strong involvement by the private sector in partnerships, not just governments or NGOs. The Tanzanian delegation to the Summit included a great many industry representatives as well as government representatives.

Overall, throughout the discussions on policy and planning, the points made at the preparatory conferences were reinforced, with the topics summarised above being the main focus of discussion. In addition, it was also said that the International Year of Eco-tourism has already stimulated some of the actions and directions identified above.

The Regulation of Eco-tourism:
Institutional Responsibilities and Frameworks

The impacts of eco-tourism on society and the environment can be positive and negative. The theme addressed by this working group was about providing the right regulatory frameworks and systems to ensure that products that are developed and marketed as eco-tourism are beneficial and not harmful to environments and communities.

Nineteen presentations were made to the working group, covering:

- Examples of regulation and control of eco-tourism—Quebec, Mexico, Japan and Seychelles.
- Certification systems—The experiences of existing and planned new certification schemes in Australia, Peru, and Costa Rica as well as the examples from the USA and Europe.
- International guidelines for eco-tourism—Austria, Germany and Europarc.
- The need for quality control and for the identification of indicators—emphasised in two Canadian presentations.
- Specific methodologies and practical examples, from Uruguay, Indonesia, India and Korea.
- Eco-tourism and ethics, presented by the representative of The Vatican.

Issues Discussed

The following were the main issues discussed by the working group.

Institutional Frameworks

Legal frameworks and regulations are not always established for eco-tourism only and very often are common to other kinds of tourism. The need to have specific legal frameworks and policies for eco-tourism was stressed by different speakers, although in some cases it has proved difficult to have the same framework in different regions of a single country.

In some cases the work of individual countries is not enough to guarantee that eco-tourism is properly developed. There were proposals in the Korean presentation to promote action for eco-tourism development at the international level.

The need to develop eco-tourism strategies at the national level through a consultation process was well demonstrated in the Seychelles.

Regulation of Eco-tourism

The role of the private sector in the establishment of regulations and in the certification process was discussed and different viewpoints were expressed. While some people felt that the private sector should take part in defining regulations, others considered that governments and NGOs should establish regulations in order to guarantee the preservation of natural and cultural resources.

Certification and Labelling

These were issues that brought a number of questions and discussions. One of the points was whether certification should be just a voluntary process, or whether it should be an instrument to complement the regulation of eco-tourism ventures. Another important point raised by different people concerned the components of certification schemes. Other aspects, beyond environmental issues, need to be taken into account and included.

The scale of certification met with a great deal of interest. How can certification schemes work at the local level and at the same time have international recognition? In relation to this, how to cover the cost of certification at the local level was a big concern in many areas and proposals were made to overcome this problem so that it can be made accessible to all sizes of business as well as to local communities. In Peru, for example, some communities receive technical and financial support from academic bodies, while in Australia, the cost of certification is proportional to the size of the business.

A final point discussed is the problem of the appearance of pseudo-eco-labels: too many labels are confusing and there was agreement that something should be done in this respect. A possible solution is the example of VISIT, a joint European initiative for the promotion of ecolabels and sustainable tourism development. VISIT has co-operated with 10 leading ecolabels in Europe and developed common basic standards for their criteria and verification procedures. These standards allow the identification of those ecolabels which guarantee a high environmental quality of their certified hotels, campsites, beaches or marinas. In 2004, VISIT will be established as a European accreditation body for ecolabels in tourism.

Sustainability Indicators and Monitoring

The need to monitor sustainability of eco-tourism products was discussed and a number of approaches were presented. The difficulty of identifying indicators for social and cultural aspects was pointed out. Surveys to determine visitor satisfaction could be used to evaluate the quality of the visitor experience. At the same time, local people should be made aware of what was being done to the environment and how this would affect them.

A good example was the "European Charter for Sustainable Tourism in Protected Areas" which has proved to be a valuable tool for ensuring that tourism in protected areas is managed according to the principles of sustainable development.

Capacity Building, Training and Education

This was considered a key issue for the sustainable development of eco-tourism. Without adequate training and education of all stakeholders, from government to the private sector and consumers, in matters relating to regulation, certification and monitoring, it is impossible to progress towards sustainability in eco-tourism. All players need to understand why some sort of regulation is necessary in many situations, why certification can help both the business and the environment, and finally why monitoring is essential to demonstrate that progress is being made towards sustainability.

Other Issues

The impact of transport in relation to eco-tourism was a key point in some of the discussions and suggestions were made on how to take it into account in eco-tourism products and in certification schemes.

Key Points and Recommendations

Institutional Frameworks

Main recommendations from the preparatory conferences:

- Ensure coordination between government ministries in the planning and regulation of eco-tourism.
- Develop a framework of cooperation between public, private and non-governmental organisations.
- Ensure institutions understand the different dimensions of sustainable tourism and eco-tourism.

There is a need to reach agreements between protected area management bodies, tourism departments or ministries as well as the tourism industry in general. A good example of this is the progress being made by the Canadian certification programme. Good coordination among protected area managers and tourism departments is extremely important.

The development of legislative frameworks at the regional level should be supported, because they can positively influence sustainability issues, including the promotion of eco-tourism and similar types of tourism harmonized with the environment. The recent establishment of quality and specifically eco-tourism product rules in Québec, Canada, is a promising example in this field.

Incentives should be set up, such as lower taxes or public land concessions at lower rates, for eco-tourism operators that promote environmentally-sensitive land use (*e.g.*, the ones working on Crown land in British Columbia, Canada). At the same time, in Ontario, Canada, regulatory requirements ensure that resource stewardship agreements are established between the State and tour operators working within an area covered by the agreement, to preserve natural areas of high tourism value. This approach reserves the most pristine areas for eco-tourism operations. The idea, in both examples, is to stimulate proper eco-tourism in sensitive and valuable natural areas with a high potential.

Regulation of Eco-tourism

Main recommendations from the preparatory conferences:

- Move gradually from optional guidelines and simple codes of conduct towards obligatory regulations.
- Establish suitable legal frameworks underpinned by effective tools for regulating eco-tourism.
- Develop guidelines and best practice information at all levels.
- Ensure protected areas are consulted and involved in regulatory procedures.

Tourism operators, local government, and conservation departments should establish regulations. They should guarantee the protection of sensitive natural resources and cultural integrity.

Legislation and regulations should be specific for eco-tourism A good example was the case study of Tourisme Quebec where a very specific legal framework is being established, clearly separating adventure tourism activities and eco-tourism with an objective of avoiding a severe impact upon natural assets.

In some areas regulations need to be compulsory since in many countries voluntary regulations do not work and very often the public asks for minimum obligatory regulations, as it was presented in the example from Mexico.

Certain laws and regulations within protected areas should be extended beyond their frontiers.

Legally binding instruments for the implementation of sustainable eco-tourism and avoidance of non-sustainable forms of tourism for sensitive areas should be established.

Strict regulations for eco-tourism at an international level should be avoided, while guidelines are acceptable.

The potential negative impact of visitors should be taken into account from the beginning of the planning process. This can be realised through some measures such as reservation systems, routing in sensitive points, zoning within the site according to carrying capacity. The Bodogol Education Center, in Indonesia, has successfully put in place some of these preventive measures.

Certification

Main recommendations from the preparatory conferences:

- Provide guidelines on certification schemes for eco-tourism.
- Avoid penalise very small scale enterprises and facilitate their access to certification schemes.
- Involve all stakeholders in developing and implementing certification processes.
- Ensure certification processes are transparent, understandable and updated.

Certification processes need to be global in concept, following international guidelines and recommendations, but local in application. An example of this is the need for ecolodge guidelines, which can always be adopted at the local level and can then be followed by some sort of international ecolodge certification.

Auditing teams must be independent and ideally should

have representatives from different countries and proper training. They should also have different cultural backgrounds.

Certification should take into account social, economic and cultural aspects, besides the environmental ones. Most of the existing concepts for eco-labels, brands and certification systems have to be enlarged by social and cultural aspects to reach the aims of sustainable eco-tourism.

NGOs should take part in the process of identifying certification schemes. In many cases NGOs have developed voluntary certification schemes which have afterwards been regulated and spread by governments.

International certification schemes must be multi-stakeholder. They should be promoted by international organisations including governments, academia, conservation NGOs, the private sector and with proper consultation with local and indigenous people. It was suggested that organisations such as WTO and UNEP could play a role in establishing an international framework for tourism certification systems and all existing certification schemes should be considered in this process.

Certification and accreditation should be industry driven and paid for by the operators, as they can use it as a marketing tool and possibly marketing advantage over competitors, therefore it can be beneficial and profitable. The case of Australia is particularly interesting with well-established eco-tourism and ecoguides certification programmes.

In the case of very small businesses in developing countries, there should be technical and financial support through grant or loans or micro-credit systems to assist in making the necessary changes and to cover the costs of certification, either from strong NGOs, local government, academic bodies, larger profitable businesses or development agencies. There was agreement that environmental certification very often leads to economic benefits since energy, water and other resources are saved.

Easily accessible funding formulae to cover the cost of international certification schemes should be explored, so that small businesses can have access to them. Other funding and capacity building mechanisms should be identified and promoted for this purpose.

Eco-tourism certifiers must be guided by social criteria geared to facilitating the integration of small businesses at preferential rates and through technical contributions or the promotion of collective certification alternatives. Financially sound NGOs should shoulder the role of a certification body at a cost more affordable for local entrepreneurs.

Certification should provide powerful incentives and guidelines for responsible business practices.

A multistakeholder Sustainable Tourism Stewardship Council, such as the one being considered by Rainforest Alliance in coordination with a range of international organisations, could help local certification programmes exchange information in a forum that allows for accreditation of certifiers, marketing and credibility.

The obligatory introduction of certification systems for eco-tourism facilities and operations should be considered at least at regional and national levels, to guarantee that the quality provided is consistent with the principles of sustainability. This is the case of the national ecocertification scheme which will become compulsory in the near future in the Seychelles.

Capacity Building, Training and Education

In the certification process, there is a need to train and educate all stakeholders, including the industry, operators and customers or consumers. This latter case is particularly important since the interest of consumers in true eco-tourism will reward good products and punish examples of "green-washing". A good example of consumer education is the brochure "Your Travel Choice Makes a Difference" from The International Eco-tourism Society.

Certification programmes should be promoted and explained to the public by both the tourism and the environmental authorities.

Education, transfer of know how, exchange and respect for local people must drive the development of eco-tourism in all destinations. In the long term, customers will reward or punish eco-tourism products according to their sustainability.

Demand from consumers and tour operators is a pre-requisite for a certification system to work. Tourists must be informed of certification schemes and therefore, the promotion by government (by both the environment and tourist departments) is essential.

Monitoring and Indicators

Main recommendations from the preparatory conferences:

- Include the economic, social and environmental impact of tourism in monitoring.
- Define targets to be achieved in a certain period of time.
- Establish continuous data collection, involving businesses and tourists.
- Ensure monitoring is a prerequisite of providing assistance to projects.

The issue of monitoring and indicators was central to the discussions of Working Group D, but the following specific points were raised within this working group.

The definition of sustainability indicators should not be left only to the private sector and should be the result of consensus among all stakeholders including local people, NGOs, government and protected area managers.

Sustainability indicators should be integrated with local planning.

Indicators must be identified at the local level and should take into account environmental, social and cultural factors.

New methods of evaluation of progress towards sustainability in eco-tourism need to be identified, that are accessible to the local population both from the technical and economic point of view.

Other Recommendations

It was suggested that World Eco-tourism Sites should be declared, where eco-tourism would be promoted by the international community in order to guarantee the conservation of high value natural resources and the well being of local people.

Travellers should be made aware of their environmental impact due to transport and its effect on global warming when travelling to remote destinations. The impact of transport in eco-tourism has not received enough attention.

Travellers should receive information on positive and relatively simple ways to compensate for their impact, such as taking part in reforestation projects in the areas visited.

The three pillars of sustainable development—public welfare, economy and environment—have to be effectively built into eco-tourism.

The development and management of sustainable eco-tourism should be promoted through not only the individual effort of a country but also through international cooperation.

Countries should develop national eco-tourism strategies through a process of consultation in order to develop eco-tourism in a sustainable manner.

Product Development, Marketing and Promotion of Eco-tourism: *Fostering Sustainable Products and Consumers*

Eco-tourism will only bring benefits to conservation and communities if good quality, viable eco-tourism products, which reflect market demand, are created and actively promoted. This working group was concerned with developing the right support structures, market knowledge, and attention to detail in product development, to enable this to happen.

The sixteen presentations at the working group covered:

- Government policies and priorities for eco-tourism development—Indonesia, Germany and Venezuela.

- The management and development of eco-tourism in protected areas—Quebec (Canada), Sao Paulo (Brazil), Italy, University of Valencia (Spain), and UNESCO.
- The position of intergovernmental, non-governmental and media organisations in eco-tourism development and marketing, and its relationship with communities and conservation—International Labour Organisation, Conservation International, Retour Foundation, National Geographic Society.
- Eco-tourism initiatives by the private sector and partnership organisations—Earth Rhythms (Canada), Native Tourism Alliance (USA), PICE (Mexico), Casa Matsiguenka (Peru).

Issues Discussed

The working group concentrated its debates on creating the right context for eco-tourism development as well as on practical development and marketing issues. Throughout, there was concern that the nature of products developed and the messages put across to visitors should reflect the need to bring economic, environmental and social benefits.

The report on the preparatory conferences identified a number of challenges for eco-tourism product development and marketing. These were:

- The failure of too many products, through lack of profitability, often due to poor feasibility assessment and business planning.
- Difficulties faced by small enterprises and community-based products in reaching markets cost effectively.
- Inconsistency in the quality of the visitor experience and in environmental management of eco-tourism products.
- The need and opportunity to gain more benefit from visitors to support conservation and local communities, for example through stimulating more spending per head and reducing leakages from the local area.

- A continuing lack of public awareness of eco-tourism issues, with few people specifically seeking out sustainable eco-tourism products.

Participants in the working group were reminded of these challenges, which provided a context for the debates that followed.

In the light of these challenges, the report on the preparatory conferences identified five priorities:

- Creating the right structures for local communities, tourism enterprises, public bodies and NGOs to work together.
- Relating supply to demand, with a better knowledge of markets and how to reach them.
- Paying attention to all aspects of product quality, including design and management for sustainability as well as visitor satisfaction.
- Providing relevant support for communities and enterprises, which is locally delivered and tailored to the needs of communities and small enterprises.
- Strengthening the promotion of eco-tourism messages and products, including promoting the concept of eco-tourism as well as specific products.

This report takes each of these priority areas in turn and sets out the points and recommendations relating to them that emerged during the working group session.

Key Points and Recommendations

Structures and Relationships for Product Development and Marketing

Main recommendations resulting from the preparatory conferences:

- Address local community needs and opportunities.

- Recognise the key role of private sector businesses and strengthen their links with local communities.
- Strengthen networking between small enterprises and projects, so assisting market outreach and promoting common standards.
- Recognise protected areas as focal points for eco-tourism products and marketing.
- Increase support from national and local government.

Recognising traditional values: Presentations at the working group emphasised that the principles of eco-tourism are often enshrined in traditional values. Such values can influence the approach at a national level. For example, in Indonesia the national tourism policy is based on the principle of the 'Balance of Life' between exploitation and preservation of resources.

At a local level, many indigenous communities have values that are based on the stewardship of the earth's resources and hospitality towards visitors. These values must be respected. They provide a positive reason for assisting local communities to take their own decisions about the development and promotion of eco-tourism and the way in which their natural resources and cultures are interpreted to visitors.

Building partnerships: The importance of establishing multi-stakeholder partnerships was underlined by many presentations and interventions. These can take various forms.

One way of assisting indigenous people to gain benefit from eco-tourism is by helping them to form partnerships with organisations which can support and fund community projects, individual enterprises and joint ventures. An example is the North American Native Tourism Alliance.

Partnerships for eco-tourism should be established between states, where appropriate. An example is the cooperation between Saharan states in a UNESCO pilot project, which is promoting cooperation in training, support for micro enterprises, and the identification and protection of natural and cultural resources.

More consideration should be given to involving tour operators, alongside communities and NGOs, in partnerships for successful eco-tourism. An example is the project for the Development of Cultural and Eco-tourism in the Mountainous Regions of Central Asia and the Himalayas. This even extends the partnership to tourists themselves—in one initiative, trekkers end their visit working with local people on social and conservation projects.

Linking conservation of biodiversity with direct economic benefits to local people: The role of eco-tourism as a stimulus for the conservation of nature was strongly emphasised at the working group. This role is best played through providing a source of livelihood for local people which encourages and empowers them to preserve the biodiversity of their local area. The presentation by Conservation International (C.I.) confirmed the importance they place on eco-tourism in their people-centred conservation approach, especially in the world's biodiversity hotspots, which contain millions of people living in poverty.

When challenged in debate about the effectiveness of eco-tourism, Conservation International cited numerous examples where it was generating significant conservation benefits. However, this requires eco-tourism products to be based on integrated, participatory processes which take time to deliver results.

Strengthening the role of protected areas in eco-tourism development: There was a specific recommendation that the key role of protected areas in the management and development of eco-tourism should be recognised. In some cases they may require more resources to fulfil this role, although eco-tourism may also provide a source of revenue.

It was recognised that protected area authorities need to work with local stakeholders on the development of eco-tourism, and that appropriate structures should be established for this. Examples of parks working with local communities were provided by the approach of Parcs Québec in extending their network, and by the long-standing UNESCO Man and Biosphere model of evolving and adaptive management. In

Italy, a national partnership for eco-tourism has been established between the Federation of Parks, NGOs and private sector representatives.

A note of caution was sounded about the level of eco-tourism activity to encourage actually within protected areas, rather than in surrounding locations, which may be more robust. There is a need for careful planning which reflects the resources and sensitivity of different areas and the type of designation. Further training and materials to improve the skills of protected area managers in eco-tourism is required; an example presented at the workshop was the Toolkit for Sustainable Tourism in Wetlands.

Seeking a greater role for provincial and local authorities: There was a specific recommendation that provincial and local authorities should play a far more active role in eco-tourism planning and support, providing a bridge between national policies and local communities. Such authorities often have responsibility for a range of services which affect eco-tourism and also provide a long-lasting structure for developing, managing and supporting initiatives. However, more guidance should be given to local authorities on how to fulfil their role in eco-tourism.

Understanding Markets

Main recommendations from the preparatory conferences:

- Use more market research.
- Take a broad view of the market, recognising different segments.
- Study current visitor flows and local market conditions before product development takes place.

Understanding visitor motivations and disseminating research results: A number of interventions pointed to the need for more market research to provide data on existing and potential visitor profiles and motivations for visiting natural areas. This research should not only take place within source markets. It is important to understand more about the kinds of people who are already responding to eco-tourism products within destinations. It was recognised that part of the answer is to ensure the better use of existing market research. There was a specific recommendation that the results of the WTO studies of seven source markets should be made accessible, to the extent possible and/or through the corresponding national tourism administrations, to small eco-tourism projects and firms in less developed countries.

Recognising eco-tourism as more than a niche market: It was pointed out at the working group session that eco-tourism should not be equated only with a niche market but also with a set of principles, especially concerning benefits to conservation and local communities. There was general agreement that too narrow a view should not be taken in identifying the potential market for eco-tourism. In a paper entitled 'Moving Eco-tourism beyond its niche' the National Geographical Society presented research that suggested that a sizeable market in the USA would respond to concepts of supporting conservation and the well-being of local people in their travel choice.

A number of the case studies presented at the working group session were catering for a domestic as well as an international market, and not only for people with a specialist interest in nature. It was suggested that it is important not to isolate eco-tourism from the mainstream of tourism. Examples were given of day visitors from coastal resorts coming to inland cultural or natural heritage sites. These may provide serious management challenges in some cases, but also a valuable source of income for eco-tourism initiatives.

The presentations and debate pointed to the need for more, well informed, market segmentation, enabling products and promotional strategies to be adapted to different requirements.

Avoiding false expectations: There was a call for better market assessment and business planning for individual projects, taking account of location, resource constraints, current visitor flows and performance of comparable products. This should help to avoid false expectations and the development of eco-tourism in areas where it is unlikely to be successful.

Key Components of Eco-tourism Products

Main recommendations from the preparatory conferences:

- Address quality, authenticity and security.
- Give top priority to effective interpretation of nature and culture.
- Design and manage service facilities, such as accommodation and catering, to maximise sustainability.
- Address destination issues, such as infrastructure and transport, as well as individual product issues.
- Relate eco-tourism to sustainable activity tourism, where appropriate.

Underlining the importance of authenticity and creative interpretation: The need for authenticity in eco-tourism projects was strongly endorsed. The advantages of creative interpretation and the use of local guides were emphasised. An imaginative example of participatory interpretation was provided by the Earth Rhythms project in Manitoba, Canada, which is all about enabling visitors to "Live the story with real people".

During the plenary discussion, attention was drawn to the value of involving environmentalists, anthropologists and other specialists to ensure the accuracy of interpretation and to add depth to it, while accepting the importance of effective, accessible presentation involving local people.

Facilitating design and management for sustainability: A fundamental point made at the Summit is that eco-tourism projects should embrace all aspects of sustainability, in the way they are developed and operated. Eco-tourism should give a lead towards more sustainable tourism generally.

A number of examples of excellent environmentally sensitive design, in terms of both aesthetics and technical factors, were presented at the workshop. It was apparent that a wealth of knowledge is available internationally on this subject. The recent publication on ecolodges by The International Eco-tourism

Society provides an example. It is recommended that priority should be given to disseminating good practice in this field.

Some concern was expressed about the cost of low impact construction but it was stressed that this need not be more expensive than traditional techniques and can bring significant savings in operational costs. It is recommended that evidence about this is put across clearly. The importance of personal security is recognised. It was pointed out that tour operators promoting eco-tourism often face high costs in meeting obligations in this respect, which have to be taken into account.

Addressing the issue of access to eco-tourism destinations and experiences: A number of interventions suggested that the issue of access is too often ignored in eco-tourism planning and development. Three aspects of this were raised.

First, in some locations there is a need to facilitate access, where communities may be isolated. It was recommended that there is a need to work more closely with transport operators in eco-tourism development.

Secondly, there is considerable concern that eco-tourism policies and products should promote the use of environmentally friendly transport options, both to and within the destination. In Germany, for example, the promotion of cycling and walking is of fundamental importance in policies towards sustainable tourism and eco-tourism.

Thirdly, there is a need to avoid discrimination against people with disabilities or other disadvantages in terms of access to eco-tourism experiences.

Technical Support for Communities and Enterprises

Main recommendations from the preparatory conferences:

- Provide relevant local training, devised with local people and enterprises to encourage participation.
- Encourage people to look together at the local resource and at eco-tourism projects elsewhere.
- Provide well-targeted, accessible financial assistance.

Giving priority to capacity building: Many presentations emphasised the importance of capacity building within local communities. For example, human resource development was seen as a priority requirement in Indonesia and Venezuela. It was emphasised that capacity building requires time and commitment. There was also a call for more financial assistance for training.

A particular point was made that, as well as supporting businesses, capacity building and specific training programmes in the field of eco-tourism could be directed at young people at the start of their working life. An example of this was provided by the Sao Paulo Green Belt Biosphere Reserve and their establishment of eco-job training centres.

Helping eco-tourism projects to learn from each other: It was agreed that a lot could be achieved by exchanging experiences between different projects. The value of the suggestion, arising from the preparatory conferences, of promoting twinning and multi-lateral links between projects, was illustrated in the presentations.

Raising the profile and knowledge of tourism within donor agencies, and the quality of applications to them: It was felt that donor agencies should take tourism more seriously. Many have no specific strategy for supporting tourism or particular skills or knowledge about eco-tourism. This should be rectified.

However, the responsibility of applicants in seeking funding was also recognised. It was pointed out that projects seeking funding must have a well-prepared business plan.

Some delegates commented that there was not enough knowledge about the various sources of financial assistance, including international donor agencies, bilateral support programmes, and assistance available from NGOs. There was a specific recommendation that a database of information on this should be created and disseminated.

Structuring financial and technical assistance to the requirements of small businesses and local communities: There was considerable debate about appropriate forms of support for eco-tourism projects.

A presentation at the workshop on the International Labour Organisation's sustainable tourism project with indigenous communities in Bolivia, Ecuador and Peru set out a structured approach, with programmes of assistance at a micro level (for community-based enterprises), at a medium level (for clusters of tourism initiatives within community networks, and for local government), and at a macro level (to strengthen organisations, certification and marketing within states).

A clear message from delegates was that assistance should be in a form that can be accessed by small and micro businesses and local communities and one that is relevant to their needs. Specific recommendations were that:

- Donor agencies should provide more schemes which channel assistance directly to enterprises and communities rather than through national governments.
- Funding should be available in small packets, with a low minimum level, relevant to the size of small enterprises.
- There is a need for micro-credit schemes.

There was a call for the application of fiscal incentives as a tool to encourage tourism service providers to develop and manage their enterprises more sustainably.

A further specific recommendation was for the establishment of a network of eco-tourism advisors or mentors as a readily available source of help for small eco-tourism businesses.

Promoting Eco-tourism Messages and Products

Main recommendations from the preparatory conferences:

- Promote eco-tourism as a concept, with an international awareness campaign.
- Grasp the significant opportunity presented by the Internet.
- Use a range of marketing techniques and partners.

- Provide comprehensive and educative information at all stages, before, during and after the visit.
- Create loyal ambassadors among tourists.

Raising public awareness of tourism impacts, eco-tourism principles and actions to take: During the working group session, a number of comments were made on the importance to promote the actual concept of eco-tourism, its ideals and values, rather than simply eco-tourism products. However, there was a little concern that the word 'eco-tourism' may actually be putting some people off. It was agreed that principles and goals are what is important; people should not get hung up on terminology.

The report on the preparatory conferences suggested that there should be a coordinated international campaign to promote eco-tourism principles and concepts, but that this might not simply be a generic campaign; rather it should promote specific action that visitors could take. As an example of this, it was recommended that the process of visitors and tour operators making financial donations to local community projects or conservation causes should be more actively promoted, with a vision of this becoming the norm rather than the exception.

A strong recommendation was made in the presentation by the Retour Foundation, an NGO working with indigenous communities, that tourists should be provided with detailed information about the effect of their travelling.

Promoting mutual understanding of cultural differences and sensitivities: It was recommended that information for visitors should include how to respect the local culture of their hosts and the sensitivity of the local environment. At the same time, there was a recommendation that indigenous and local communities should be provided with information about the culture and expectations of their visitors.

Working effectively with tour operators and the media: The importance of tour operators was referred to on several occasions. There was a specific recommendation that priority should be given to involving and educating local incoming tour operators and agents within destinations. On the other hand, some delegates recommended that eco-tourism principles should be promoted more heavily amongst international tour operators, including the larger companies.

The strong influence of media reports and travel guides, which can be both damaging and highly beneficial to eco-tourism, was emphasised during the plenary session. It was recommended that travel writers should be introduced to genuine, interesting stories about real people and experiences, rather than bland details of product.

Using the Internet as a communication medium at all points in the tourism chain: There was widespread agreement about the importance of the Internet for promoting eco-tourism products. One comment highlighted its value amongst the large market of independent travellers, where it can be used for exchange of information and testimonials amongst visitors and for providing information within destinations as well as prior to departure. A high priority should be given to helping small enterprises and community initiatives link to appropriate technology.

Raising confidence through branded products: Branding of eco-tourism products was considered to offer more opportunities. An example was a proposal to establish a world-wide brand of ecolodges with strong conservation credentials.

Gaining support for eco-tourism amongst future visitors: Discussion at the workshop echoed the need, expressed in the preparatory conferences, to promote the concept of eco-tourism to children and young people, as a receptive audience and as the travellers of the future.

Finally, the results from many successful projects presented during the Summit reaffirmed the importance of delivering a quality experience, leading to word of mouth recommendation, as the best form of marketing. This will increase the volume of tourists who are committed to eco-tourism principles, who become ambassadors for conservation, and who have a greater understanding of different cultures around the world.

Monitoring Costs and Benefits of Eco-tourism:
Ensuring Equitable Distribution Among All Stakeholders

In many eco-tourism strategies the aim is to reduce the costs of eco-tourism and ensuring that a whole range of benefits are obtained for local communities, the environment, visitors and other stakeholders. However, unless there is a system for monitoring the impacts of eco-tourism, then the success of new strategies and actions will not be known. This working group was concerned with effective processes for checking on impacts and improving the distribution of benefits.

Presentations were made to the working group, covering:

- The relationship between indigenous people and eco-tourism—Quebec, Equations (India), U.S.A.
- Poverty and managing equitable distribution—South Africa, Sri Lanka, Ghana.
- International guidelines for monitoring costs and benefits—UNCTAD, IBST (International Bureau of Social tourism), Australia, Canada.
- World heritage protection—UNESCO, Indonesia, Uganda.
- Monitoring small and medium enterprises—Ethiopia, Madagascar.
- Public sector role—Balearics (Spain).
- Specific methodologies and national examples—Kenya, Brazil, Yugoslavia.
- Social aspects and better access to eco-tourism—IBST, Equations (India).

Issues Discussed

The following points were debated during the working group session.

- New eco-tourism cost/benefit evaluation methods that would highlight the social and economic benefits for local populations, as well as the limitations of the financial benefits generated compared to other forms of tourism, notably mass tourism.

■ Appropriate legal and institutional mechanisms to facilitate and make effective the systematic participation of local communities in the overall eco-tourism process, including policy definition, planning, management and monitoring.

■ Financial and fiscal mechanisms to ensure that a significant proportion of the income generated from eco-tourism remains with the local community or serves conservation purposes.

■ Methods to ensure the permanent control of impacts through the adaptation of carrying capacity methodologies to eco-tourism development, including the definition of damage warning indicators and disturbance gauges for protected sites and other natural areas.

■ Distribution mechanisms to share the benefits of eco-tourism development in order to reinvest a proportion of the revenues generated in protected areas.

■ Methods to assist understanding and measurement of social costs, benefits and change (*i.e.* changes in the behaviour and habits of the local population) so as to limit the negative consequences, to maximise social benefits for host communities and to improve attitudes, awareness and respect towards the protection of the environment.

■ Specific management and monitoring procedures for different types of eco-tourism sites, (*i.e.* desert zones and islands), concerning such aspects as water and waste management, the management of scarce resources, and others.

■ Evaluation of appropriate price levels to ensure sufficient returns for firms, suitable redistribution in favour of local populations and that correspond to the purchasing power of tourism demand.

- Ensuring that the principles of "polluter pays" and "user pays" will ensure genuine protection of the environment whilst guaranteeing eco-tourism development.

The working group endeavoured to bring together development strategies aimed at differentiating eco-tourism from traditional tourism and creating a real balance to achieve the desired equitable distribution between all the stakeholders.

As a result of the presentations and the debates during the working group session, guidelines and directions towards concrete solutions were devised. These solutions challenge traditional tourism development policies that, as was emphasised by the contributors, must not merely consider eco-tourism as a priority but as a tourism development catalyst, thus providing a new approach to tourism development as a whole. This was particularly highlighted in the contributions by the delegates from Kenya, Brazil, India and Serbia.

Key Points and Recommendations

For this catalytic role of eco-tourism to really be effective, it is necessary to consider recommendations relating to the main pillars of this topic, namely monitoring costs, monitoring benefits, and equitable distribution. Some global recommendations also emerged from the working group.

Monitoring Costs of Eco-tourism

Main recommendations from the preparatory conferences:

- Determine the economic costs of providing suitable infrastructure, including energy and transport, resources such as water, and waste treatment.
- Use indicators such as site stress to monitor environmental costs.
- Consider factors such as the disturbance of traditional lifestyles in determining social costs.

- Take an integrated approach to determining costs, such as effect on employment in other sectors, such as agriculture.
- Research specific management and monitoring procedures for different types of eco-tourism sites, *e.g.* deserts and islands.
- Research methods to ensure the permanent control of impacts, including damage warning indicators for protected sites and other natural areas.

The presentations showed that for ecoutourism to develop sustainably it needs direct as well as indirect support from the public sector at the national and local levels.

Recognising costs relating to environmental management: The conflict between protecting nature and eco-tourism development induces extra costs which eco-tourism operators must bear. In the case of Sri Lanka for example, with respect to wildlife, the problems associated with the protection of the elephants must be managed in such a way that the local population could also be able to live in total security, particularly the farmers. In this particular case specific planning guidelines must be drawn up, which include protection barriers, requiring very heavy investment. This need for large financial resources impedes the development of eco-tourism and can rupture the sustainable development process in these destinations.

This situation can be particularly serious in mass tourism destinations as illustrated by the presentation on the Balearic Islands in which it was argued that there is a direct relationship between high tourist numbers and the attractiveness of the destination. In this case, there is a conflict between tourism development and economic development because of the extra costs on the environment, resulting in the deterioration of the tourism situation in these destinations.

Taking all development and operational costs into account, including training: Eco-tourism itself engenders extra costs, notably in terms of funding training. This important point was much discussed during the sessions. Indeed, eco-tourism often implies heavier equipment expenditure and more skilled personnel than are required in traditional tourism. Therefore, preliminary training funding programmes must be introduced, and this can harm the competitiveness of the eco-tourism product in a very competitive market. As a result, the profitability of eco-tourism projects may be deemed insufficient. Examples from France for instance show that quite often the financing of training must come from public funds, which implies that in certain developing countries, the financing of eco-tourism training must be included in international cooperation programmes.

Considering the full costs of transition to eco-tourism: The cost of protecting nature generally implies very high expenditure and can be the cause of usage conflict in economic terms but also in social terms. This is the case in India for example where, in some highly populated regions, eco-tourism development replaces certain agricultural production activities that must be abandoned to safeguard the endowments of protected areas. In such cases, the creation of jobs for tour guides and wardens does not compensate for the jobs lost in the agricultural sector, and this can cause tension between the local population and eco-tourism operators when the cost of reconversion of agricultural populations are not taken into account in public policies.

Monitoring Benefits of Eco-tourism

Main recommendations from the preparatory conferences:

- Take account of local income benefits and tax receipts.
- Consider improvement in local employment, living conditions and social services.
- Measure the local population's satisfaction through surveys.
- Use tourism satellite accounting to show impacts on different sectors.
- Develop new evaluation methods to take account of wider benefits and costs

The discussions during the working group session showed that the benefits of eco-tourism are not as obvious as might be first thought. These benefits can be the cause of problems and sometimes controversy.

Being realistic about financial benefits: The financial benefits, in terms of fiscal and parafiscal receipts, must be considered as particularly important for local populations. However, the examples presented during the sessions show that these benefits only become significant after many years. Case studies from Madagascar demonstrate that in the short term fiscal and parafiscal receipts generated by eco-tourism activity are weak and cannot finance the environmental protection that is necessary for high quality tourism products. Furthermore, these examples show that these benefits are very difficult to distribute amongst public and private stakeholders.

Using eco-tourism benefits to alleviate poverty: The benefits of eco-tourism should be orientated principally towards the poorest local populations. This is the objective of the many programmes presented during the Summit such as those in South Africa, Ghana and Uganda. From this point of view, eco-tourism is better adapted than traditional commercial tourism to achieve this objective. However, as the presentation from India emphasised, eco-tourism is a type of tourism development that can harm the traditional activities of the poorer populations (*i.e.* agriculture). This means that the benefits of eco-tourism are not always sufficient to provide a significant contribution to the problems of extreme poverty and even in certain cases it can harm the very means of subsistence of very poor rural populations. Therefore, the assertion that developing eco-tourism is a good method of solving the problems of poverty in developing countries should be expressed with caution, spelling out the conditions for this to occur.

Emphasising the merits of eco-tourism in benefiting small enterprises: The benefits in terms of liberalisation of international exchanges in the GATS agreement framework should facilitate access to tourism development for all countries including LCDs (Least Developed Countries). However, as the speaker from

UNCTAD pointed out during the debates and during the presentations at the Summit, traditional tourism tends to mostly benefit large enterprises. This is not the case of eco-tourism, which should therefore be favoured in commercial international negotiations. Furthermore, this was emphasised during the session on international cooperation, which clearly demonstrated that tourism was a privileged element of regional cooperation benefiting primarily small and medium size enterprises.

Taking full account of associated benefits: The presentations and debates showed that the balance between costs and benefits are not always obvious to justify eco-tourism development in economic and social development polices. However, several new points were brought to the debates proving that the benefits of eco-tourism are much more numerous and important if some major elements which are often forgotten or ignored are considered.

In particular, two very positive points concerning eco-tourism were discussed after the presentations by the IBST (International Bureau of Social Tourism):

- On the one hand, eco-tourism benefits tourists by giving them the choice to enjoy a different type of tourism than traditional tourism. However, this benefit is only fully accountable if it is available to the whole population such as the young, the elderly and insofar as it is possible for the handicapped.
- On the other hand, eco-tourism favours the initiatives of non-profit organisations and cooperatives, which generally have important direct and indirect impacts, benefiting local and indigenous communities.

The Equitable Distribution of Benefits Amongst Stakeholders

Main recommendations from the preparatory conferences:

- Establish financial and fiscal mechanisms to ensure that a significant proportion of income generated from eco-tourism remains in the local community or serves conservation.

- Put in place distribution mechanisms which reinvest a proportion of the revenues generated in the protected areas.
- Consider the impact of price levels on the distribution of benefits.

It emerged from the presentations and debates that the principles of eco-tourism are more of an aspiration than a reality for many countries, regions and local and indigenous populations, despite significant progress.

Equitable distribution is an aspiration for many stakeholders because there exist today a multitude of initiatives and eco-tourism product development projects everywhere in the world. Nevertheless, a survey carried out in Australia showed that there are thousands of eco-tourism schemes, which would suggest that the economic weight of eco-tourism in world tourism is becoming increasingly important and could support the efforts to achieve a better distribution between all stakeholders of the benefits of tourism development.

The equitable distribution between all stakeholders is strengthened because of the prevalence of small and medium sized enterprises in the development of eco-tourism. The example provided by Ethiopia, discussing the role of SMEs in the development of eco-tourism, shows that the benefits of eco-tourism can be turned from aspiration into reality if tourism development associated with eco-tourism is sufficiently important.

The equitable distribution between all stakeholders will only become a significant reality when the benefits to be distributed are great enough. However, the contributions from the representatives of the poorest regions and countries emphasised that this is not the case everywhere in the world. One of the reasons put forward by UNCTAD is the lack of comparative studies to provide useful information on the successes and failures of different methods of equitable distribution amongst stakeholders. The aim would be to establish demonstration projects which would serve as references to ensure that the development of eco-tourism will also provide real equitable distribution between all stakeholders.

Global Recommendations

Main recommendations from the preparatory conferences:

- Ensure a constant monitoring of eco-tourism activities to ensure they are meeting the required objectives.
- Determine distinct quantitative evaluation criteria or a range of standards, in cooperation with national and local authorities.
- Establish an evolutionary management system, including monitoring, based on public-private partnership.

The following overall conclusions were drawn from the presentations and the debates in the working group and were presented during the plenary session:

- The existing eco-tourism cost, benefit and impact evaluation methods, should be reviewed and new methods should be devised which would highlight the social and economic benefits for local populations and compare these with the costs, benefits and impacts of other forms of tourism and other economic alternatives.
- Appropriate legal, political, institutional and funding mechanisms should be established in order to facilitate and make effective the participation of local communities in the overall eco-tourism process, including definition, planning, management, monitoring and conflict resolution.
- Indigenous communities and groups should be involved from the very beginning in the decision process about eco-tourism including the assessment and monitoring of costs, benefits and impacts in particular with respect to their culture and traditions.

- Financial and fiscal mechanisms should be implemented to ensure that a significant proportion of the income generated from eco-tourism remains with the local community and is reinvested for environmental and cultural conservation purposes.

A permanent and consistent monitoring of eco-tourism impacts should be implemented as an integral part of the overall management for protected sites and other natural areas, and therefore the existing approaches such as carrying capacity methodologies, damage warning indicators and other monitoring instruments should be adapted.

In addition, the participants in the working group proposed a recommendation to the plenary session of the World Ecotourism Summit to affirm the clear and inalienable rights of indigenous communities, in terms of international legal instruments, to self-determination and prior informed consent in eco-tourism development.

Reports from the Special Forums

On the final day of the Summit, two special forums were held in order to discuss the perspective of eco-tourism businesses (Forum 1) and the issue of development cooperation (Forum 2). The results of these forums are presented in the pages which follow.

In addition, a Ministerial Forum was held. This forum enabled a wide range of countries to describe their policies and activities in the field of eco-tourism. The majority of speakers were Ministers of Tourism or senior officials from the ministry of tourism in the respective countries, but some countries were represented by their environment ministry or their diplomatic representative in Canada.

The countries making interventions at the Ministerial Forum included:

- Andorra

- Algeria
- Bangladesh
- Cambodia
- Cuba
- Cyprus
- Ecuador
- Egypt
- India
- Malawi
- Nigeria
- Pakistan
- Paraguay
- Philippines
- Romania
- Sri Lanka
- Uruguay

Each country representative explained the state of development of eco-tourism in their country and the problems and challenges being faced. All of them reiterated their commitment to sustainability principles in tourism and set out the steps being taken to develop and promote eco-tourism.

Forum 1: *The Eco-tourism Business Perspective*

This forum concerned the practical experiences and needs of private sector businesses operating in eco-tourism. It centred on four presentations from enterprises based in the US Virgin Islands, Canada, Panama and India. There was also a considerable period for discussion with many points raised from the floor.

Isssues Discussed

· The Need for Government Support for Small Eco-tourism Operators

Eco-tourism operators often find themselves at a disadvantage because of specific government regulations. For example, in destination countries where business visas have a limited time before expiry, this may result in on-ground tour leaders or facilitators having to leave the country prematurely.

Other problems result from a lack of government action. One example is the lack of assistance for operators to develop new tours in destinations. This is a big problem for operators, since research and testing potential products on the ground may take some years, but once products are developed, other companies may replicate this new package, with no research costs. Developing new packages is becoming increasingly difficult.

Some problems occur when the ethics of the destination government are in conflict with the principles of eco-tourism. Some ethically minded operators pull out of the destination, which ironically leaves the field (and their repeat clients and developmental groundwork) available to less ethically-oriented tour operators.

Problems of Financing Eco-tourism Operations

It was generally agreed that obtaining finance to initiate eco-tourism operations is extremely difficult; it is often non-existent. Many operations are only possible by using personal savings or obtaining personal loans. The conventional banking sector is not currently helpful until after success is achieved, when assistance is least necessary.

Other costs concerns are related to proposed certification programmes, which operators fear they will not be able to buy into; additionally, they do not have the time to engage in the often lengthy and difficult certification procedure.

Cost and Lack of Support for Research and Development

Operators agreed that it is difficult and expensive to research and develop new eco-tourism packages in many destinations. Also, that when established, there are no mechanisms to prevent other operators from copying their packages.

Lack of Integrated Objectives

Some eco-tourism operators started with worthy but limited motivations, such as a strong desire for environmental conservation or protection of endangered places or species. However, they discover that unless local jobs are created and operational profitability is an objective, the business will have difficulties or will fail, thus also failing to achieve the original objective. It was felt that entrepreneurs need to internalise the principles of sustainability in their business, and that if they emphasise only one or two perspectives, they will not achieve sustainability over the long term. Those businesses focusing on economic perspectives also need to integrate community and environmental perspectives; reciprocally, those businesses focusing on community benefits also need to consider environmental issues relating both to the community and their business. In this way, there is a greater likelihood that the business will be sustainable over the long term, whereas if other perspectives are not considered, long-term business viability is unlikely.

Environmental Destruction

Operators expressed that poaching is an issue in a number of destinations, as well as slash-and-burn agriculture and other practices, which destroy forests and other habitats. These unsustainable land use practices are greatly affecting the quality of some destinations. Operators could improve environmental conditions at destinations by involving more local communities, bringing economic alternatives, and by this way providing incentives to preserve the environment; however, without government support it is difficult for them to tackle these problems alone.

Conclusions and Recommendations

Separate Policies are Required for Eco-tourism, Distinguishing it from Mainstream Tourism Operations

Mechanisms should be developed to facilitate start-up funding for small tourism operations.

Governments or other agencies at the destinations should examine ways to provide assistance to eco-tourism operations researching and introducing new packages. As an example, the Malaysia Tourism Commission has cost-shared advertising of new packages for a certain time period, which benefited both the operator and the destination.

It was recommended that NGOs should play a stronger role in providing up to date research information (destinations or markets) to operators.

Involve those who are Part of a Problem in the Solution

It is recommended that all stakeholders should be involved in solving eco-tourism-related problems, especially those who are part of a problem. For example, in India, there has been recent interaction between poachers, NGOs, forest officials, and the eco-tourism facilitator.

Take an Integrated Approach

Eco-tourism operators should take an integrated operational perspective from the outset. This will involve: protecting the environment that visitors wish to experience; providing local jobs so that the environment is not endangered by unsustainable local use (*e.g.*, slash and burn agriculture); providing desired visitor interactions with local people; and focusing on business profitability to sustain the other objectives.

It was suggested that creative businesses can create profit streams within their operations through applying sustainability principles. For example, in Maho Bay Camps (US Virgin Islands), sustainable technologies contribute to cost savings as well as to guest satisfaction. Waste aluminium, glass and plastic is used in craft workshops and converted into products for sale, thus employing locals, providing guest entertainment, generating revenues, and removing waste from the island.

It is recommended that public-private partnerships be encouraged as a method of assisting business start-ups, as well as meeting joint objectives, involving business, government,

NGOs, or development agencies.

Provide Adequate Remuneration to Local Employees at Destinations

It was recommended that local people be paid significant wages by operators. This helps ensure ongoing reliability and quality performance, and acts as a model for others. For example, in India, slash and burn agriculture is reducing, unused cargo boats are being converted to viable house-boat operations, and poachers are being transformed into respected, well-paid employees.

The portion of total consumer package costs which destinations receive should be critically examined, since at present the average percentage is relatively low.

Forum 2: *Development Cooperation for Eco-tourism*

The development cooperation forum concentrated on the role of development agencies in providing financial and technical support for eco-tourism.

Most of the speakers were representing international or bilaterial donor agencies or consultancies, including: GEF/ UNDP Small Grants Programme, SNV Netherlands, Swiss Association for International Cooperation, German Technical Cooperation Agency (GTZ), and the Inter-American Development ment Bank, besides the World Tourism Organisation. The Minister of Tourism from Angola provided a recipient country perspective.

Issues Discussed

The Need for International Cooperation

The WTO and government representatives emphasised the crucial role of international cooperation in promoting a sustainable development of eco-tourism, particularly in less developed countries.

The WTO, as the UNDP's executing agency for tourism development, is a·catalyst for generating finance and can organise international cooperation. With its technical expertise WTO can provide guidelines and solutions to achieve an appropriate balance between the economic development of tourism and sustainability. Thus WTO can facilitate the development of new types of international cooperation, motivating other agencies towards a common objective with public/private sector partnerships.

This need for regional cooperation on eco-tourism projects, particularly in Africa, was pointed out by Angola's Minister of Tourism. An example of this kind of support was given through the RETOSA/SADEC tourism projects.

Speakers looked in turn at issues relating to bilateral, regional and international cooperation.

New Objectives for International Cooperation

There has been a notable change in the way development agencies are treating tourism projects. Whereas previously there was an emphasis on the quantity of tourism development and revenue generated, there is now greater concern for the quality of the end result and a range of social and environmental as well as purely economic objectives. The revision of tourism master plans has reflected this change of emphasis. This has led to a focus on the capacity of local communities to engage in, and benefit from, tourism.

A Growing Number of Players

In the past development cooperation was mainly provided by a small number of international organisations dealing with states at a government level. Now there are many more agencies providing relevant assistance, including NGOs, regional organisations, bilateral aid schemes and private sector bodies. Some of these new forms of cooperation are particularly appropriate for eco-tourism as they are often focused on generating self-help in communities (*e.g.* the approach of SNV

Netherlands).

New Structures and Levels for Cooperation

International cooperation itself has changed. Cooperation is now located in an inter-regional context and its focus is on decentralised programmes. This regional cooperation is well adapted to eco-tourism. A new priority is given to training and capacity building, as key issues to strengthen eco-tourism, and to providing support for indigenous organisations.

Conclusions and Recommendations

Provide More Support for Capacity Building

The recognition of the need to support capacity building, mentioned above, is important. A further focus on this in all assistance programmes should be encouraged.

Ensure that Projects Assisted are Viable

Too frequently in the past assistance has been provided for eco-tourism projects which may not be viable in the long term, after assistance has come to a end. More attention should be given to feasibility assessment.

Make Sure that Local Communities are Involved and Benefiting

Development agencies should pay attention to organisational and participatory structures in recipient destinations. It is very important that there is local participation in programmes supported. A number of comments made stressed the importance of organisational strengthening and the role of local authorities.

Raise the Profile of Eco-tourism within Development Agencies

In general, development agencies are still paying too little attention to eco-tourism. They should be encouraged to develop strategies for their work in this sector. This should apply to individual agencies and collectively, as there is a need for more coordination between agencies in their work in this area.

Provide a Range of Levels of Financial Support

In the past financial assistance has tended to be provided in large amounts, relevant to larger scale projects. There is now a need for a full range of types and levels of assistance, including programmes suitable for very small enterprises and community-based initiatives, and for medium sized projects which are locally owned, yet with significant costs as well as local impacts.

Preparing and Adopting the Final Declaration

The Summit closed with a final plenary session which addressed the text of the Quebec Declaration on Eco-tourism.

An initial draft of the declaration had been circulated to delegates at the start of the Summit. All delegates were invited to submit written comments on the text, including specific recommendations for amendments, improvements and additions. A total of 160 written comments were received by the deadline at the end of the second full day of the Summit. WTO and UNEP also received verbal representation from a number of individuals and groups, including representatives of indigenous communities and of NGOs working with such communities. All these comments were carefully assessed by WTO and UNEP and taken into consideration in the preparation of a second draft.

The second draft of the declaration was circulated to delegates at the start of the third day. This draft formed the basis of the debate during the final plenary session. Many delegates made further comments and recommendations on it from the floor. These interventions were recorded. All of them were assessed and used by WTO and UNEP to produce a final text of the declaration on the day following the Summit. This text was then made available to delegates and others on the Internet.

WORLD ECO-TOURISM SUMMIT

THEME A
Eco-tourism Policy And Planning:
The Sustainability Challenge

Main outputs of the preparatory conferences leading up to the World Eco-tourism Summit. The outputs discussed policies and planning at a range of scales, from international and national, to local and site specific. In addition, although there are 3 reports covering the other conference themes, a number of these themes were also addressed within some of the planning and policy development themed discussions, including; product development, regulations, costs and benefits, monitoring, and marketing. This seems to reinforce both the complexity of the subject and the interdependent nature of the themes.

Issues Discussed

Key Overarching Issues and Challenges for Planning and Policy Development

A wide range of issues/challenges formed the major outputs of this Theme. In many cases, conference summaries seemed to direct outputs/recommendations to higher government levels. It is normally governments which develop most plans and policies, and it is these very plans and policies which impact the eco-tourism operator or communities most (no conference summaries examined planning and policy development of eco-tourism businesses or projects). Also, those at the "grass roots" tend to feel un-empowered, or less involved than they feel they should be. So it may be only natural for participants to address their recommendations upward to those public, private or non-governmental organisations who are in charge, or should be in charge of planning and policy development at the different levels.

A number of issues and challenges were of broad relevance across conference themes, and across most preparatory conferences. These tend to be within the mandate of national levels of government, and to involve multiple agencies, particularly those with protected areas mandates. Conferences indicated that to date, there has been little development and management of the community sector by authorities and managers of protected areas. In addition, strategies tend to be driven externally—so are not implemented because they are not developed and owned locally.

Need for Transboundary Management: It was recognised internationally and regionally, that eco-tourism activities and resources do not necessarily adhere to administrative boundaries. This is a challenge for parks and protected areas. Eco-systems form a better basis for planning and policy making, yet are rarely the administrative units. Biological resources clearly cross administrative boundaries, but cultures also cross these boundaries, including indigenous cultures. The movement of visitors also crosses boundaries, and these flows are being impeded by administrative requirements in some regions (*e.g.,* in CIS countries for both ship and land tourism). There is a need for better co-operation between countries sharing trans-boundary natural resources and protected areas to set up joint legislative and institutional frameworks that facilitate planning and management processes for conservation and tourism.

Lacking or Conflicting National Planning and Policy Objectives: This was probably the largest issue that emerged. It was specifically highlighted at every regional preparatory conference. Challenges are multi-layered, and relate particularly to a lack of overall vision, a lack of integration of various sector/ ministry policies, and frequently unspecified and unclear government department roles. The challenge is rooted in a lack of overarching sustainable development goals, perspectives, and mandates at senior government levels. The issue is exacerbated by intersecting responsibilities of many government ministries in developmental, planning and marketing issues related to eco-tourism. Often, there are conflicting goals and mandates within individual ministries or agencies, which may lead to arbitrary or uncoordinated decision-making.

Inconsistent or Nonexistent Policy/Institutional Frameworks for Eco-tourism: A common problem in many parts of the world is the lack of an institutional framework for the development of eco-tourism, which is partly related to low recognition and value given to eco-tourism. A number of regional conferences discussed the need for eco-tourism policy frameworks. Policies are not consistent because they are generated within individual departments, or even within one arm of an agency, so policies further some agency objectives, without necessarily supporting the objectives of other agencies. This essentially means that sustainability objectives are not supported (*e.g.*, some agencies have development mandates, while others have conservation mandates). Overarching policy frameworks are needed. In addition, some countries view eco-tourism as one of many subsets of tourism, and do not therefore develop specific policy and institutional frameworks for eco-tourism. All conferences felt it was senior Government's responsibility to develop national strategic plans and polices for eco-tourism, while specific guidelines and tools are required at the regional or local level.

Need for Models of Successful Planning and Policy Development: Most conferences indicated that there was a lack of successful models related to: protected areas which function successfully as eco-tourism products; practical planning and management tools; a range of policy-related options for local needs and circumstances; ways of integrating different agencies' and stakeholders' perspectives. The general need is for good examples of practical applications for eco-tourism.

Lack of Fiscal Commitment: Every regional conference mentioned the lack of financial resources for: protected areas planning and management; community education, empowerment and training; research; and partnershipping activities. Budgets may reflect lack of ministry support or priorities, or politicians' priorities. Entrepreneurs also lack funding sources, particularly in difficult economic climates, (*e.g.*, regions with developing economies, such as Andean and Meso-America, African, Asian and Pacific regions). With a slightly different perspective, CIS countries feel that tourism should not be taxed more than other industries (*e.g.*, through border fees, etc.) and the Arctic conference agreed.

Information is Lacking: Information is lacking for appropriate planning and development, and about trends in environmental and socio-economic implications of tourism and eco-tourism. Key aspects identified as lacking included: quality research and analysis, resource inventories and other baseline data, and appropriate tools for planning and management of resources, impact, visitors, supply and demand (*e.g.*, biodiversity/threat/ infrastructure/services/ cultural resource inventories, visitor information and education techniques, use-intensity management, traffic management, niche market information, etc.).

Lack of Human Resource Capacity: There are many types of education, training and capacity building required, including of government staff, due to lack of appropriate expertise and to high staff turnover (*e.g.*, increased planning skills needed). Capacity is required in individual entrepreneurs, particularly with respect to a broad range of business functions, knowledge of markets, hospitality, environmental issues, and the importance of socio-cultural perspectives and resource management. Capacity building is required among a range of community members with respect to such topics as hospitality, fulfilling visitor expectations, and how to become directly involved in eco-tourism.

Land Tenure: A particularly important issue, especially in Africa, is the need to identify land tenure. It is difficult or impossible for indigenous peoples to develop land or facility based eco-tourism if they cannot establish rights to the land. Legal mechanisms need to be in place for land rights to be recorded and established.

Empowerment of Local Communities Needed: Communities need to be able to take more control of the management of eco-tourism, and should be involved in managing resources and benefits (directly and indirectly). Many regional conferences felt that eco-tourism projects could be used to complement intensively-used destinations, reducing visitor pressures (which reduces disadvantages in other areas, *e.g.*, Mountain areas,

Europe). This included showing communities how they could be involved in planning and policy making processes, and the benefits that might accrue, as well as how to benefit: from ownership and control of eco-tourism; from eco-tourism planning and policy making initiatives; from galvanising local economies through a range of products; or from important conservation functions.

Enabling Participation of all Stakeholders: It was felt that planning and policy development is not carried out with much stakeholder involvement, and that often stakeholder participation tends to be unmeaningful. So strategies are often not implemented because they are not developed and "owned" locally. Meaningful involvement would lessen such concerns as maintaining authenticity of social systems, indigenous and other cultures. Not only should stakeholders be consulted, but planners and policy developers should develop creative and culturally appropriate ways to encourage a diversity of stakeholder input (*e.g.*, obtaining advice from community workers, enabling verbal (vs. written) input, holding focussed discussions with diverse sub-groups, or working through school/church/sports/ women's' groups, etc.).

Recommendations

Key Crosscutting Recommendations

Use National and International Transboundary Management Approaches

- International eco-tourism planning and policies should be integrated across national and international boundaries, with respect to resource planning and management, and to visitor movement. Eco-systems are the appropriate management units, even if outside protected area boundaries.
- Adjacent jurisdictions should develop mechanisms to ease border movements, particularly in CIS and adjacent countries (*e.g.*, creating tourist cards to facilitate travel;

relaxing visa procedures or currency/exchange regulations; influencing airfare changes).

Governments Should Take Responsibility in Planning and Policy Development

- National level leadership and guidance should be demonstrated through consistent departmental and interdepartmental vision and objectives. Planning and policy development for eco-tourism should be in the context of sustainable development objectives, and integrated with other economic, social and conservation activities (*e.g.*, national policy co-ordination could be facilitated by Inter-Ministerial co-ordination committees at appropriate levels, and chaired by senior personnel).

- In some regional conferences, it was felt that eco-tourism planning should be part of a larger sustainable tourism planning perspective, or integrated into other sectors' planning, while in other conferences it was recommended that specific corridors and areas be delimited for eco-tourism (*e.g.*, in the Meso-American conference, it was felt that protected area management plans should include clear goals for biological corridors and should analyse the potential of border areas to develop eco-tourism corridors through land use plans.).

Plan Systematically for Protected Areas

- Protection of critical areas was considered a primary goal of protected areas management and fundamental to eco-tourism planning and development. This reflects the view that management of supply (resources) should be the core concern. Visitor satisfaction (demand) should be considered, but in such a way as to support resource conservation rather than to be the primary driver of protected areas management. A protected areas planning framework should be developed for all countries/regions, within the context of an overall vision.

- Zoning is a strong tool that should be used in protected areas planning (including incorporating core areas and reserves, low and medium impact areas, and buffers). Zones should have strict regulations with enforcement, and infrastructure and facilities should be in peripheral areas.

Formulate and Implement Policy and Planning Processes

- Some conferences recommended that public sector agencies, NGOs and other stakeholders involved in environmental and community matters establish co-operative agreements and set up an umbrella organisation to plan, regulate and monitor eco-tourism activities.

- Tourism planning and policy development should involve many sectors/departments, particularly for protected areas (*e.g.*, coastal area planning and management should include integrated strategies for air and water; eco-tourism/tourism should be integrated into other sectors' planning and policy-making, using such tools as land use planning, transportation planning, town planning, infrastructure development, and socio-economic planning at all scales). Similarly, the tourism and culture sectors should collaborate (*e.g.*, archaeological site conservation or presentation).

- Tourism planning (and protected area planning) should include clear goals and facilitation mechanisms for community development (*e.g.*, community-owned micro-enterprise creation and development). Tourism policy development should ensure rules are not overly complex for either visitors or for communities.

- The development of plans and polices for eco-tourism should involve:
  - Vision and long-term perspectives at all levels.
  - Appropriate policies for different scales, based on better information/data.

- ❑ A balance of voluntary and legislated regulation and activities.
- ❑ Definition of government's role with respect to eco-tourism enterprises.
- ❑ Good integration of traditional mechanisms and institutions (already in place).
- Good examples of practical policies and plans should be disseminated, particularly those that demonstrate site-specific realities, monitoring, regulatory enforcement, and accountability.

Develop Appropriate Tools for Planning and Management

- International agencies should increase their collaboration and contribute to appropriate tools (*e.g.* developing policies, guidelines and codes of conduct. The World Tourism Organisation and other intergovernmental agencies could strengthen their role in sharing international experiences in eco-tourism (*e.g.*, producing publications, organizing forums, or identifying and disseminating best practices on eco-tourism planning, policy development and management).
- Develop an inventory of tourism assets, together with appropriate research, including biodiversity, threats, and endangered species, should be part of eco-tourism planning and development.
- Incorporate a range of appropriate tools in tourism planning and management (*e.g.*, environmental assessments, vision development, determining acceptable numbers/types of visitors in protected areas, land use planning, appropriate places/timing of visitors, pricing policies, zoning mechanisms, facility controls, interpretive tools, guidelines and codes). Conditions of operation should be established for both marine and terrestrial operators.

Commit Adequate Financial Resources and Develop Appropriate Funding Mechanisms

- International funding agencies need to be encouraged to support eco-tourism development projects. Funding mechanisms are also required for planning and co-operation at sub-regional levels.

- Government should view small-scale projects particularly favourably, through loans, grants, or other mechanisms, so as to ease/enable the entry of these enterprises into the marketplace. Support or subsidies should be done conditional on performance or impact monitoring related to eco-tourism goals (*e.g.*, defining targets, indicators, data collection, or biological conservation efforts). Such conditions of assistance should be appropriate to the size of the projects.

- Adequate core funding should be provided to protected areas, and government policies and regulatory mechanisms should mandate returning a portion of tourist revenues to conservation of the protected areas (rather than to general revenues).

- Create appropriate funding mechanisms to help sustain partnerships (*e.g.*, NGOs could act as a conduit for funding projects or partnerships; or eco-tourism projects eligible for international funding could be linked with international pro-poor and biodiversity agendas). It was suggested that regional research centres should be established for research and education on eco-tourism, which would require a partnership approach.

Governments, Development Agencies, NGOs, Private Businesses and Others Should Build Local Capacity

- Capacity building should be a focus (especially in Africa and South America) to enable better participation in planning and policy development processes. Mechanisms should be developed to translate/explain the meaning and implications of proposed policies and plans to stakeholders.

■ Training is the prime mechanism recommended to increase local employment, to add to product value, and to increase local business capabilities. It should be developed appropriately in terms of content, to reflect destination needs (*e.g.*, CIS countries suggested accommodation management, guiding, languages). Similarly, the manner of delivery, training methods, and time frames, should be developed to suit the destination/recipient's cultural and learning style and needs (*e.g.*, hands-on, or train-the-trainer).

■ Private businesses should favour employing locals, and for this provide on-the-job training opportunities.

Build Multi-Stakeholder Participation into Planning and Policy Development Processes

■ Consulting a wide range of stakeholders (both inside and outside the destination) should be built into any planning, policy, or regulatory processes, to develop a sense of community and ownership. Consultation processes should be inclusive and transparent, with particular efforts to include the disadvantaged or the traditionally voiceless (*e.g.*, indigenous groups, women, elders or youth). Planning should incorporate a range of benefits and goals for the community, and should ensure a bottom-up approach.

■ The manner of consultation and participation mechanisms should be culturally appropriate to the target groups, and may vary within one planning or policy development process.

■ Businesses and agencies should proactively contact stakeholders (*e.g.*, cruise ships could initiate contact with stakeholders, to ensure measures are implemented to realise environmental protection and community benefits—Arctic conference). Similarly, central levels of government should initiate involving other levels.

Recommendations for Environmental Conservation

Conserve Material Resources at All Levels

- Plans and policies should ensure that resources are conserved and used more effectively. Use incentives, education, or other measures to encourage energy conservation (use of renewable sources); water conservation (and storage); waste management (3Rs: reduce, reuse, recycle); sustainable biological resource use; and reduced imported materials (especially into islands).

- In Mountain regions and Europe particularly, sustainable transportation should be built into destinations, vacation resorts, and other areas by planners and policy makers. Similarly, tour packagers should feature sustainable transportation in their products as a consumer benefit and a conservation approach.

Educate Communities about Biodiversity and Conservation

- Participatory processes should be used to educate local people about the value of biological and cultural diversity in eco-tourism development, and on how they can both conserve and derive benefits from natural and cultural resources.

- Private companies should pursue voluntary initiatives with stakeholders to promote consumer awareness of environmentally and socially responsible tourism.

Manage Impacts

- Apply a range of approaches and tools for impact management. Carrying capacity studies were recommended to manage impact. Although many conferences focussed on this approach, they did not seem aware of the very large number of alternative tools to address problems of growth, impact or visitor activities and behaviour. Recommendations generally mentioned such specific and limited resource variables as water supply (in desert or island areas) or numbers of beds available locally, where carrying capacity (*i.e.,* identifying the limiting variable threshold) might be a valuable tool.

■ Curb unbridled growth through a range of mechanisms (other than a numbers limit). This was recommended as appropriate to deal with specific problems, such as managing group size, or group frequency, or other use-intensity management tools.

■ Promote sustainable transportation through renting low, or emission-free vehicles, street redesign, traffic speed regulation, cycling and rental spots, routes and information, and other non-motorised traffic modes. Companies should offer comprehensive sustainable transport packages, car free areas, and good intermodal transfer, through multi-stakeholder collaboration.

■ Develop environmental or community standards/ guidelines (*e.g.,* for eco-accommodation in Asia-Pacific, or for activity limits in Andean South America).

Manage Visitors

■ On the one hand, visitor management was recommended to reduce/manage impact, while on the other, it was recommended that protected areas or even countries/regions not have such complex rules that visitation is deterred. Demand management (in terms of type, numbers, concentration, and spread) was recommended. Thus some areas might be developed as tourist nodes or compact tourist destinations to develop a critical mass and increase development feasibility; while other areas may encourage more visitor spread (*e.g.,* to disadvantaged rural or mountain areas). A related recommendation was identification of appropriate markets using alliances of NGOs to perform focus group and other survey work.

■ Use economic policies to manage visitors (*e.g.,* entrance fee policies to help channel seasonal traffic, lower stress on infrastructure, and help pay for services offered).

- Use information and education as strong management tools (*e.g.*, via signposts, alternative routes, different entry points, information centres, interpretive centres, guides, interpretation).
- Use interpretation as both a visitor education and management tool. To increase interpretation capabilities, introduce eco-tourism interpretation programmes in universities, tourism and hotel schools, tourism training and capacity building programmes.

Recommendations for Economic Development

Build Small Business Capabilities and Provide Incentives for Sustainable Practices

- Strengthen small and medium sized (SME) and micro enterprises, to position them for success (particularly recommended in Africa). Such training programmes might include business start-up, hospitality, investment, entrepreneurial activities, management, accommodations management, market analysis, marketing and sustainability. Other types of training programmes should include tour guiding, interpretation, and responses to specific local needs.
- Develop incentives for small eco-tourism businesses that ensure environmental protection and local sustainability (*e.g.*, through financial mechanisms, provision of exclusive access to key areas, provision of guarantees or long-term leases, adjustment of conditions of operation, sharing research findings, joint marketing incentives, etc.).

Provide Government and other Support for Community Level Eco-tourism

- Infrastructural support should be provided (adjacent to parks and protected areas or within designated zones) that assist local communities in eco-tourism development (*e.g.*, signage, accommodation, routes, transportation, telecommunication, electricity, water, waste and sewage treatment facilities, etc.).

■ Build on existing subsistence or economic activities. Eco-tourism activities should be used to support development of disadvantaged areas and alleviate poverty (*e.g.*, on islands, or in rural poor areas) through planning and decision-making. Means could include resource use/development policies, affirmative action policies, capacity building, and focussed education. Micro-credit programmes should be developed to assist small scale enterprises. Some conferences recommended that local eco-tourism businesses with community involvement should be favoured over multi-national tourism companies.

■ The role of governments should be more as a facilitator of eco-tourism operations and businesses developing public-private co-operation mechanisms, rather than being operators themselves. This allows government to develop multistakeholder frameworks for monitoring and regulatory activities, and enables entrepreneurial capabilities to flourish.

Educate Destinations about Sustainable Means to Increase Economic Benefits

■ The misconception that increased visitation is the way to increase economic benefits is in part responsible for some of the negative impacts of tourism. Inform stakeholders about other ways to increase economic benefits (*e.g.*, by retaining the same visitor for longer, or providing opportunities for visitors to spend more, such as by identifying more festivals, enhancing cultural tours with add-ons, expanding local crafts, enhancing packages with additional activities or opportunities to induce visitors to purchase longer tours).

Recommendations for Social and Cultural Benefits

Enhance Use of Heritage Resources

- By protecting and rehabilitating historic/heritage buildings, monuments, and structure through policy, and use them for tourism purposes (*e.g.* accommodation, catering, information centre, exhibitions, etc).

Involve Communities and Give Ownership

- Encourage community involvement in social and cultural programming, to provide direct economic and cultural benefits, as well as to enhance visitor experiences and authenticity.
- Involve communities and all operators in monitoring impacts, or other feedback requirements.
- Obtain community input about traditional and cultural activities, to determine the activities of value and sustain these via planning and policies, and to preserve critical elements of a culture (*e.g.*, aboriginal land based economic activities).

Education and Awareness Building

- Education and awareness-building need to be directed to the full range of stakeholders, and should address all elements of sustainability—conservation and protection; economic feasibility; and socio-cultural benefits of eco-tourism. Community awareness campaigns are needed about eco-tourism regulations and policies, and training about tourism pros and cons, hospitality, how to obtain increased added value from visitors, and how to manage and take control of tourism locally. Obtain leverage by focussing initially on community decision-makers.
- Ensure that governments, agencies, tour operators, and outside companies know that they have some responsibilities/opportunities in preventing/resolving certain

problems which communities may have (problems which originate outside the communities, since locals are often only in control of internal elements of their current condition).

■ NGOs should develop more short-term planning processes that could be transferred effectively to communities for their future use.

Recommendations for Multi-Stakeholder Participation

Joint Ventures

Facilitation of community level joint ventures should occur, particularly with the private sector. Examples suggested in preparatory conference summaries include: community co-management of protected areas to enable community-developed products with protected areas agencies; strategic alliances between private businesses and local communities to enable benefit-sharing such as through providing local goods or services; non-governmental organisation support for and assistance with community-level projects; arrangements between inbound operators and destinations to include sustainable package elements in their offerings, such as sustainable transportation. Support for joint ventures could be built into planning (*e.g.*, the development of guidelines for agreements between communities and all other stakeholders) or into policy initiatives (*e.g.*, through incentives, subsidies, demonstrations, training programmes, etc.).

Points for Further Debate

Many of the preparatory conference planning and policy development recommendations summarised above identify issues, challenges and problems in eco-tourism planning and policy, but they don't define specific solutions for most of them. The recommendations are often directed at senior levels of government, especially with respect to coordinating activities both horizontally (between agencies), and vertically (from national to community levels). Discussions at the World Eco-tourism Summit may wish to consider the fact that there is a need for good practices to be highlighted in this area, as well as specific tools to enable appropriate implementation. Suggested topics for discussion might include:

- The need to manage impact or to limit tourists, and how to do this, is a difficult issue. More specific discussion or examples of multiple approaches and mechanisms would be useful (*e.g.*, using a range of voluntary, educational, and incentive-based approaches, as well as the conventional regulatory mechanisms).

- The approach of participatory and adaptive (co)-management could be a fruitful line of discussion.

- Practical ways to integrate eco-tourism planning into broader regional or local development policies and plans. This could involve how to encourage diverse agencies to co-operate; how to integrate policies into other community, regional, or enterprise support initiatives; or how government should be involved in a range of activities from support for new eco-tourism initiatives to research activities.

- There is a need for good practices to be highlighted in development of legislative, regulatory and policy tools, which address community-based problems.

- Practical suggestions for how communities can take control of their future.

- While discussions focussed strongly on communities, the needs and perspectives of indigenous peoples were not always differentiated from those of mainstream communities. How to involve indigenous minorities meaningfully in planning and policy development could be a fruitful discussion.

- Those mechanisms which achieve both environmental and socio-cultural benefits could be explored.

- How to constructively involve those who are related to eco-tourism activities and part of current problems/solutions, but are not necessarily aware of this, should be addressed, since all players have useful contributions to solutions.

■ How to involve politicians, persuade them of the benefits of a more integrated approach, and to make them care about environmental and socio-cultural values, and about eco-tourism.

■ There is a need for more examples of good eco-tourism policy-making and planning, and for practical examples of the implementation of plans and policies, especially those which demonstrate a good balance between centralised policies and site-specific realities, and those which successfully demonstrate accountability and monitoring.

THEME B
Regulation of Eco-tourism:
Institutional Responsibilities And Frameworks

Prepared by Mr. Francesc Giro

Introduction

A number of issues were discussed at the different preparatory conferences in relation to the need to monitor and regulate eco-tourism, and stressing the need and importance of evaluating progress towards sustainability. There is a wide range of situations, depending on which part of the world we are talking about. In some areas eco-tourism is well developed, the governments have set up regulations, a number of certification systems are available and there is only a need to evaluate if there is a real progress towards sustainability. On the other hand, there are regions where eco-tourism is just appearing, there is a lack of institutional support and regulations are inexistent. In between these two extreme cases, there are a number of varied situations in the different continents, with different needs and with one common issue, which is the development of eco-tourism.

WTO has been devoting a great effort to the development and dissemination of methodologies for the identification and use of sustainability indicators in tourism development. The WTO publication *"A Practical Guide to the Development and Use of Indicators of Sustainable Tourism"* defines a set of core indicators, which would be of potential use in all destinations, together with supplementary indicators for specific types of destinations (*e.g.*, coastal resorts, small islands, eco-, cultural and community tourism sites). Another very interesting development related to evaluation is The Global Reporting Initiative, set up by UNEP and other institutions, which is producing specific indicators for reporting on the activity of Tour Operators, within the UNEP/WTO/UNESCO Tour Operator Initiative for Sustainable Tourism Development.

Issues Discussed

Institutional Framework

A common problem in many parts of the world is the lack of an institutional framework for the development of eco-tourism. Besides that, in many countries the presence of many governmental ministries who have intersecting responsibilities regarding the developmental, planning and marketing issues relating to eco-tourism, can become a problem since such bodies have contradicting agendas: balancing development of tourism (in this case eco-tourism) and conservation of the natural and cultural assets. The need to develop umbrella mechanisms that allow such bodies to work successfully together in order to create the balance necessary for the development of eco-tourism was also stressed. In some areas there was an agreement in the fact that Governmental commitment to conservation and eco-tourism development is one of the most important factors for operational success. Since the natural environment is the primary attraction in many eco-tourism destinations, it is imperative that public, private and non-governmental organisations co-operate in regulating the industry and enforcing the institutional framework. In some areas such as

Europe in general, and the Mediterranean countries, the situation is different. Institutional frameworks are in place to guarantee proper development of eco-tourism. However, in general there is confusion between eco-tourism and other kinds of sustainable tourism and also the situation and real potential for eco-tourism is very different depending on which country we are talking about.

Regulation

There has been a general agreement in pointing Eco-tourism Certification and regulation as key factors of evaluation with a view to sustainability. An important point discussed was the need for public-private sector cooperation with a view to establishing policies, strategies and regulations relative to sustainable tourism development. Emphasis was made on how important it is to consult with all the players in protected areas, including the administrative bodies on the matter of regulating eco-tourism flows. In desert countries where borders very often have nothing to do with geographical limits, there was an agreement in the fact that regulations for eco-tourism in protected areas should be extended beyond the frontiers of the neighbour countries. In some cases there was some resistance against the definition of regulations and it was suggested that a better approach would be to establish guidelines, and only after, a next step could be to transform a list of optional guidelines into obligatory regulations. In general, it was recognised that a variety of regulations need to be developed such as codes of conduct, guidelines and so on, together with legal regulations that help reduce negative impacts. Finally, in many cases there was agreement on the need and interest and very often there was not more regulation because of a lack of financial and technical resources.

Certification and Labelling

In continents where eco-tourism is well developed, one of the main issues that were discussed was certification and labelling.

The experiences analysed during these conferences confirmed the need for basic guidelines, which should be adapted by each country to meet its specific conditions. Attention was drawn to the risk of certification being used as a non-tariff barrier by external buyers, which would have a particularly detrimental effect on small businesses.

Quality labels such as The European Charter for sustainable tourism in protected areas are very useful tools for helping such areas/destinations and tourism business/enterprises to define their sustainable tourism strategy by means of a strategic and participatory approach. Such labels aim to ensure the development and management of tourism in protected areas in a sustainable way, taking into account the needs of the environment (efficient protection), local residents (economic benefits and living standards improvements), local business (higher profits due to a high selling value of the labelled area) and visitors (high quality tourism experience). Labelling was agreed to be one of the ways to regulate eco-tourism. In countries where eco-tourism and certification are less developed, there was some resistance to it, with the belief that small-scale eco-tourism products could not reach the standards.

Definition of Evaluation and Monitoring Criteria

There are few examples of monitoring of eco-tourism in order to evaluate progress towards sustainability. Communities need to identify what needs they have, the ways in which tourism can meet those needs and the delivery of those needs then need to be time lined in order to define evaluation and monitoring criteria. In a number of preparatory meetings, there was an agreement in the fact that there is a need for some kind of monitoring and evaluation of the degree of success of eco-tourism projects, which can be used as case studies in the region to show, in a practical manner, the benefits of eco-tourism development both for local people and for conservation.

The situation is very different in each country but the experiences presented have shown that there is a need for basic guidelines for eco-tourism development that can then be adapted to the context of each country. Evaluation and accreditation where found to be important tools for the improvement of eco-tourism products and also for making easier the process of progress monitoring.

Identification of Indicators

The identification of indicators and its difficulty was a subject of debate in a number of meetings. One of the indicators used was the collective welfare of the community, as it covers both community and individual benefits from eco-tourism. One important point was to find out what proportion of income is going to individuals, households and to community projects and then how to monitor this. It was pointed out how important it is to secure information about community benefits from eco-tourism. Sometimes the indicators set by governments are difficult to use, particularly where the indicators suggested by government are intrusive, such as the monitoring of household earnings in rural communities, which can have constraints. Other indicators are more suitable, in that they are in the public domain: for example the number of bicycles, better housing, ability to send children to school etc.

Another possible approach shown was to measure household income and other community indicators from the demand side. Surveys of tourist expenditure can reveal a great deal about community benefits without having to investigate household earnings in rural communities. It is possible to discover from tourists what they have been spending and where, and from this information to make good estimates of the amount of money flowing into local communities from tourism. Similarly it is a relatively easy matter to identify from the tourism industry the amount of money that is being spent in the local community. It was finally pointed out that performance indicators needed to be determined and agreed in the design phase of programmes and projects and to be related to clear development objectives.

Recommendations

Regulation of Eco-tourism

- Move gradually from optional guidelines and simple codes of conduct, into obligatory regulations.

- Governments should provide leadership, coordinate planning and set the legislative and regulatory framework needed for successful eco-tourism.

- Establishment of suitable legal frameworks under-pinned by effective tools for controlling and monitoring eco-tourism activities, along with other instruments, such as certification and accreditation, which contribute to improving the quality of eco-tourism products.

- In order to become credible, certification processes must be transparent, readily understandable and broadly publicized, in addition, to which they should be subject to periodic updates.

- It is essential to consult with all the players in nature parks and with the administrative bodies involved on the matter of regulating eco-tourism flows, safe-guarding threatened sites and training guides while also creating awareness.

- Development of International, Regional and National Policies in order to address issues affecting the development of eco-tourism. They should include guidelines, codes of conduct and best practices that define eco-tourism.

- Establishment of management plans in protected areas which include sustainable development of tourism, zoning, codes of conduct, and land use planning, etc, in order to regulate eco-tourism activities.

Labelling

- The enforcement of control mechanisms and monitoring of eco-quality has to be done with the participation of all stakeholders involved.

- Accommodation classification should include an ecolabel or eco-certification scheme in order to improve sustainability performance of accommodation facilities in eco-tourism and provide consumers with reliable expectations and advice before booking.

- Involve all stakeholders in the acceptance and use of all tools for achieving sustainability in eco-tourism (eco-labels, brands, indicators, carrying capacity assessment, even the legislation).

- Compliance with general tourism regulations and codes should be stricter in the case of eco-tourism, combining supervision and monitoring, with awareness raising campaigns among business people and tourists, training of service suppliers and possibly sanctions against those who do not comply.

- The participatory design and implementation of a voluntary certification system of sustainability of eco-tourism activities should be promoted.

Monitoring

- The monitoring of the benefits of eco-tourism for the local community should not be solely based on monetary indicators but also on socio-cultural factors such as infrastructure development, education and health services, as well as the community's changed perception of its natural assets and their conservation.

- It is also important to measure changes in the level of awareness and acceptance of conservation in particular communities over periods of time.

- There needs to be transparency and independent review of the performance of projects in their contributions to both conservation and local communities.

- Setting targets and monitoring performance against the targets is important in assessing the scale of the achievement. This requires a record keeping system *e.g.* numbers of visitors, visitor satisfaction and expenditure etc.

- Effective monitoring needs defining targets, which should be achieved in a certain time period (*e.g.* the number of tourists, ratios between modes of transport in terms of arrivals, water purification, reduction of noise and traffic, raising local generated income of people, employment etc.).

- Indicators to measure performance and impacts should be defined. The range of indicators should include the social, ecological and economic development. They should cover those elements which are most crucial for local sustainability (*e.g.* water, area, bio-diversity, transport, employment, local income, local quality of life, security, crime).

- There should be continuous data collection involving business and tourists (*e.g.* questionnaires); the involvement of all stakeholders in the monitoring process and monitoring institutions; and regular revision of the local eco-tourism strategy taking account of the results of the monitoring process.

- Local governments need to strengthen their technical capabilities to be able to monitor the performance of commercial tourism companies and of tourists within protected and non-protected mountain areas.

- National subsidies and support for local projects and strategies must ensure that monitoring is a prerequisite of the projects, and that adequate financial resources are devoted to the monitoring process after the life of the aid programme.

- NGOs should be involved in monitoring progress, since they can play an important role in order to guarantee the benefits of eco-tourism development, both for local people and for the conservation of the diverse natural resources of the region. At the same time, taking charge of these operational activities allows a high level of control and monitoring of eco-tourism.

- Monitoring systems should be established in order to evaluate the economic, social and environmental impact of eco-tourism.

■ Local communities should be supported so that they could take part in the process of monitoring the impact of eco-tourism.

Evaluation

Evaluation systems for sustainability of tourism have to choose indicators and criteria for an assessment scheme that balances between indicators for state of society and state of environment, socio-economic driving forces, socio-economic and environmental pressures and driving forces and indicators for institutional frames. Such evaluations should be done and published on a regular basis, allowing for voluntary benchmarking of destinations.

Issues for Further Debate

■ The reduction of the uncontrolled launch of pseudo-eco-labels. Creation of an "umbrella" eco-brand by joining tourism, environment and consumer associations.

■ Extend Certification to other aspects of eco-tourism activity such as service quality and the participation of local communities in the management of eco-tourism and the benefits thereof, besides environmental issues.

■ To establish Certification on a voluntary basis or as an instrument to complement the regulation of eco-tourism ventures.

■ The certification of eco-tourism products should pave the way for benefits and incentives for certified companies.

■ To explore easily accessible funding formulae to cover the cost of international certification systems which makes them inaccessible to small businesses.

■ Eco-tourism certifiers must be guided by social criteria geared to facilitating the integration of small businesses at preferential rates and through technical contributions or the promotion of collective certification alternatives.

- Financially sound NGOs should shoulder the role of a certification body at a cost more affordable for local entrepreneurs.

- Local certification initiatives must be extended with a view to promoting the creation of regional networks, which could in turn be recognized (accredited) by international systems.

- In the light of the proliferation of "eco-labels" and certification systems, steps must be taken to promote the establishment of an equivalent system or certification based on international parameters, which involves the concept of accreditation.

- Certain laws and regulations within protected areas should be extended beyond their frontiers.

- To promote a constructive public-private sector relationship. Private sector operators should take responsibility for the economic, social and environmental impact of their activities.

- The private sector should be included in the process of designing regulations.

- Establishment of an international award scheme for eco-tourism destinations, associated with the UNESCO world heritage site designation, as an incentive for improved eco-tourism planning and management.

- Most of the existing concepts for eco-labels, brands and certification systems have to be enlarged by social and cultural aspects to reach the aims of sustainable eco-tourism.

- To establish legally binding instruments for the implementation of sustainable eco-tourism and avoidance of non-sustainable forms of tourism for sensitive areas, especially mountain regions, if the implementation is accompanied by specific regional strategies and measures.

- The development of legislative frameworks at the regional level should be supported, because they can positively influence sustainability issues, including the promotion of eco-tourism and similar types of tourism harmonized with the environment.

- Some countries have suggested that strict regulations for eco-tourism at an international level should be avoided, while guidelines are acceptable.

- Consideration of the obligatory introduction of certification systems for eco-tourism facilities and operations, at least at regional and possibly at worldwide level, to guarantee that the quality provided is consistent with the principles of sustainability.

- One proposal was made in order to raise financial resources from visitors in order to fund conservation and management the natural environment and cultural heritage, as in many countries in Asia this proved to be one of the problems limiting the proper development of eco-tourism.

THEME C
Product Development, Marketing and Promotion of Eco-tourism: Fostering Sustainable Products And Consumers

Prepared by Dr. Richard Denman

Abstract

This report by Dr. Richard Denman, one of four experts appointed by WTO and UNEP for the World Eco-tourism Summit, summarises key themes, issues and recommendations for product development and marketing of eco-tourism, arising from the preparatory conferences. It starts by listing some challenges to be faced, especially by small projects which find it hard to reach markets. Priority areas for action are identified as:

- Creating the right structures for working together.
- Relating products to markets from the outset.
- Paying attention to all aspects of product quality.
- Providing relevant support for communities and enterprises.
- Strengthening the promotion of eco-tourism messages and products.

The report presents broad recommendations in each of these areas and provides a list of key topics for further debate at the Summit.

Product Development, Marketing and Promotion of Eco-tourism: Summary Report

This report is a summary of the main conclusions of the preparatory conferences held in 2001 and 2002 in advance of the World Eco-tourism Summit. The report covers issues relating to product development, marketing and promotion of eco-tourism, which is the third of the four Summit themes. Parallel reports have been prepared on the other themes: policy and planning; regulation; and monitoring.

Issues Discussed

The Context of Eco-tourism Development and Marketing

During the preparatory conferences many case studies were presented of eco-tourism projects from around the world, established by a wide range of private, voluntary and public bodies. Each had its own story to tell. Lessons learned from this practical experience were debated and discussed and then reflected in the conference reports.

Looking across all the regions, although there are notable differences in the type of eco-tourism experience on offer, in the level of resources available and the challenges faced, there are striking similarities in the objectives behind eco-tourism development and in the issues involved in establishing and maintaining sustainable products. This gives legitimacy to drawing global conclusions from the Summit.

There is still great variation in the understanding of what constitutes an eco-tourism product. While it is broadly accepted that we are talking about a nature-based experience that is managed in a sustainable way, many presentations covered other types of product and wider issues of sustainable tourism. There are regional differences here: a strong focus on wildlife and wilderness is apparent in the Americas and Africa, while in Asia there is particular interest in the associated cultural dimension and in Europe eco-tourism is often linked to rural tourism and landscapes shaped by man. A common thread is the concept of a product that provides the visitor with an authentic understanding of the area's natural and cultural heritage, and involves and benefits local people.

In all regions, the purpose behind the development of eco-tourism products can be equated with sustainable development objectives. In some situations the underlying motive may be to benefit conservation, through generating more resources or providing an alternative, more environmentally sustainable, local economic base. Elsewhere, the motivation may be more to do with diversifying the economy and the tourism market, or tackling rural poverty. Many products are developed for a multitude of reasons. In all cases, the principles behind successful product development and marketing are similar.

Although there may be similarities in objectives and principles, the starting point and individual circumstances of each project may be vastly different. Current levels of visitation, inherent attractiveness of the area, accessibility and infrastructure, ecological sensitivity, local skills base, and community structure and aspirations, will vary. These differences exist within all regions as well as between them. Therefore each individual project needs to be very carefully assessed and planned.

Key Challenges and Priorities

The preparatory conferences have demonstrated that in all regions of the world there are many excellent eco-tourism projects delivering positive benefits to local communities and the conservation of the environments in which they are located, as well as a fulfilling experience for visitors. However, there are also many challenges for product development and marketing.

Too Many Products Fail

There are examples in most regions of eco-tourism products which have failed through lack of profitability, or are likely to do so when donor support is no longer available. Often these are community-based and perhaps started primarily for conservation reasons. A common problem is lack of market response and poor feasibility assessment and business planning.

Small Enterprises and Community-based Products Find it Hard to Reach Markets

Cost effective promotion is a challenge for many eco-tourism enterprises because of their isolation, small size and lack of resources and skills.

The Quality of Visitor Experience and Environmental Performance Can be Inconsistent

Excellent eco-tourism products are to be found in every region, but the sector can be let down by products with an insufficient quality of service or environmental management. Sometimes the problem may lie in the surrounding destination, its infrastructure and planning control, rather than in the eco-tourism project itself.

Visitors to Natural Areas Could Contribute More to Conservation and Local Communities

Many natural environments, including protected areas, are already receiving significant visitor numbers. The challenge and opportunity for product development and marketing is to stimulate more visitor spending per head, minimise leakage away from the local area, reduce environmental impact and increase support for conservation.

The Public is Still Relatively Unaware of, or Unresponsive to, Sustainability Issues

Despite the growth in demand for nature-based tourism, only a small proportion of travellers, including those from specialist niche markets, appear to be specifically seeking out sustainable products. Many suppliers and host communities are also still not sufficiently aware of sustainability issues.

In the face of these challenges, the following priority areas for action can be identified:

- *Creating the right structures for working together*: All the preparatory conferences stressed the need for stakeholders to work together on the development and marketing of eco-tourism products. None of the successful case study examples were operating in isolation.

- *Relating products to markets from the outset*: A common call has been to relate supply to demand, with a better understanding of markets and how to reach them.

- *Paying attention to all aspects of product quality*: Attention to detail is needed in product design and management in order to meet market interests and sustainability objectives.

- *Providing relevant support for communities and enterprises*: Small enterprises and local communities require technical and financial assistance, which is locally delivered and tailored to their needs.

- *Strengthening the promotion of eco-tourism messages and products*: More can be done globally and locally to promote the concept of eco-tourism and help products reach their customers.

The remainder of this report looks at the main points arising from the preparatory conferences within each of these areas.

Recommendations

Structures and Relationships for Product Development and Marketing

Local communities, private sector enterprises, NGOs, local authorities and protected areas, national governments and international agencies all have a role to play in eco-tourism development and marketing.

- *Address local community needs and opportunities*: All preparatory conferences have emphasised the importance of working with local and indigenous communities in determining the level and type of tourism development in their area and in encouraging individual entrepreneurship, community-based enterprise and employment opportunities for local people.

- *Recognise the key role of private sector businesses*: Fostering and working with successful private sector operations, encouraging and helping them to meet a combination of commercial, social and environmental objectives, has proved to be a sound strategy. It is important to strengthen links between private operators and local communities. International and incoming tour operators have an important role to play, not only in promoting eco-tourism but also in advising on product development and the overall quality of a destination, relating this to customer requirements.

- *Strengthen networking between small enterprises and projects*: There was a frequent call for small eco-tourism enterprises to work together, to strengthen their marketing outreach and encourage common standards. Examples vary from associations of village community eco-tourism products in a number of Asian and African countries, to branded small farm based accommodation enterprises in Europe with central booking services. Two conferences put forward the concept of local clusters of eco-tourism initiatives, thereby establishing a critical mass of product in one area which would provide a composite visitor experience, be more able to attract business and justify investment in supporting infrastructure.

■ *Recognise protected areas as focal points for eco-tourism products and marketing*: Often parks and other protected areas provide the main draw for visitors, creating an opportunity for local communities to gain economic benefit through the provision of facilities and services. The relationship between protected area authorities and local communities and tourism enterprises can be a critical one. There are various examples of stakeholder groups or wider liaison forums attached to national or nature parks, enabling the park to influence standards, marketing messages and new projects, while also supporting and coordinating enterprises and reflecting their needs. The quality of a park's own facilities and services, and the relationship between visitor management and conservation policies, is obviously of major importance in its own right.

■ *Increase support from national and local government for product development and marketing of eco-tourism*: Priorities may include infrastructure improvement, including sustainable transport, and featuring eco-tourism more strongly in destination and thematic promotional campaigns.

Understanding Eco-tourism Markets

The preparatory conferences recognised the importance of a realistic market assessment when developing and promoting eco-tourism products.

■ *Use more market research*: There was a general agreement that not enough is known about eco-tourism markets and more research is needed. This has been partly addressed by WTO studies of the eco-tourism market in the seven main generating countries, prepared for the International Year and presented at most preparatory conferences. These studies used quite a narrow definition of eco-tourism, characterised by its size, impacts, educational components as well as visitor interest in nature and culture in natural areas. Results have pointed to this being a small niche market yet strongly growing. Although specialist tour operators are important in this market, the majority of ecotourists are individual travellers making their own arrangements.

- *Take a broad view of the market, recognising different segments*: Many individual enterprises and destinations have suggested that they are attracting a range of different types of visitor, including people enjoying an eco-tourism experience as part of a more general holiday, domestic tourists and schools groups as well as more specialist nature tourism niche markets. More informed market segmentation will enable products and promotional strategies to be adapted to different expectations and requirements.

- *Study current visitor flows and local market conditions*: The pattern and distribution of tourism demand in the area, the performance of comparable operations, and the strengths and weaknesses of the location, should be carefully assessed, before product development takes place.

Key Components of Eco-tourism Products

The composition of eco-tourism products should vary in order to satisfy different market segments and local conditions. However, some general priorities were identified at the preparatory conferences.

- *Address quality, authenticity and security*: Throughout the preparatory conferences, the importance of these three attributes was underlined. Quality does not necessarily mean luxury, but attention to detail and understanding customer needs. Authenticity is about meeting a visitor aspiration of 'seeing the real thing' while respecting the sensitivities of local communities and environments. Security is about visitor safety, perceived and real, but can also be applied to wider issues of reliability.

- *Give top priority to the interpretation of nature and culture*: The most essential component of an eco-tourism product is the inherent quality of the landscape and wildlife. The WTO market studies confirmed this as the main visitor motivation, but closely followed by the opportunity to meet local people and experience cultural traditions and lifestyles. Eco-tourism is distinguished by providing an experience that is both educative and enjoyable. Quality of interpretation is of paramount importance; within this, the value of good local guides, who know their subject and how to put it over, has been strongly emphasised.

- *Design and manage service facilities to maximise sustainability*: Although not the driving force in an eco-tourism offer, accommodation, catering, and opportunities to make purchases are essential components of the product. There is a whole host of planning, design and management issues here that affect viability, environmental impact, enterprise and employment opportunities for local people, value retained in the local economy and the quality of the visitor experience. Case studies presented during the preparatory conferences have demonstrated a wealth of good practice in this area and a growing body of knowledge internationally, on topics such as: eco-lodge design and management; village based accommodation and homestay programmes; use of local produce and traditional dishes; and handicraft production and sales.

- *Address destination as well as individual product issues*: Successful and sustainable product development in eco-tourism also needs to take account of infrastructure, environmental management and visitor services in the destination as a whole. For example, the need for more sustainable transport options to and within the destination was stressed at the European preparatory conference.

- *Relate eco-tourism to sustainable activity tourism, where appropriate*: Although eco-tourism is clearly distinguished from activity tourism, it is apparent that some ecotourists are looking for activities such as hiking or trail riding to complement the product offer. This appears to be particularly true in mountain areas, in regions like Europe and Central Asia. In maritime locations, such as small island states, making activities like diving and yachting more environmentally sustainable was seen as an issue for eco-tourism. Three conferences also raised the controversial question of the relationship between hunting and eco-tourism, recognising that this activity, when carefully controlled, can provide resources for wildlife management and raise the perceived value of certain species within local communities.

Technical Support for Communities and Enterprises

In all regions there is a recognised need for local communities and small enterprises to receive relevant technical support to assist product development and marketing.

- *Provide relevant local training*: Locally available skills training is required, covering guiding, environmental management, customer care, catering, languages, promotion and information technology. It has also been emphasised that people from indigenous and local communities should be supported in taking up management positions in eco-tourism. Capacity building of this kind has been assisted by governments, NGOs, donor agencies, educational institutions and the private sector, often working fruitfully in partnership. The importance of developing such programmes with local people and private enterprises, to ensure they are tailored to need and have local ownership, has been stressed. Some projects have demonstrated the advantage of including local government officials and NGOs in training programmes.

- *Encourage people to look together at the local resource and at other projects*: A number of conferences pointed to the value of local study tours to raise people's awareness of conservation issues and the opportunities of eco-tourism. Projects were also presented where the stimulation and sound practical knowledge came from visits to successful eco-tourism projects elsewhere. There may be opportunities to develop more twinning and multi-lateral links between projects.

- *Provide targeted, accessible financial assistance*: The important contribution of micro-credit and small grant schemes for eco-tourism was demonstrated by a number of projects, and there has been a call for more financial support that is within the reach of local entrepreneurs, including resources for marketing. However, one preparatory conference emphasised the need to avoid developing eco-tourism products that will remain dependent on public subsidy in the long term.

Promoting Eco-tourism Messages and Products

In general the preparatory conferences have called for more promotion of eco-tourism, while recognising that the level of promotion of any one location should be determined by its carrying capacity and take account of the views of the local community.

- *Promote eco-tourism as a concept*: There is a particular desire to see more active promotion of the principles and values of eco-tourism, to recipient communities and to the travelling public. There is a need for a stronger international campaign to make tourists aware of both the harmful and the beneficial impacts of their activities, and how this depends on their travel choice. This could go beyond simply the generic message, with promotional support for relevant certification schemes and for activities such as donating to conservation causes in destinations visited. One conference emphasised the need to focus on the promotion of eco-tourism to young people, as a receptive audience and the travellers of the future.

- *Grasp the significant opportunity presented by the Internet*: The Internet has had a major impact as a medium for promoting individual eco-tourism products and the considerable potential it presents is widely recognised. It lends itself well to the eco-tourism market, which is particularly responsive to up to date, detailed information and reports from previous travellers. A cautionary note was sounded about the lack of consumer trust in making bookings through the Internet, but this is being overcome as specific sites and brands are becoming better known. The advent of IT based Destination Management Systems will help to link demand to supply more efficiently.

- *Use a range of techniques and partners*: Despite the growth in Internet use, there was general recognition that eco-tourism products should continue to use a range of promotional tools in their marketing, including working with specialist media and tour operators. There was a strong call for national and local tourist organisations to become more actively engaged in promoting eco-tourism themes and products, in their publications and through travel fairs and familiarisation trips.

- *Provide comprehensive and educative information at all stages*: The detail and accuracy of information supplied to visitors in advance of their stay is particularly important in this sector. Ecotourists need to know what to expect. As well as covering travel details and facilities, this should include information on the ecology and culture of the area and how to respect it. Likewise, the quality of information supplied during their stay, for example by hosts, protected area authorities or local tour operators, can greatly affect the visitors' experience and their impact on the local community.

■ *Create loyal ambassadors*: Almost all conferences stressed the importance of 'word of mouth' recommendation as the most potent form of marketing. Providing visitors with a quality experience, getting feedback from them and maintaining some post-visit contact, will help to turn them into committed ecotourists and ambassadors for conservation.

Points for Further Debate

From the discussion and recommendations arising from the preparatory conferences, summarised above, it is possible to pull out some substantial issues in the area of product development and marketing for further debate at the World Eco-tourism Summit.

■ Strengthening the involvement of local and indigenous communities in product development, and the benefits they gain from it.

■ Generating more conservation benefits from eco-tourism product development and marketing.

■ Helping protected areas support, and gain benefit from, the development and marketing of eco-tourism products associated with them

■ Finding the best ways of linking together eco-tourism products for mutual benefit, such as geographical clusters, associations of operators, vertical linkages between products and tour operators and transnational consortia.

■ Understanding the breadth of the market for eco-tourism products and its main components.

■ Strengthening the delivery of technical and financial support for small eco-tourism enterprises and community-based initiatives.

- Improving the exchange of know-how and good practice between projects.
- Encouraging national and local government and tourist organisations to do more to promote eco-tourism and improve the conditions for its development and success in destinations.
- Strengthening the application of web-based marketing tools.
- Making sure that tourists are getting the right level of information, including what is expected of them as well as what they should expect.
- Raising the profile of eco-tourism, and the principles it embodies, through a promotional campaign at an international level.

THEME D
Monitoring the Costs and Benefits of Eco-tourism: Equitable Distribution Between All Actors

Prepared by Prof. François Vellas

Monitoring the costs and benefits of eco-tourism is vital to the success of a tourism development strategy based on the equitable distribution of benefits between all actors. Such a strategy must be built on the will of the international, national and local public sector agencies to support a tourism development approach based on eco-tourism principles as well as on strong (*i.e.* profitable) tourism firms for which eco-tourism is not just a slogan but a means of ensuring the sustainability of their activities and of developing new opportunities for growth.

Issues Discussed

Eco-tourism encompasses all forms of tourism focused on nature where the principal motivation is to observe and appreciate nature and traditional cultures living in natural areas. Therefore, eco-tourism is generally organized for small groups and involves an element of education and interpretation. It must provide positive impacts on the natural and socio-cultural environment, and any negative impacts must be limited and controlled.

Thus, the measurement of economic, ecological and social costs and benefits of eco-tourism is different from that of traditional tourism. The ratios used in these measurements, particularly those evaluating economic profitability, must go beyond merely measuring financial profitability and take into account the impact on the local population's income, activities, and social conditions.

Measuring Economic Costs and Benefits of Eco-tourism

The measurement of the economic costs and benefits of traditional tourism is based on a ratio of estimated profitability of the tourism investment using a methodology of market surveys and of load factor/occupancy determination. Calculating the appropriate coefficient of occupancy determines the profitability of tourism investments. Therefore operators aim to achieve and exceed a breakeven occupancy to ensure return-on-investment and maximum profit.

The Gross Operating Result (GOR) is the basic indicator used to measure the economic costs and benefits of tourism investments. The decision to go ahead with a tourism project will be made by comparing the budget available for financing the investment and with the total amount of the investment without taking into account the environmental costs or the social impact of the project.

For eco-tourism projects, this type of economic and financial analysis is not generally sufficient. The cost benefit analysis of eco-tourism projects cannot be just calculated in terms of potential profitability but must also take into account costs and benefits for local populations.

The many examples of cost benefit analyses of eco-tourism projects presented during various regional seminars show that even with an accommodation occupancy rate of only 20 per cent, local population income increases substantially, and often provides more than double the income derived from agriculture.

Yet traditional financial analysis would indicate that such occupancy rates would be too low compared to the norm and therefore the investment would be abandoned. Based on the conclusions of these regional seminars, in particular those in the Seychelles, Mozambique and Belize, it is recommended that whilst profitability is vital the measurement of economic costs and benefits must be taken into account. The following factors must be considered:

in term of economic costs as for instance:

- The cost of energy infrastructure (existence or lack of renewable energy sources).
- The cost of transport infrastructure and access to eco-tourism sites (roads and access roads).
- The cost of providing drinkable water.
- The cost of waste treatment (solid and sewage).

In term of economic benefits, as for instance:

- Increased income benefits for the local populations.
- Tax receipt benefits for the national public authorities.
- Royalties and access right benefits for the local public authorities.

Measuring Ecological Costs and Benefits of Eco-tourism

The measurement of the ecological costs and benefits of tourism projects is a keystone of eco-tourism development. Indeed, eco-tourism development is one of the rare forms of tourism development, which under certain conditions can support the protection of the natural zones through conservation programmes that it may initiate and finance.

The instruments used to measure the ecological costs and benefits are mainly composite indicators to determine the pressure and intensity of use on eco-tourism sites. The WTO defines three composite indicators particularly well adapted to measure ecological costs and benefits:

- *Carrying capacity*: this composite indicator determines the maximum number tourists that a site can hold, particularly during intensive use in peak period. This indicator can be calculated using indices of protection of the natural sites and indicates the capacity of the site to support different volumes of visitors.

- *Site stress*: this composite indicator measures impact levels on the site taking into account its natural and ecological characteristics. Despite all precautions taken to limit damage to the natural environment, eco-tourism still produces some negative impacts, this indicator measures the extent of these negative impacts and signals when action must be taken to minimise these.

- *Attractiveness*: this measures the ecological characteristics of the site that are attractive for eco-tourism and which may change over time and with increasing intensity of tourist visits. This is a qualitative indicator, which plays a very important part in ensuring the sustainability of eco-tourism investments.

These indicators contribute to the efficient ecological monitoring of eco-tourism products and provide an overall vision of the various products created in the same geographical area by all the different operators.

The Measurement of Social Costs and Benefits of Eco-tourism

The measurement of social costs and benefits of eco-tourism projects indicates the extent that eco-tourism achieves one of its principal goals *i.e.* the equitable distribution of benefits between all the actors. The conclusions of the majority of the regional seminars on the subject, in particular those in Brazil, Kazakhstan and Maldives, clearly show that one of the main priorities of eco-tourism is to provide local populations with economic and social benefits.

However, eco-tourism may also have social costs, which are rarely taken into account. It is not just sufficient to measure the tourist/resident ratio; the degree of local population satisfaction must also be evaluated. The following indices are used to measure this:

In term of social cost:

- Disturbance to the rate/rhythm of the local population's working lives (time of work related to tourism compared to normal schedules of work);
- Disturbance to the traditional use of space by the local population because of the routes used by the ecotourists; and
- Disturbance of the local population's eating habits and everyday life as a result of contact with tourists.

In term of social benefits:

- Creation of employment and new activities related to eco-tourism;
- Improvement in comfort, living conditions and social services (electricity, access to healthcare and education, etc.); and
- Measurement of the local population's degree of satisfaction through surveys.

These indicators provide the tools to evaluate the potential and real impacts of eco-tourism and its contribution to nature conservation.

The Contribution to Nature Conservation and Evaluation of the Impact of Eco-tourism on the Environment, Society and Culture

Eco-tourism contributes to nature conservation by providing economic benefits to host communities, and organisations and administrations in charge of environmental protection and natural areas. As such, eco-tourism not only creates jobs and provides local populations with sources of income, but it also creates awareness amongst both inhabitants and tourists of the need to preserve the natural and cultural capital.

As frequently emphasised by participants at regional conferences the assessment of potential and real impacts of eco-tourism on the environment, society and culture and the need for evaluation tools are vital. Thus, the Tourism Satellite Account (TSA) model could be adapted to measure the impact of the eco-tourism on the environment and society.

The TSA implementation project published by the WTO in 2001 states clearly that the conceptual framework of the TSA can be widened to integrate a sectoral and spatial focus to include environmental and social costs of tourism as well as economic benefits. Therefore, the TSA could become the most appropriate tool to measure the impact of tourism, in particular:

- The cost of employment lost in agriculture caused by the increase in tourism activity;
- The damage caused to the ecosystem;
- The damage to biodiversity; and
- Goods and services which become too expensive for the local population because of inflation as a result of demand by tourists and their suppliers.

TSA are based on Input/Output tables (I/O) which show the relationship between different sectors and activities of production and how benefits are used and redistributed. The impact of eco-tourism could be compared with that of other forms of tourism development using TSA I/O tables.

However, because of the qualitative aspects linked to culture, the impact of eco-tourism on culture requires specific analysis. Thus a case-by-case approach must be adopted.

Tourism activities in rural communities should be conceived as complementary to traditional economic activities. This needs to be so for two main reasons: firstly, to multiply the linkages of eco-tourism with other, traditional economic activities, such as agriculture, fishing, handicrafts and others; and secondly, to avoid overdependence of the local economy and jobs on tourism alone.

Recommendations

Adopting precautionary measures at the local, national, regional and international levels: The objective of precautionary measures is not to discourage the development of eco-tourism, but to ensure efficient coordination between the local, national, regional and international levels in order to guarantee the sustainability of eco-tourism sites. However, as reported in discussions during the regional seminars, in particular those in the Seychelles, Algeria and Greece, the total cost of the environmental protection of eco-tourism destinations may exceed the financial benefits.

In this case applying the principle of the "polluter pays" and the principle of the "user pays" may not guarantee that all the costs of environmental protection will be covered and it is the responsibility of the public authorities to make up the rest. Five types of measures may be considered:

- *Increasing the resistance of sites*: With international assistance, national and local authorities in charge of the environmental protection of natural sites can artificially increase their resistance by protecting them with barriers and routings that prevent direct visitor access to in the most sensitive zones where conservation problems may occur, as is the case in small islands.
- *Varying eco-tourism activity in time and space* so that visitors are not always directed towards the same places at the same time, for example in arid and desert regions. This requires precise coordination between local and national authorities.
- *Strictly reducing the number of visitors admitted to certain sites*, in particular mountain sites, even (and especially) in high tourist season. This measure can cause conflicts

between international, regional, national and especially local partners because of the economic stakes involved.

■ *Regulating the amount of time allowed for visits to the sites as well as schedules* according to the frequency of visitation and the period of the year, in particular in certain islands of the Mediterranean, which receive a large number of ecotourists.

■ *Restricting access according to tourists groups and their sensitivity toward the protection of sites*: This measure can be implemented by imposing guides with competencies specific to the sites visited. It also requires tight coordination between national and local authorities, particularly in the case of wildlife conservation parks in Africa, as mentioned during the seminar organized in Mozambique.

Concrete Proposals

Integrating monitoring and evaluation methods: concrete proposals

Evaluation methodology must be based on the constant monitoring of eco-tourism activities in order to ensure that they are meeting the required objectives. This entails the use of environmental, social and economic evaluation indicators as the most appropriate tools for monitoring.

Integrating Monitoring

A selection of indicators that can be used to evaluate projects and eco-tourism activities include:

■ Local resident per capita budget allocated by government to nature conservation and the management of the environment;

■ The surface area of protected zones expressed as a percentage of the country's or area surface area in which eco-tourism projects are developed;

- The number of rare species in the eco-systems of eco-tourism destination;
- Number of tourists in proportion to the number of residents;
- Number of tourists by surface area of the protected zone;
- Trend in number of firms in the area over time;
- Number of tourist firms using an ecolabel;
- Impact on local production indicator;
- Development control indicator; and
- Mechanisms to reinvest eco-tourism receipts for site protection.

Evaluation Methods

Selecting the appropriate indicators to be used in the evaluation and monitoring of eco-tourism projects can be problematic. Indeed, for greater effectiveness, it is advisable to determine distinct quantitative evaluation criteria or at least a range as standards for each type of tourism or area. These standards for the selected indicators must be elaborated in co-operation with the national and local authorities responsible for tourism so that they become operational in each country and in each area.

- Quantitative and qualitative liquid and solid waste processing indicators with a system adapted to process waste produced by tourists;
- Cultural impact indicator;
- Training indicator;
- Job creation indicator;
- Water and energy consumption indicators (use of renewable energy);
- Indicator of visits by the local population; and
- New technology usage indicator.

These can be used as references by the authorities in charge of tourism development and are an effective method to check whether the objectives of sustainable tourism planning are being met by private tourism development projects and whether these projects should be encouraged to be continued or held back.

The proposed ratios for the evaluation indicators must be balanced according to their perceived importance for each area or tourist zone. Furthermore, it has been suggested at the regional conferences and seminars that monitoring itself is not sufficient without responsive measures and management actions, and that it must be accompanied by mechanisms to recover the capital invested in eco-tourism projects to benefit ecological projects and nature conservation, so that the development of eco-tourism is truly compatible with better protection of natural zones.

The Need for Studies and Evolutionary Management Systems

To ensure accurate monitoring of the costs and benefits of eco-tourism, an equitable distribution of these benefits and to guarantee long-term success a management system based on public/private sector partnership is vital. Evolutionary, management systems for eco-tourism are based on an institutional framework comprising long-term policies to facilitate the development of tourism investments. This framework should include a consultation mechanism with operators and the local population to review the design and implementation of eco-tourism projects. Local people should participate more as entrepreneurs and decision-makers in tourism and not only as employees as now is often the case. Small scale, locally owned tourism is considered the most appropriate means to achieve this given that benefits could flow directly to the local populations. This often requires appropriate support and mentoring together with training opportunities.

The framework should also comprise a strict control system for tourism investments to ensure that the projects that are developed respect environmental protection criteria for the area.

From the discussion and recommendations arising from Theme D of the preparatory meetings and regional conferences, the main issues related to monitoring eco-tourism's costs and benefits and to ensuring an equitable distribution among all stakeholders can be highlighted.

Points for Further Debate

The following issues could be discussed at the World Eco-tourism Summit:

- Devising new eco-tourism cost/benefit evaluation methods which would highlight the social and economic benefits for local populations, as well as the limitations of the financial benefits generated compared to other forms of tourism, notably mass tourism.

- Finding appropriate legal and institutional mechanisms to facilitate and make effective the systematic participation of local communities in the overall eco-tourism process, including policy definition, planning, management and monitoring.

- Establishing financial and fiscal mechanisms to ensure that a significant proportion of the income generated from eco-tourism remains with the local community or serves conservation purposes.

- Researching methods to ensure the permanent control of impacts through the adaptation of carrying capacity methodologies to eco-tourism development, including the definition of damage warning indicators and disturbance gauges for protected sites and other natural areas.

- Putting in place distribution mechanisms to share the benefits of eco-tourism development in order to reinvest a proportion of the revenues generated in the protected areas.

- Understanding and measuring social costs, benefits and change (*i.e.* changes in the behaviour and habits of the local population) so as to limit the negative consequences, maximising social benefits for host communities and to improve attitudes, awareness and respect towards the protection of the environment.

- Researching specific management and monitoring procedures for different types of eco-tourism sites, (*i.e.* desert zones and islands), concerning such aspects as water and waste management, the management of scarce resources, and others.

- Determining appropriate price levels to ensure sufficient returns for firms, suitable redistribution in favour of local populations and that correspond to the purchasing power of tourism demand.

- Ensuring that the principles of "polluter pays" and "user pays" will ensure genuine protection of the environment whilst guaranteeing eco-tourism development.

Bibliography

A.V. Seaton (ed.) (1994). *Tourism: The State of Art*, John Wiley, New York.

Airey, D. and Johnson, S. (1998). *The Profile of Tourism Studies Degree Courses in the UK: 1997-98*. London: National Liaison Group.

Aldous, T. (1972) *Battle for the Environment*, London: Fontana/ Collins.

Anderson A. Barbara, Provis Chris, and Chappel J. Shirley (2004). "The Selection and Training of Workers in the Tourism and Hospitality Industries for the Performance of Emotional Labour", *Journal of Hospitality and Tourism Management*.

Anderson, N. (1961). *Work and Leisure*, London: Routledge and Kegam Paul.

Archer, B.H. (1973). *The Impact of Domestic Tourism*, Cardiff: University of Wales Press.

Arvil, R. (1967), *Man and Environment*, Crisis and the Strategy of Choice, Penguin, Hamondsworth.

Ash, M. (1972), *Planners and Ecologists*, Town and Country Planning, Vol. 40.

Ashworth, G. (1984) *Recreation and Tourism*, London: Bell and Hayman.

Astin, A. (1990). *Assessment for Excellence*. New York: Maxwell McMillan, Inc.

Atkinson, B.W. (1981), *Precipitation in Man and Environmental Processes*, edited by K.J. Gregony and D.E. Wailing, Butterworths.

Avvill, R. (1967) *Man and Environment*, London: Penguin.

Balsdon, J.P.V.D. (1966). *Life and Leisure in Ancient Rome*, London: Bodley Head.

Bell, R. and S. Weitman (1995). "Increasing Applied Skills in an Introductory Marketing Course", Hospitability and Tourism Educator, 7(2), pp. 11-13.

Bharucha, M.P. (1994), Environment Compliance Litigation, *Chartered Secretary.*

Bhatt A.K. (1997). 'Human Resource Development in India' in *I.I.T.T.M. Journal of Travel and Tourism*, 1(1): 36–44.

Billings, W.D. (1964), *"Plants and Ecosystem'*, MacMillan and Co., London.

Bird, E.C.F. (1981), *Coastal Processes in Man and Environmental Processes*, edited by K.J. Gegory and D.E. Wareling, Butterworths, pp. 82-101.

Bosselman, Robert H. (1999). 'Curriculum and Instruction' in Clayton W. Barrows & Robert (editors), *Hospitality Management Education*. The Howarth Hospitality Press, New York.

Botkin, D.B. and Keller, E.A. (1982). *Environmental Studies*, C.E. Merrill Publishing Company, A Bell and Howell Company, Columbus, p. 505.

Bryan, R.B. (1981), *Soil Erosion and Conservation in Man and Environmental Processes*, edited by K.J. Gegory and D.E. Walling, Butterworths.

Bubsy, G. and P. Brunt (1997). "Tourism Sandwich Placements: An Appraisal," *Tourism Management*, Vol. 18(2).

Buhalis, D. (2003). *eTourism–Information Technology for Strategic Tourism Management*, Prentice Hall, Harlow, U.K.

Bull, A. (1991). *The Economics of Travel and Tourism*, London: Pitman.

Burkart, A.J., and S. Medlik (1974). *Tourism Past Present and Future*, Butterworth Heinemann: London.

Burton, P.E. (1988). "Building Bridges between Industry and Educations." Paper presented to Teaching Tourism into 1990, Conference University of Survey.

Butler, R.W., *"The Social Implication of Tourism Development"*, Tourism Research 2, 2(1974).

Carter, R. and Richer, P. (1999). *Marketing Tourism Destinations Online*, WTO Business Council, Madrid.

Charistou, E.S. (1999). "Hospitality Management Education in Greece", *Tourism Management*, 20:683-691.

Chidambaram R.M. (1999). Enrichment of Commerce Curriculum, University News, Vol. 137, No. 44, Nov. 1st.

Christan, E. and J. Eaton, (2000). "Management Competencies for Graduate Trainees", *Annals of Tourism Research*, Vol. 27, No. 4, pp. 1058-1061.

Chuck, Y. Gee. (1989). *The Travel Industry*, New York: Van Nostrand Reinhold.

Clapham, W.B. (1973). *'Natural Ecosystem'*, MacMillan, London.

Cloud, P.E. (1969). *'Resources and Man'*, W.H. Freeman and Company, San Francisco.

Cohen, Eric., *"Towards a Sociology of International Tourism"*, Social Research 39, 1 (1972).

Cole, M. (1971), *Plants, Animals and Environments*, Geographical Magazine, Vol. 44, pp. 230-31.

Concept C. and J. West Lake (1989). Tourism Teaching into the 1990 Tourism Management, 10(1), pp. 69-73.

Cooper, C., Scales, R. and Westlake, J. (1992). "The Anatomy of Tourism and Hospitality Educators in the UK," *Tourism Management*, 13,: 234-247.

Cosgrove, Isabel and Jackson, R. (1972). *The Geography of Recreation and Leisure*, London: Hutchinson.

Crampon, L.T. (1963). *The Development of Tourism*, Colorado: University of Colorado Press.

Cullen, Thomas P. (1988). "Filling China's Staffing Gap". The Cornell Hotel and Restaurant Administration Quarterly, 29(2), pp. 76-78.

Curtis, J.T. and McIntosh, R.P. (1950). "The Interrelations of Certain Analytical and Synthetic Phyto-sociological Characters to Study Ecology", pp. 314-34.

Dassaman, R.D. (1976), *Environmental Conservation*, Wiley, New York.

Daubernmire, R.F. (1974), *Plants and Environment*, 3rd ed., John Wiley, New York.

David Airey (1994). "Informal Tourism Employment: Vendors in Boli, Indonesia", Tourism Management 1994, 15(6) pp. 464-467.

Davis, H.D., *Potentials for Tourism of Developing Countries*, London: Finance and Development, 1968.

Det Wyler, T.R. (1971), *Man's Impact on Environment*, McGraw-Hill, New York.

Donald Hawkins and John D. Hunt, "Travel and Tourism Professional Education" *International Journal of Management and Tourism*, pp. 349-362.

Donald, E. Hawking (Eds.), *Tourism Planning and Development Issues*, Washington: George Washington University, 1980.

Dumazedier, J. (1967). *Towards a Society of Leisure*, New York: Free Press.

Eaton, J., and Christau, E. (1997). "Hospitality Management Competencies for Graduate Trainees: Employers' View", *Journal of European Business Education*, 7(1), pp. 60-68.

Edgell, D. (1990). "International Tourism Policy," New Work: Van Nostrand.

Edmunds, *Environmental Administration*, New York: McGraw-Hill, 1973.

Edward, J. Mayo (1981). *The Psychology of Leisure Travel*, Boston: CBI Publishing Company.

Evangelos Christou (1999). "Hospitality Management Education in Greece–An Exploratory Study", Tourism Management, 20 (1999), pp. 683-691.

Fitzgerald, M.J. and Cullen, T.P. (1991). "Learning through a "Read World" experience, The Cornell Hotel and Restaurant Adminis-tration Quarterly, August, pp. 85-88.

Foster, D. (1985). *Travel and Tourism Management*, London: Macmillan.

Furley, P.A. and Newey, W.W. (1983), *Man and the Biosphere*, Butterworths, London.

Gamble, P.R. (1992). "The Educational Challenge for Hospitality and Tourism", *Tourism Management*, March: 6-10.

Gearing Charles, E. (1976). *Planning for Tourism Development*, New York: Praeger Publishers.

George E. (2004). Medical Tourism: Tamil Nadu's Top Agenda. By Laxmi Subramanian. *Express Travel and Tourism*. Vol. 17, No. 10, October.

Ghodsee Kristen (2003). Executive Summary of Research Present-ation: Women Employment, and Tourism in Post Totalitarian Bulgaria.

Go, E.M., (1994). Emerging Issues in Tourism Education, in W. Theobald (ed.) Global. Tourism–The Next Decade, Oxford, Butterworth–Heinemann.

Hammarskjold, K. (1972). *"Economics of Air Transport and Tourism"*, Montreal: I.C.A.O.

Hawkins, D.E. and Hunt, T.D., (1980). Travel and Tourism Professional Education, Hospitality and Tourism Educator (1), pp. 7–13.

Haywood, K.M. and K. Maki (1992). "A Conceptual Model of the Education/Employment Interface for Tourism Industry", pp. 237-248 in Ritchie. JRB and Hawkins, D(eds), World Travel and Tourism Review CAB, Oxford.

Heath, E. (1992). *Marketing Tourism Destinations*, New York: Wiley.

Hegarts Joseph A. (1990). "Challenges and Tourism Education Programmes in Developing Countries", Hospitality and Tourism Educator 2(3): pp. 12–15.

Higgins, R.B., (1996). The Global Structure of the Nature tourism industry: Ecotourist, tour operators, and local businesses, *Journal of Travel Research*, 32(2), pp. 11–18.

Hodyson, A. (1987). *The Travel and Tourism Industry*, Oxford: Pergamon.

Hollander, S. (1968). *Passenger Transportation*, Michigan: Michigan State University.

Holliman, J. (1974), *Consumer's Guide to the Protection of the Environment*, Ballanine, London.

Hospitality Training Foundations, Labor Market Review (2000). "The Scene in the UK".

Hunt, J.D., and Higgins, B. (1981). "Proposed Undergraduate Programs in Travel and Tourism". The George Washington University.

Hunziker, W. (1951). *Social Tourism: Its Nature and Problems,* Geneva: Aliance International de Turisme.

Hurdman, L.E. (1980). *Tourism: A Shrinking World,* New York: Wiley.

Imandar D.B. (2003). Karnataka Tourism Taps Healthcare Sector, *Express Travel and Tourism,* Vol. 6, No. 18, July 16-31.

Inkpen, G. (1998). *Information Technology for Travel and Tourism,* Addison Wesley Longman, Essex UK.

Jafari, J. (1990). Research and Scholarship: The Basis of Tourism Education. The *Journal of Tourism Studies,* Vol. 1, No. 1.

Jenkins, C.L., (1980). Education for Tourism Policy Makers in Developing Countries, *International Journal of Tourism Management,* Dec., 1980, pp. 238-42.

Joseph, D. Firdgen, *Dimensions of Tourism,* East Lansing, Michigan: American Hotel and Motel Association, 1991.

Joshi Anuradha, (1999). *Value Development among Youths,* University News, Vol. 37, No. 43, Oct. 25th.

Kerry Godrey and Jackie Clarke (2000). *The Tourism Development Handbook,* London: Cassell.

Khan, Olsen Var (ed.) (1993). *VNR's Encyclopedia of Hospitality and Tourism,* New York.

Ladki, M. (1993). "Hospitality Education: the Identity Struggle", *International Journal of Hospitality Management,* Vol. 12 No., 3, pp. 243-251.

Law, C. (1993). *Urban Tourism: Attracting Visitors to Large Cities,* London: Mansell.

Laws, E. (Ed.) (1997). *The ATTT Tourism Education Handbook,* Tourism Society, London.

Laws, E.C. (1995). *Tourist Destination Management: Issues,*

Analysis and Policies, London: Routledge.

Lawson, Maclom (1975). *Teaching Tourism Education and Training in Western Europe: A Comparative Study*, London: Tourism International Press.

Lee, N. and Wood, C. (1972), *Planning and Pollution*, The Planner, Vol. 58, pp. 153-58.

Leslie D., MewAleenan, M. (1990). The Indo Trial Placement Experience in the U.K. Students, *Journal of Industry and Higher Education*, 4(1), pp. 15-22.

Lickorish, L.J. (1953). *Tourism and International Balance of Payments*, Geneva: International Institute of Scientific Travel Research.

Lieper, N. (1995). *Tourism Management*, RIMT Publishing, Melbourne.

Luke, D., and A. Ingold, (1990). "Planning for Industry: A Study in Curriculum Design." *International Journal of Contemporary Hospitality Management*, 2(2), pp. 20-23.

Marsh, G.P. (1984), *Man and Nature* (Physical Geography as modified by Human Action), Charles Scribner, New York.

Mash, R. (1989). *The Rights of Nature*, University of Wisconsin Press, Madison.

Matsieson, A. (1982). *Tourism: Economic, Physical and Social Impacts*, London, Longman.

Medlik, S. (1972). *Economic Importance of Tourism*, Surrey: University of Surrey.

Middleton V.T.C., Ladkin, A. (1996). *The Profiles of Tourism Studies Degree Courses in UK: 1995/6*, National Liaison Group, London.

Mill, R.C. and Morrison, A.M. (1986). "The Tourism System." Englewood.

Milman Ady, Peter Ricci (2004). "Predicting Job Retention of Hourly Employees in the Lodging Industry", *Journal of Hospitality and Tourism Research*, Vol. No. 21(2), pp. 28-40.

Murphy, P.E. (1985). *Tourism: A Community Approach, Methuen*, New York.

Nelson, I.G. and Byrne, A.B. (1986), *Man as an Instrument of Landscape Change*, Alberta Geog. Rev., Vol. 58, pp. 226-38.

Nicholson, M. (1977). The Environmental Revolution, London: Penguin.

O'Connor, P. (1999). Electronic Information Distribution in Tourism and Hospitality, CABI Publishing, U.K.

Odum, H.T. (1971), *Environment, Power and Society*, Wiley Interscience, New York.

Okeivi, F.D. Fruley and Postel, R.T. (1994). "Food and Beverage Management Education, 6(4), pp. 37-40.

Parker, S. (1971). *The Future of Work and Leisure*, London: Mac Gibbon and Kee.

Peaker, A. (1973). *"Holiday Spending by the British at Home and Abroad"*, National Westminster Bank Quarterly Review, August.

Pearce, Sales, J. (1959). *Travel and Tourism Encyclopedia*, London: Blandford.

Philips E.A. (1959). "Methods of Vegetation Study", A Holt Dryden Book. Henry Hott and Co. Inc., p. 107.

Raymond, F. (1978). *Ecological Principles for Economic Development*, London: John Wiley.

Rebecca Shephered and Chris Cooper (1995). "Innovations in Tourism Educating and Training", Tourism Recreational Research, Vol. 20 (2), 1995, pp. 14-42.

Richards, G. (1972). *Tourism and the Economy*, Surrey: University of Surrey.

Ritche, J.R.B. (1988). "Alternative approaches to teaching tourism", paper presented at Teaching Tourism in to the work-based 1990s Conference, University of Survey.

Robinson, H.A. (1976). *Geography of Tourism*, London: MacDonald and Evans.

Ross, G.F. (1994). *The Psychology of Tourism*, Melbourne: Hospitality Press.

Ryan, C. (1991). *Recreational Tourism: A Social Science Perspective*, London: Routledge.

Sanes, C. (1996). Employees Impact on Service Delivery, Management Development Review, 9(2), pp. 15-20.

Seldin, P. (1988). Evaluating College Teaching. College Teaching and Learning: Preparing for New Commitments. *In New Directions for Teaching and Learning*. Young, R.E. and Eble, K.E. (Eds.) San Francisco: Jossey-Bass Publishers.

Sharpley Richard, Foster Gill, (2003). "The Implications of Hotel Employee Attitudes for the Development of Quality Tourism: The Case of Cyprus", *Tourism Management*, Vol. 24, pp. 687-697.

Sheldon, P. (1997). *Tourism Information Technology*, CA International, Wallingford, UK and New York, USA.

Shen B., and Z. Liu (1999). *Principles of Tourism Studies*, Xue Lin Publishing House, Shanghai.

Simmons, I.G. (1974), *The Ecology and Natural Resources*, Edward Arnold, London.

Smith, K.S. and Simpson, R.D. (1995). Validating Teaching Competencies for Faculty Members in Higher Education: A National Study Using the Delphi Method. *Innovative Higher Education, 19*.

Sophee Elias (1992). The future of Tourism and Hospitality Management Courses. Tourism Management, March 1992, pp. 137-140.

Sorensen (1973). "Environment Impact Assessment", Wild Life Institute of India, D.Dun. (U.P.); Selected readings—A Review General, Version 2000.

Stuart A. Schulman and Joseph A. Greenburg "Two Year College Tourism Education: A Study of Institution Satisfaction and Linkage, *International Journal of Management and Tourism.*Z pp. 101-108.

Tas, R. (1988). "Teaching Future Managers", *The Cornell Hotel and Restaurant Administration Quarterly*, 29(2), pp. 41-43.

Tribe J. (1997). "The Indiscipline of Tourism," *Annals of Tourism Research*, Vol. 24(3), pp. 638-657.

Turgut Var and Dr. Sang-Mu Kim, "Tourism Education in Korea", International Journal of Management and Tourism.

Umbreit, W.T. (1992). "In search for Hospitality Curriculum Relevance for the 1990's," *Hospitality and Tourism Educator*, 15(1), pp. 71-74.

Verma Shashi (2004). Towards an Effective University—*Industry Interaction: A Tripod Approach*, University New, Vol. 42, No. 32, August.

Vose, Richard (1995). Tourism: The Human Perspective, Hodder and Stoughtan Educational, London.

Wahab S., Hammam, A. and Jafari, J. (1998). "Tourism Education and Training", *Annals of Tourism Research*, Vol. 25(2), pp. 527-528.

Walle, A.H., (1997). A Conference Report, "Graduate Education and Research" Annals of Tourism Research, Vol. 24 (3), pp. 754-756.

Whittaker, R.H. (1975), *Communities and Ecosystem*, 2nd ed. MacMillan, New York.

Wong Simon, Pang Loretta, (2003). "Motivators to creativity in the hotel industry-perspectives of Managers and Supervisors", *Journal of Tourism Management*, Vol. 24, pp. 551-559.

Woods, H., Robert, Viehland Douglas, "Women in Hotel Management", *Cornel Hotel and Restaurant Administration Quartely*, US.

World Travel and Tourism Council (2004). Travel and Tourism in India. *The Economic Impact and Potential*, London.

Index